Come Climb The Ladder And Rejoice

Welcome

A Spiritual Guide

Volume One

By

Louise D'Angelo

Published By
THE MARYHEART CRUSADERS, INC.
Meriden, Conn. 06450

Printed in U.S.A.

Nihil Obstat: The Reverend Norman Belval, S.T.D.
                       Censor Deputatis

Imprimatur: ✠ The Most Reverend John F. Whealon
                       Archbishop of Hartford, Conn.
                       April 15, 1990

The Nihil Obstat and Imprimatur are official declarations that a book or pamphlet is free of doctrinal or moral error.

1st Printing 1993

Library of Congress Catalog Card No.: 88-92302

ISBN Vol. 1: 1-878886-01-0

Printed and bound in the United States of America.

TABLE OF CONTENTS

PART ONE
Understanding The Spiritual Life

PART TWO
The Life Of Grace

PART THREE
God Draws The Soul To Closer Union With Him

PART FOUR
Beginning The Prayer Life

Dedicated To All
Who Seek A Closer
Union With God

My Sincere Thanks
To Everyone Whose
Encouragement Made
This Book Possible

L. D.

ABOUT THE AUTHOR

Louise D'Angelo

Louise D'Angelo is the founder and president of an approved Catholic lay apostolate called "The Maryheart Crusaders." This non-profit organization has been in existence since 1964, and has received the acknowledgment of many Bishops in the United States. The main goal of The Maryheart Crusaders is to bring back fallen-away Catholics through a program of adult religious education; in addition, the organization strives to help improve the spiritual lives of Catholic lay people. The Crusaders' program includes meetings, lectures, classes for adults and distribution of free Catholic literature. Crusaders also defend the Pope, Bishops, priests, religious and deacons in various ways, for example, by letters to editors or to T.V. stations if and when these might attack the Catholic Church or its moral stands.

They participated in the Forty-first International Eucharistic Congress held in Philadelphia in 1976, at the Evangelization Conference in Washington D.C. in 1980, at several Marian congresses in the Bostom area, and one in Hartford, Connecticut.

Mrs. Louise D'Angelo is a nationally known writer and lecturer who has spoken at church affairs for many years. Her articles have appeared in such publications as *Marian Helpers Bulletin, Our Sunday Vistitor, Immaculata* magazine, *The Mary-Heart Crusaders* newspaper, and *House of Loretto* magazine.

In addition, Mrs. D'Angelo is the author of the following books: *Too Busy for God? Think Again, Come Home...The Door Is Open* and *Mary's Light of Grace,* all published by The Maryheart Crusaders.

In keeping with her work as a Crusader, Louise has written against many cults, often doing extensive research. She is well qualified to bring to light the teachings of the Witnesses and to expose such teachings for all to see.

Her book, *The Catholic Answer to the Jehovah's Witnesses,* is her greatest effort concerning cults, and is presented to the public at a time when it is very much needed in order to challenge the Witnesses and their so-called "Bible truths."

PREFACE

With my books *Too Busy For God? Think Again* and *Come Home...The Door Is Open*, I tried to create a desire so that the average lay person can start a spiritual climb up THE LADDER OF PERFECTION to a closer union with God. This book is a continuation of the spiritual teachings contained in my other two books. This book explains in greater detail what it means to live a most active spiritual life and what it means to reach a closer union with God. This book also explains how this union can be obtained. You will find here a wealth of spiritual information which can be put to good use in everyday living for the lay person or a religious.

L. D.

INTRODUCTION

One day a favored soul received from our Lord certain praises which she felt she did not deserve. She looked at the vision before her and cried out: "Please do not say anymore...You know that I am nothing!" Our Lord gently smiled and replied: "But do I not have the power to make a something out of a nothing?"

Often, people came to me, very upset because of the evil and corruption found in our society. They felt and believed that the only thing God could do about such a situation was to destroy the whole world and in that way eliminate all sin and evil (as well as the whole world). My standard answer would be: "You have seen the power of the devil and his evil, you have yet to see the power of God's grace!"

If one has ever seen the power of the ocean's waves as they pounded upon the cliffs of the seashore, if one has ever been awed by the power of lightning flashing across the summer sky, if one has ever felt small and insignificant as he viewed the mighty power of the whole solar system, then one has seen only a tiny fraction of the power of God's precious gift to man, called grace.

Grace has a power which far exceeds the combined forces of the whole universe and of nature, because it has the power to bring an eternal happiness, to change night into day, to bring peace where there is no peace, to bring love where there is hate, to bring hope, when all hope has faded, to encourage, to strengthen, to heal. Grace has the power to raise a fallen man from the depths of his own miseries to the heights of sanctity.

Grace has the power to heal the wounds which sin stamps upon souls. Grace has the power to destroy evil, sin, corruption and temptation. Grace has the power to reunite fallen mankind with its Creator. Grace has the power to change a Mary Magdalene or an Augustine into a saint. Grace has the power to transfer a soul from the emptiness of a materialistic world to the fullness of a life lived with God and for God. Grace has a power which is endless, constant, ever flowing from the Heart of God outward to His beloved children. Grace has a brightness which far exceeds the glow of the noonday sun.

Grace is all these things and more, much more. And the most marvelous part about grace is that it is ours for the asking. Grace is not reserved only for the great ones, the fortunate ones, the wealthy, the famous, the chosen ones. Grace is for all, for you and for me, for the poor, the lowly, the ones the world casts aside: and it is this grace which makes a "something" out of a "nothing."

L. D.

PART ONE

UNDERSTANDING THE SPIRITUAL LIFE

Chapter 1

LET US BEGIN

The main problem with people who fail to live an active spiritual life is confusion about religion. This confusion is understandable when a person is confronted by all sorts of religious views, from the oversimplified to the "way out."

Those people who tend to oversimplify religion try to make you believe that only a short prayer consisting of "I believe in Christ" is all that is needed. Those who complicate religion, by getting involved in deep theological problems and solving them their "own way," try to make you believe that it is impossible to save your soul unless you become a "living Bible."

However, religion is neither simple nor complicated. Saving your soul is not a simple task but it is also not a complicated one. You need much more than a simple statement of belief in Christ; yet, you do not need unmeaningful complex answers to basic religious problems.

The climb to union with Christ, also, is by no means simple nor easy; still it can be done with the correct basic religious knowledge which is sensible and uncomplicated.

Within these pages, I will tell you what you need, and do not need, to know in order to attempt the climb up THE LADDER OF PERFECTION to a more perfect, a more complete union with Christ. I will also explain why you should make the attempt.

To know what the rewards are when your personal union with Christ brings you a certain amount of perfection is as important as to know how to climb THE LADDER OF PERFECTION.

There are two words which sum up these rewards: peace and joy. The spiritual peace and joy found when one has a most wondrous union with Christ is worth all the effort it takes to begin and to continue the climb. So, as the title of this book proclaims: COME CLIMB THE LADDER...AND REJOICE.

Chapter 2

IDENTIFY YOURSELF TO CHRIST

Everyone has an identity. First of all, we have a name, we belong to a certain race, and to a certain country. When we meet a stranger or answer a phone, we identify ourself. We say, for example: "I am Mary Smith," or "I am John Brown."

There are other signs of a personal identity besides a name. Our voice identifies us. When we call a friend or loved one on the phone, we do not have to give our name; the person, who answers, knows us by our voice.

The way we dress, or fix our hair, or decorate our home, as well as our mannerisms are marks of identification. Just being in the home of someone you know well tells you who lives there.

Each person has a oneness with himself or herself which belongs to no other.

In much the same way, a Christian has an identity which belongs only to a Christian. After Christ's death and Resurrection, after He left His Church for the first Christians, those people had an identity which belonged only to the followers of Christ. They were known for their pure love: "Look at the Christians, see how they love each other."

A Catholic has many marks of identity which belong only to Catholics. At one time, for example, on Fridays, everyone knew who the Catholics were (the practicing Catholics, that is). They were the ones who never ordered a hamburger or had meat on the table in their homes. If someone went into a strange Church and wasn't sure what kind of a Church it was, when they saw the confessionals, they knew: here was a Catholic Church. On

5

Saturday evenings or Sunday morning, Catholics go to Mass, never to a service.

Now, the point of all this talk about identity is: how do you identify yourself as a Catholic to Christ? or does He just know you for what you are or for what you pretend that you are? Must you identify yourself to Christ as a Catholic? The answer is: yes, you must. Why?

Well, for one thing, listen to Christ speaking to this group of people, as they try to identify themselves to Him: "When the Master of the house has entered. . .they will say: 'Lord, open for us. . .we ate and drank in thy presence. . .' He said to them: 'I do not know where you are from, depart from me" (*Luke* 13:25-27).

"But, I know you not," Christ replied. "I am not sure who you are or what you are." Christ is also saying: "Because I do not see marks of identification within your life or within your actions, how can I be sure that you are what you tell me you are?"

When you tell Christ that you are a Christian, a Catholic, how can you be sure that He will see you as a Christian, as a Catholic? Are the marks of Catholicism visible in all you do and say, or have they slowly but surely faded away?

As a Catholic, you were baptized into the Church. You became a member of the Church. But more so, you became a child of the family which Christ, Himself, founded when He started His Church. As a child of the Church, you were given the mark of baptism the first mark which identifies you as a Catholic. But, in addition, you were given other identifications which consist of Catholic duties and responsibilities. In other words, it is not enough just to say you are a Catholic; you must show by your words, deeds and actions that you are the Catholic you say you are. Being a Catholic and being identified as a Catholic are two different things.

If you were to stand before Christ and declare: "I am a Catholic," would He look puzzled and state: "But I know you not"? Can you be identified as a Catholic by your faith, your beliefs, your obedience to the Church and acceptance of what she teaches? Or have you failed to live and think and act as Christ expects you, a Cathoic, to think, live and act?

Would Christ recognize you if you have decided to accept and believe only what you have chosen to accept and believe, rejecting what you feel will somehow interfere with your plans for your life? No, He would not recognize you as a Catholic, a Roman Catholic.

Baptism makes you a member of the Catholic family. However, your deeds and actions keep you a member recognized as such or a member no longer in the state of recognition.

A father who confronts a son who has brought disgrace and dishonor to the family name will say to that boy: "You are no son of mine! I don't know you anymore!" In much the same way, Christ will say to a Catholic who is a fallen member of the Church: "I don't know you."

So, the very first step to take when one seeks a union with Christ, by climbing THE LADDER OF PERFECTION is to make sure that you will be recognized by Christ for what you say you are: a Roman Catholic.

Christ said: "But why do you call me 'Lord, Lord,' yet do not do what I say? Not everyone who says to me, 'Lord, Lord' shall enter the kingdom of heaven, but only the one who does the will of my Father in heaven" (*Matt.* 7:21).

No Catholic can seek perfection or attempt to start the climb to union with Christ, unless or until this Catholic shows that he or she is a true, faithful member of Christ's Church. Any Catholic who attempts the "climb" may never reach the goal if the person tries to reach union with Christ away from or outside of the Church.

"Doing your own thing" became a popular saying during the 60's and 70's (and may still be around today). The words meant that a person no longer needed rules or laws to follow because it was more important to be self-choosing or self-made into your own image and likeness. It meant to do anything you wanted to do whatever suited your own way of life. So the homosexuals, the drug addicts, women who wanted abortions, couples living together without marriage, all became signs that a person had cast aside safe modes of living and was doing his or her own "thing."

This "doing your own thing" even invaded religion and the Church. It became fashionable for people to turn religion into one that was most comfortable for their own needs. Rules, laws, teachings, doctrines were cast aside if these interfered with the plans the person made for daily living.

As well might be imagined, utter chaos and confusion became the ultimate result of this type of philosophy. People just did not find that illusive "Garden of Eden" which they thought they would find by doing their own "thing."

It is easy to understand why. Disobedience was the foundation upon which people built that type of lifestyle. "Doing my own thing" was nothing more than "I will not obey."

If there is one virtue above all others which is needed before one can climb THE LADDER OF PERFECTION, it is the virtue of humility which allows the person to say: "I will obey," "I will accept," "I will believe."

Humility, obedience, love for God, these are some of the marks of a Catholic, whom Christ will recognize as being a Catholic; because, their words, deeds and actions show that they are a Catholic.

So, do not make the mistake of thinking that you can climb the "Ladder" your "own way." That is impossible. Why? Because you need grace, lots of grace, to do that. And where do you find the grace which you need? It is to be found in and through the Church and her teachings and her sacraments.

Chapter 3

THE TIME IS NOW

One day, a fallen-away Catholic was trying to tell me that there is such a thing as reincarnation. He firmly believed that when he died, he would "come back again" as another person, and this process would continue many times until he finally reached the state of "perfection" and allowed into heaven. He tried to explain to me that reincarnation was a "proven" fact and told me a little story of how a small child, on his death bed, told everyone in the room that he would "return" as a different person.

I asked him: "If there really is this reincarnation, then tell me why you are making so many mistakes now in this life or why there are so many people in the world doing such terrible things as committing crimes? Did they not learn anything from past lives?"

He quickly replied: "Oh! well you see, for some it is their first life. They correct their mistakes in the next life."

I answered: "And for you? Is this your first life—or your last?"

He did not answer.

Of course, I informed the misguided Catholic that there is no such thing as reincarnation. If there were, then there would have been no need for Christ to redeem us. Then our salvation would come about merely from a long series of different lives wherein we could rise above our own failings without the need or help of a Savior. Then we would not need grace nor the sacraments, nor our Church. There in that statement, we would not need the Church nor the sacraments, is the key to why a person wants to believe in reincarnation. It becomes such a great comfort to them to believe that there is no such thing as a judgment at death as the Church teaches. They prefer to think that if they don't make it to heaven after this life, they will merely be given another life or a "second chance" as I was told by my fallen-away relative.

The most amazing thing about all who want to believe in reincarnation is that they do *believe in a heaven* of perfect joy and happiness! They are not like the atheists who refuse to believe in God or in a heaven. They not only firmly believe that there is a God and His heaven, but they sincerely want to end up in this magnificent place of everlasting joy and happiness.

Another amazing fact about those Catholics who believe in reincarnation is that they do have some understanding of the need for a perfection which will enable them to enter into their heaven after a series of lives on earth. They, in a very limited way, do associate God, perfection and heaven with what they do while on earth.

However, at the same time they are too lazy, too proud, or too unconcerned to act now, while they are alive, to do what God tells them has to be done so that they can attempt to reach perfection and enter heaven. They find an excellent excuse for not accepting the truths of God, the sacraments and a way to self-improvement by simply telling themselves that if they don't make heaven after this life ends, they will merely be given another chance to do so. When they reason or rationalize in that way, it is very easy for them to give up the practice of their religion or to accept un-Catholic beliefs, or if they are already a fallen-away Catholic, they find a dandy excuse for staying a fallen-away Catholic.

However, one thing which is very wrong with this mixed-up way of thinking is (as I asked my relative) how can they be so sure that they are in their first life and not their last? For some unknown reason, a fallen-away Catholic who does believe in reincarnation seems to "just know" that he will be handed another life to play with at the moment of death; wherein, he will "perfect" himself. Alas, if the fallen-away Catholic sincerely believes that he is not yet perfect and must have another life in which to find perfection, that Catholic is very loudly proclaiming the fact that he is *not now* living as a good Catholic should live. He is in reality saying, "Look at me! I am a very poor Catholic now, but don't worry, when I die I will be given another life and I will become a better Catholic in my second or third or fourth life!" Of course such a belief is nonsense.

My first thoughts, when I hear anyone express a belief in the false teachings of reincarnation are: what is this person doing *now* to gain perfection? Why wait for the so-called "next" life or the "next" or the "next"?

The time for perfection is now, today, this very moment. We can never begin too soon to start the climb up THE LADDER OF PERFECTION to a closer union with God. We are given by Almighty God one life—and only one life—in which to cooperate with the grace of salvation. This life is here at this very moment.

The belief in reincarnation is only one of the many excuses which Catholics give for not living a holy, active spiritual life. Yet, ninety percent of such people really and truly want to go to heaven. Some of them even claim to love God. Others merely say that they do not want to go to hell. All of them make the same mistake. They overlook most of the opportunities which are present in their daily lives which could be used to bring grace and holiness to their souls and in that way reach the heaven which they desire.

Saving one's soul and purifying it is a very "now" responsibility. It is not something which can be put off until a later date. Why? There may be no "later date." There is no absolute guarantee given to anyone that he or she will have another day, week, year of life. A person cannot place the awesome obligation of saving his soul in the uncertain future. Young and old, men and women, teenagers, babies and little children have all died unexpectedly. No one knows for sure what a tomorrow will bring or even if a tomorrow will exist for him or her.

One day eight teenagers happily went to a party. On their way home, they saw a train wreck. Excited, they stopped their autos and rushed to view the accident as close as possible. As they ran to the wreck, they suddenly fell dead. Emitting from the crushed freight cars was a deadly chlorine gas. There was no tomorrow for them. How sad!

Our Lord tells us of a similar example of the shortness of time on earth: ". . .and the rich man will say to himself: 'Soul, you have many good things laid up for many years; take your ease, eat, drink, be merry!' But God said to him: 'You fool! this night do I demand your soul of you and the things that you have provided, whose will they be?' So is he who lays up treasures for himself and is not rich as regards God" (*Luke* 12:16-21).

To be "rich as regards God," what does that mean? It means that you should gather for your soul the spiritual treasures which can only be found in living an active spiritual life. When do you do that? The time is now, today. Start today because tomorrow may be too late. Learn today how to climb THE LADDER OF PERFECTION to a closer union with God; and you will find that this union will last forever.

Chapter 4

WHAT IS THE SPIRITUAL LIFE?

Before a person can attempt the climb up THE LADDER OF PERFECTION, he must understand what the spiritual life is all about.

Some people, especially because of the increase in interest about the occult, think that spiritualism and living an active spiritual life are one and the same. At one time I confused these two terms and when I came across the words "the spiritual life" in a book, I wondered why the author was talking about such a non-Catholic subject as spiritualism. However, the author was not talking about spiritualism.

Spiritualism is the science or the belief that the dead can be contacted through a series of weird actions upon the part of the living. This is strictly condemned by the Church. In the "Maryknoll Catholic Dictionary" (by Albert J. Nevins, M.M.), we find these words concerning spiritualism. "The attempt to communicate with spirits of another world, who are dead. The Church forbids unnatural and useless communication with the spirits of another world. Therefore, it is forbidden to be present at a seance, even out of curiosity or to take part in this act" (page 545).

Living a good, an active spiritual life is far different. It means to live your material life for the benefit of your soul. It means to live a life filled with goodness, virtue and faith so that after death the soul stands before God filled with the splendor of His magnificent grace.

Many people forget that they have a complete life to live: a material life and a spiritual life. Others are far more concerned with the material life of the body than with the spiritual life of the soul; forgetting that both the material and spiritual life become part of one human nature or one reality, which cannot in all essence be separated.

Living a material life consists of everyday activities: eating, sleeping, working, talking, acquiring material possessions, visiting friends, taking vacations, getting an education, going to parties, watching T.V., etc.

Living an active spiritual life consists of: going to Church, praying, penance, loving God, devotions to Mary and the saints, receiving the sacraments, reading spiritual books (such as this one), acquiring virtues, especially the virtue of charity for others, and so forth.

When a person lives a good spiritual life, as well as a good material life, then the person can be sure that this goodness will last forever; for he or she has lived a complete life.

So many people, who refuse to go to Church, or to believe in God, will say: "I am a good person, I don't hurt anyone, what do I need the Church for? I love my family. I do good to my family. I help them. Why should I go to Church?"

Such people are living only a material life and not a spiritual life as well. Such people are living only half a life, walking around with their souls in the stagnant waters of spiritual neglect. Such people are not doing God's holy will nor following the teachings of Christ. This type of goodness alone cannot help the soul nor purify the soul. Christ said: "For, if you love those who love you, what reward shall you have? Do not even the publicans do that? And if you salute your brethren only, what are you doing more than others? Do not even the Gentiles do that? You, therefore, are to be perfect, even as your heavenly Father is perfect" (*Matt.* 5:46-48).

"You, therefore, are to be perfect, even as your heavenly Father is perfect" (*Matt.* 5:48).

What is this perfection that Christ speaks about? Does He mean that we should make for ourselves a perfect life of material happiness? Does He mean that we should perfect our intellect, our talents, our abilities, our artistic inclinations? Does He mean that we should have perfect fun, no matter how, as long as we enjoy ourselves? No, Christ does not mean such things when He tells us to strive for perfection. What does He mean?

Well, He looks beyond the frail shell of a human, called the body, and sees the eternal soul within this body. His words are spoken to that soul. "Be perfect" is His command. "Shine forth with the same light which shines forth from the Being of your heavenly Father!"

What is this heavenly light of perfection? It is called grace. A soul, in the state of grace, is a soul worthy to stand by God and to share all the eternal joys of His kingdom called heaven. A soul, without grace, in the state of mortal sin, is a soul not in the condition required by God to enter His kingdom of heaven.

However, the command to be "perfect" does not mean merely to have the soul in the state of grace. It means much more. It means that the soul, filled with this light, called grace, must live a most active spiritual life. This grace can be and must be increased. This grace can be and must be constantly in motion, ever reaching out to bring to the soul more spiritual gifts. It means that the soul, filled with grace, must ever seek a closer, a more intimate union with God.

That is what the spiritual life is all about: a soul ever striving to increase its own grace, ever striving to reach a closer union with God by ever striving to climb THE LADDER OF PERFECTION towards this closer union with God.

Chapter 5

SPIRITUAL INACTIVITY

One of the saddest wastes of grace happens when a person makes no attempt to improve his or her spiritual life. A sinner, who is content living away from God and the sacraments, allows magnificent graces to die in stagnant waters. But in this chapter I wish to speak about an even sadder situation. This involves the person who is no longer a sinner in the sense of committing grave, serious sins, but who has reached a certain low level of union with God...and stays there! In other words, he makes no attempt to improve his spiritual life, rather imagining that he has reached the top of the ladder.

In one way, a sinner who stays in the stagnant waters has an advantage over the person who reaches a certain spiritual level and stays there. The sinner constantly is given numerous powerful graces, which if used, could rise him out of his spiritual hibernation. But, on the other hand, when a person turns his back on the graces which are necessary for spiritual advancement, these graces may one day cease. God knowing that a person has no intentions of improving his spiritual life will leave the person in the state which the person desires to be in. Remember that, in climbing THE LADDER OF PERFECTION, there must be a constant desire for self-knowledge and self-improvement. Without such desires, God will leave the soul in the spiritual state which the soul creates for itself. If God notices that the soul does not even appreciate His graces, which could raise the person to a higher state, then such graces will be withdrawn.

It is very important to realize that during the early stages of spiritual advancement, the person must, of his or her own free will, unite the will with God's. In other words, the person must exhibit great desires to advance towards union with God; and these desires must be absolutely genuine and sincere. There must be, in addition, a most profound motivation. God does not play games with His graces; even though, some people would like Him to. They might desire such and such a grace, but not to reach a closer union with Him. Their motivation could even be purely material. Also, God, very quickly knows when a person is sincere about desiring a closer union with Him. He, also, is in reality very shy about exposing the depths and secrets of His love. He does not grant such extra special graces to just anyone. A person must well prepare his heart and soul in advance so that God can bring to the spiritual life the sweet wine of intimate union with Him. The first steps taken towards such a union must be taken by the person himself; and often must continue for a long period of time before God is ready to reveal to the soul special treasures of His love and union.

The problem is that most people, who start the climb to perfection or union with God, stop this spiritual process long before they reach the point of having God open up the depths of His Heart to expose its treasures and secrets to them. They become far more concerned about the progress *which they made* rather than about the progress which they could make if only they continue.

While it is notable for a person to reach the point of spirituality wherein he absolutely refuses to commit another mortal sin, that person must realize that this accomplishment is only the beginning of union with God and it is not the beginning and end all wrapped up in one. The fact is, there is really no end to the process of spiritual union with God. The beginning is always the beginning of a new stage or level and the true, complete, perfect end can only be union with God in heaven. However, in between all the beginnings and the end, there are numerous stages or degrees of this union. I can compare this to a beautiful rose, first a bud (the first beginning), then the gradual opening up of the petals. Yet notice how jealously the rose protects its innermost beauties. Only towards the end of its life, does it open wide its portals so that its full beauty and splendor can be seen. Often, the rose will die before this final stage is reached. When this happens, then no one can catch a glimpse of its full, complete grandeur.

This is what happens in the majority of cases when a person wants some sort of a union with God. Although their first intentions are good, they often give up before their complete, full capabilities are utilized. They might taste the first sweet nectar of spiritual consolations and decide that there is no reason to continue the struggle towards a greater union with God. They might not even know about or care about the fact that it is quite possible to advance towards a closer union with God. So they settle for the least union which is just to have the soul in the state of grace.

I know numerous people, and I can imagine that there are a great many more, who settle for the least union with God. The sad part of this fixed or stationary attitude is that the soul can stay on this elementary stage of union with God for an entire lifetime. Although the person does love God, does receive the sacraments, does increase grace through prayer and the sacraments, the personal union with God remains a very impersonal (even cold) relationship. The person never fully knows or understands the God who dwells within his or her soul.

St. Teresa of Avila in her book INTERIOR CASTLE explains this very well. She describes the soul as being filled with many mansions and explains how a person enters each separate mansion. It is only in the innermost mansion, deep within the soul, where one finds the King and Lord. Until the person enters the last or seventh mansion, this person does not even know who the King is who dwells within this mansion. And as I said, this King will not reveal His true identity unless and until the person prepares his soul for this overpowering revelation.

The word "overpowering" is the key to why the King will not of Himself reveal His true identity. So great an experience would this "overpowering" be for a soul *not prepared* to receive this gift that the person would simply die of fright being totally unable to comprehend the meaning of such a revelation. Only by an enormous increase of sanctifying grace can such a revelation work the desired effect upon the soul; for God's true identity can be seen, known and understood only with oceans of grace.

Most people do not possess these "oceans of grace." They are very much lacking in this grace; even if they do possess sanctifying grace. The saddest part of such a lack of grace is that this lack is the person's own fault. God has this "ocean of grace" to give to everyone who needs it to increase union with Him; however, the majority of people do not even bother to make this grace available to themselves.

As I said, most people are content to live a very shallow spiritual life. Even men and women who say daily prayers, go to Mass and support their Churches, etc. do not live the type of a spiritual life which they could be living: daily climbing the ladder to closer union with God. They do keep away from mortal sin, which is, of course, commendable; however, they seldom if ever do extra penances, say extra prayers, do extra spiritual reading, practice extra acts of charity or visit the Church during the week to keep Christ company. I do not mean that they should neglect daily duties and responsibilities to follow a more active spiritual schedule but they are too involved in unnecessary material pursuits and distractions. For example, they will spend long hours watching T.V. programs and then be "too tired" to go to a worthwhile Bible class. They will go to Mass on Saturday night because they feel this is an obligation, but they will not say the Rosary every day because they feel this is not an obligation. They will gladly help a friend in need, whom they like, but refuse to help someone whom they dislike. They will make sure that they receive their "Easter Duty," but they will not be bothered by a few "white lies" or cheating on their income tax. They will make no attempts to overcome their weaknesses and bad habits because they will reason that they are a good person and do not need self-improvement.

They are indeed good because they keep their souls in the state of grace; however, many of these good people are very much lacking in basic virtues. They may speak unkindly about people, they hold grudges, they express sentiments of anger, hate, jealousy. In other words, they remain far more human than spiritual in their words, deeds and thoughts. For that reason, they fail to advance to closer union with God and, as I said, they can remain in this state of spiritual inactivity for a lifetime.

What a shame that is! I become truly upset to know that so many good people are simply not advancing up THE LADDER OF PERFECTION when they could be if only they would try. All they would have to do, in order to start the climb to a closer union with God is to take an honest look at their daily spiritual lives and to discover what they lack in the way of doing things for God with His grace. They have merely to come to the conclusion that they are far more human in their actions, deeds and thoughts than spiritual. Then they would have to find out how to include in the human part of their daily lives a true spiritual program. This would include acquiring, using and increasing virtues and graces, as well as overcoming faults and weaknesses.

The time to begin such a spiritual revisal is *now* not next week or next year. Precious time has already been lost. The decision to begin a true spiritual program may be difficult to make at first; and actually putting the program into action may seem impossible at first. I remember that when I began to include a spiritual program in my daily life, I found it almost impossible to complete one extra Our Father during an eight hour working day. However, with perseverance and the help of God's grace, you can begin to form a solid spiritual program of love for God and overcoming sins, faults and weaknesses.

Chapter 6

BECOMING "TOO RELIGIOUS"

I have discovered much to my surprise, that many lay people fail to live an active spiritual life or else fail to increase their spiritual activities because they are afraid of becoming what they call "too religious."

I hear remarks about this "too religious" way of thinking. Some people actually desire a more active spiritual life but, as they told me, if they start to pray more or go to Church more they will be called "too religious."

What exactly do they mean by this term "too religious"? They mean that they do not want to become a religious fanatic and I don't blame them.

Becoming a religious fanatic is a spiritual illness which is the direct opposite of spiritual apathy and in spite of the person's apparent enthusiasm about religion, this illness does more harm than good. I have seen this illness actually destroy families. I have also seen it place a person on the road to mental illness or keep him there.

So, a person must guard against falling into this illness of becoming "too religious" as well as falling into the illness of spiritual apathy. However, at the same time, a person must strive to increase holiness and union with God. This is not a contradictory statement.

There is a vast difference between becoming a religious fanatic (by becoming "too religious") and becoming a person who reaches a holy union with God. While a person, who is striving for holiness or sanctity does become more religious and begins to live a life which is Christ-centered, this way of life is not the life of a religious fanatic. Why? Because there is one basic or fundamental difference between holiness and becoming a fanatic. That is found in the difference between humility and pride.

A fanatic's whole approach to religion is based upon pride. This pride tells the fanatic that he (or she) is the greatest, most perfect person on earth. This pride makes the person look down on all others who are not doing what he is doing or living as he is living. This person wants to be noticed and praised for his many religious activities. This person wants to believe that no one on earth (or very few people) are as good and as holy as he is. This person will perform unbelievable acts of piety—and make sure that others find out about these acts.

For example: a religious fanatic will say ten Rosaries a day and then condemn others who can scarcely find the time for only one Rosary a day, as he (or she) brags about the fact that his ten Rosaries make him truly saintly. Or a religious fanatic, who manages to go to three Masses every morning, will have no sympathy for the overworked housewife and mother who cannot go to even one daily Mass because she also has to go to work eight hours a day.

I know of one such person, who was most fanatical, who tried to always outdo the devotions of others. I know of another such person who would question others about their personal relationships with God and then remark: "Well, I do the same thing!" Or "I think that way, too!" All the while this person wanted to appear equal or better than the one who was trying to live a hidden life of sanctity.

This is *not* the way to union with Christ!

As I have always stated, THE LADDER OF PERFECTION must be built upon a solid base of humility. There can be no spiritual advancement unless there is first the humility which is needed for spiritual advancement.

Outward spiritual activity does not always mean that a person is growing in holiness and grace. Outward spiritual activity could mean that a person is *not* growing in holiness and grace.

However, a well-planned program of spiritual activity, which is based upon a true, humble desire to seek a closer union with Christ, will lead a person into holiness and union with Christ.

So do not become frightened by the thoughts that if you seek a closer union with Christ that you will become "too religious." Do not think that the more you learn about your beautiful Catholic religion and the more you practice it, the more fanatical you will become. That is not true. You may become more enthusiastic as you discover the beauties of true holiness, but you will not become fanatical as long as you keep in mind that your spiritual program must be based upon humility. With humility and a healthy knowledge of your dependence upon God and His grace, there is no reason why you cannot daily grow in holiness and reach a closer union with God.

Chapter 7

EMOTIONS AND RELIGION

One of the worst types of religious faith is the one which emotions alone created. Many people base their whole religious experience only upon feelings of deep emotions. Many religious groups or sects or cults hold their followers because their teachings become a tight grip or trap upon the emotions of these followers. One well-known religion is a good example of that. They hold their believers in a trap of fear making them believe that they are the only ones, who ever lived or who will ever live, who will be saved. If the members of this sect leave, they would join the billions of condemned, so they are taught. Other religious groups can only "worship" God after a period of wild dances and songs.

Still others cannot worship God unless they have personal deep emotions which prove to them that God exists. Others (and many Catholics fall into this category) will not go to Church because they get "nothing" emotional out of living a good active spiritual life.

The youth who search for Christ and can see Him only as a "Super Star" or can draw near to Him only through loud music are relying upon an emotional experience to find their religion.

Even a group such as the Pentecostal Movement, has as the base of its religious acceptance a very deep personal emotional experience. Without the outward signs, such as the speaking in tongues and the so-called healings, a person finds religion to be very dull and meaningless.

Many Preachers, whom I have personally heard, attract followers and "believers" through what they proclaim as testimonies of healings. With loud words of deep emotion they proclaim religion to be merely one long, never-ending series of healings, which they, of course, are capable of performing—but more— which anyone can accomplish if they had the same faith in the "Mighty Healer, Christ."

While some good might come from what I call "Emotional Faith," as a whole, this type of faith is very shallow and can cause far more damage to a person's spiritual life than good. Why do I say that? Well, for one thing, when the emotions of excitement, enthusiasm, ambition and the "I am saved" type of religion disappear, the person is left in a worse spiritual condition than he or she was in before this type of an encounter with Christ.

Once the person is alone with himself or herself, away from the emotion-exciting events, there descends upon this person a feeling of aloneness which can lead to many disastrous spiritual reactions. I have only to think of someone I know who became very emotionally involved in the Pentecostal Movement. Her whole life and religion became caught up in the happenings of this group; so much so, that a great feeling of guilt crept over her if she missed one weekly meeting. As a result her life and especially her spiritual life began to suffer, until she had the courage (and by the way, the correct knowledge) to break away from the group. When she did, she found the spiritual peace and stability which are impossible to find in religious experiences which are based solely upon overemphasized emotional experiences.

The very first thing to remember about religion is that it is based upon *faith* not *emotions* and more often than not this faith has to be a blind faith.

For good reason, Christ said to the doubting Thomas: "Ah, but blessed are they who *have not* seen and yet have believed" (*John* 20:29).

Do not misunderstand. I am not saying that there are no emotions in religion. There are many emotions to be found when one is trying to live a more active spiritual life. There are emotions, such as pure, holy love for God, great joy when God sends a special gift or favor, deep spiritual turmoil when one is forced to pass through the dark night of the soul and so forth. What I am saying is that religion and the practice of religion *must not be based upon personal private emotions or upon moods.* If it is, then the moods and emotions decide what one is to believe and how active one must make his or her personal spiritual life. For example: if you feel "in the mood" to go to Mass, then you go. If, on the other hand, you are not "in the mood" to go to Mass, you stay home. Or, another example: if you think you will have a deep spiritual emotional awakening, such as happens when one witnesses a miracle, then you go to Mass. If you do not have this emotional feeling, then you stay home. Or, another example: if some teaching or doctrine of the Church does not appeal to you or interest you or excite your emotions, then you may feel free to cast aside such teachings or doctrines. Many Catholics refuse to go to Confession, although Confession is a doctrine of the Church, simply because Confession does not appeal to them. Or, if they feel that all they need as far as religion is concerned is a wild, emotional outburst of "I believe in Christ, I am saved" and then cast aside all the teachings and truths of God, then they have a very poor foundation for an active spiritual life or for true, pure union with God.

I can give another good example of the way people base their own religion upon personal emotions. This is a very common example and I, unfortunately, find this example in many Catholics' spiritual lives. Even practicing Catholics, ones who had a habit of never missing Mass or Confession or Communion, fall into this emotional bit about religion when they suffer a severe emotional crisis. If a loved one dies, for example, or if the person suffers an incurable illness, the person leaves God and the Church then blames God for the sorrows and crosses.

One can see here that such people based their religion only upon personal, private emotions. When days were happy and sunny, they gladly and faithfully practiced their religion. However, when the storm clouds of life came, the practice of their religion disappeared.

All such emotional encounters with God must be avoided. Faith and religion are built upon and around the truths of God, the teachings of Christ and of the Church. Religion then becomes a solid beam of light which shines brightly through all the storms and emotional crises of life. Religion must never fall into the pitfalls and traps of what is known as "doing your own thing," or believing only what you want to believe and treating God only as you wish to treat Him.

In other words, the foundation for a good spiritual life must be built upon what *God* wants you to do and what *God* wants you to believe. Instead of saying: "I will do what I want to do and believe only what I want to believe," you must say: "What does God want me to do and to believe?" You find the answer from the Church. That is the foundation of faith.

Chapter 8

LESS HUMAN, MORE SUPERNATURAL

As your climb towards union with God up THE LADDER OF PERFECTION continues, you will discover that more often than not the climb brings many unexpected crosses and sufferings. Many people, as soon as they discover this truth, begin to lose interest in a more complete union with God and give up. Others think that they are doing "something wrong" and become very upset about this situation. However, the truth of the matter is that you must remember such crosses and sufferings are part of the climb and belong within the person's spiritual life.

The very fact that purification of the soul can only be accomplished through the fires of inner battles, tells you that there is nothing wrong with the climb when the sufferings and battles are there. The fact is, the encounters with such conflicts should be a sign of encouragement. It means that you are proceeding in the right direction towards a closer union with God.

Of course it is not easy to accept this fact nor to continue when the going gets rough. That is where the help of God's graces come in. You will constantly, without letup, need the supernatural help of God's supernatural graces. Why? Because what you are attempting to do by climbing THE LADDER OF PERFECTION becomes a supernatural thing to do!

Right at the beginning of the climb, you must clearly understand that what you desire to do, by trying to reach a closer union with God, is not a *human* but a *supernatural* endeavor. That little bit of understanding and knowledge will save you many moments of torment and anxiety. To gain holiness, which is to gain virtue, which is to overcome weaknesses, faults and sins, is to go against human nature!

If a person is allowed to give in to all human desires, demands and whims, that person automatically becomes a selfish, sinful human being. The seven capital sins or vices of human nature are deeply embedded within each and every one of us. Theologians tell us that these human "flaws" are ready and able to surface at any time and to enslave us. A closer look at these seven natural enemies of goodness and virtue show quite clearly that such is more than true. They are: *pride,* which is the base for almost all sins including, disobedience to the laws of God and the Church. *Covetousness,* which is desires for material goods. Within covetousness you will clearly see such sins as stealing, lying, cheating, deceiving, murder, greed, selfishness, etc. Then there is *lust* which produces a vast assortment of sins of the flesh. Next there is *anger* which in itself is a springboard for numerous sins of violence, revenge, hate, profanity, malicious gossip and destroying the property of others. Then there are *envy* and *gluttony* which brings out the worst of ourselves when allowed to dominate our lives. Finally, there is *sloth* which if allowed to run our lives makes a human being lazy, unwilling to carry out the duties and responsibilities of daily life and unable to live an active spiritual life giving to God the love and worship which He has a right to claim.

Human nature demands that each and everyone of us follow the tainted paths created by these seven capital sins. On the other hand, holiness demands that we turn away from such paths and fight the temptations to be an entirely *human* person devoid of God's grace. So there has to constantly be the struggle between temptations and God's grace. There has to constantly be a turning away from the human side of man to the supernatural side. Living an active spiritual life, trying to have a closer union with God, climbing THE LADDER OF PERFECTION becomes then, a *supernatural* task which carries a person above and beyond human nature and human desires.

A purely *worldly human* person cannot see any reasons for giving up pet sins so that he or she can please God. Such a person lives only by the standards set by the demands of a very weak, selfish human nature. On the other hand, living an active spiritual life becomes taking upon oneself the awesome obligations of living a Christ-centered life. Then one's goal becomes *supernatural* and not *human*, requiring a supernatural outlook on life and daily living.

Make no mistake about it, reaching a closer union with God means tearing one's own self away from being what weak human nature wants one to be. As I said, reaching a closer union with God means to become less human in ways and actions and more supernatural.

How could such be possible—to become less human and more supernatural? The answer is, once again, grace: the supernatural gift of sanctifying grace. When Christ told us to be as perfect as His heavenly Father is, Christ knew that weak human beings could never accomplish such a feat. However, Christ also knew that with the help of supernatural grace man could accomplish supernatural deeds and become as perfect as His heavenly Father (*Matt.* 5:48). It is within this perfection, or the attempts to reach this perfection, where human, natural desires fade away and become supernatural, Christ-like desires which are expressed in deeds and actions which deserve supernatural rewards called merits.

So, when you are confronted with the different degrees of sufferings and battles within your spiritual life, remember that you are dealing with a *supernatural desire for holiness*. This desire rises you above and beyond purely human, materialistic desires and goals. That being the case, you must view all your words, thoughts, deeds and desires in a different way or light. Your very first thought should be: how can I please God?

It is this part of trying to please God every moment of every day which holds the secret of sanctity.

Theologians teach us that if we accept God's will every moment of every day, we cannot but help but be a saint. That is logical because if we do accept everything in our lives as God's holy will, we would automatically do nothing to displease Him. We would faithfully fulfill all the duties and obligations of our state of life. We would have a well-formed daily spiritual program. We would accept and believe all which Holy Mother Church teaches. We would increase grace within our souls by the means of prayer and the sacraments. We would do all that is possible for us to do to extend to others charity and brotherly-love, etc. In other words, we would live a more active, a most pure spiritual life and use grace to keep us on the paths to union with God.

Know also that when you select to live a more active spiritual life so that you can climb THE LADDER OF PERFECTION to a closer union with God, you chose to accept all the commitment implies. That "all" includes the sufferings of the climb as well as the consolations; and there will be far more crosses than consolations. Why? Because Christ chose the cross as the means of our salvation and He has asked His followers to also choose and carry a cross: "If anyone wishes to come after me, let him deny himself and take up his cross and follow me" (*Matt.* 16:24).

In these words you can clearly see the difference between being *human* with human desires and being *supernatural* with supernatural desires. No purely human person would actually want to carry crosses. However, on the other hand, no purely human person would want to follow Christ.

If you truly want to follow Christ up THE LADDER OF PER-FECTION, you must expect to find many heavy crosses along the way. But do not allow yourself to become dispirited. Also along this same way, you will find all the supernatural help you will need by and through grace so that your supernatural goal of union with God can be accomplished.

Chapter 9

HOW FREE WILL WORKS

Before you can start to climb towards a closer union with God, you must clearly understand the way your own free will operates. Otherwise you will run into difficult problems especially when you realize that for every step you take up THE LADDER OF PERFECTION there has to be some sort of a choice made such as a choice between using or not using a certain grace. More often than not, such a choice will bring a conflict or a spiritual battle. Often the battles become so severe that you may find yourself crying out: "Why, oh, why do I always have to be tempted not to do the good deed I want to do?" "Why must I always struggle so hard to be the kind of a person I want to be?"

If you do not understand what is happening to your spiritual life at such times you may very well just give up and forget about your goal of obtaining a closer union with God. If you understand how your own free will acts, then you will save yourself a lot of personal doubts, fears and agonies and you will be less tempted to give up.

First of all, what exactly is free will? Free will exists within the souls of men and women. It became a pure gift from God to us when He created men and women. God bestows upon us an immortal soul. Within this soul, God places an intellect and a free will so that we can know God, can know the difference between right and wrong, good and evil and can freely choose good or evil, virtue or sin. With these two gifts comes our conscience which guides our free will and also responsibility for the deeds and actions resulting from the use of free will.

The best way to understand your own free will is to realize

that a flower or a tree has no free will. They cannot change the rules or laws of nature which govern their existence. They grow as nature demands. You, on the other hand, can control your own deeds and actions and even your own salvation. If you save your soul, that will be done by an act of faith and love on your part which came from your free will. You freely chose to follow the ways and teachings of God. Why do I say that this is your free will acting? Because you have a choice. You could have chosen *not* to follow God and His teachings. You could have chosen the opposite paths which lead to eternal sufferings. Because it is within your own power to make such a choice, that means you have the freedom to do so: a freedom which God does not and cannot interfere with. God can teach, through His Church. He can offer Himself to you in the Sacrament of the Eucharist. He can send you oceans of grace, and so forth; however, the final decision is up to you and your free will. You can listen to His Church or not listen. You can believe the truths of God or not believe. You can follow Christ or not follow Him. You can use grace or not use it. The choice is always there and it is within your power of free will to make.

That is why, it cannot be truthfully said that God *sends* a person to hell. God *sends* no one to hell. The person, who is unfortunately cast into hell, ends up there because he freely chose a life of sin and evil. He wanted to live without God and grace while on earth so after death God gives him what the foolish man wants: to live for all eternity without God, His love and His grace. The person's free choice sent him to hell, not God.

Now, if God gave to man this gift of free will, then free will had to be put into use. So there has to constantly be two different, diverse ways or paths to follow which enable man to use his free will such as: temptation or grace, goodness or evil, material ways or spiritual ways, virtue or sin, etc. If there existed only one way, for example only goodness, grace and virtue, that one way would allow no choice and thus it would destroy man's free will.

You might bring forth an argument here and say, "Well, would not that be best for all men? Why does there have to be a free will that could turn a man away from God and place him into the heart of hell?"

It is true that free will can turn a man away from God and can lead him to hell; however, free will was never meant to do that. It would be more correct to say that free will when *misused* can lead a man to hell, rather than to say that free will can *be used* to do that. When free will is properly used, along with grace, it is meant to guide a man to the heights of sanctity and union with God. Free will can and does make a man a child of God's *by his own choice!* That is very important: by his own choice. In that case, this choice not only becomes a free one on the part of man but it also becomes a choice of love. It is in reality the one and only way for man to love God and to fully respond to His love for man. Without free will, no one could really love God as He so desires them to love Him or act as He commands them to act.

Consider, if you will, these commandments from Christ: "If anyone wishes to come after me, let him deny himself, and take up his cross and follow me. For he who would save his life will lose it; but he who loses his life for my sake will find it" (*Matt.* 16:24-25).

And this: "What will a man give in exchange for his soul?" (*Matt.* 16:26). Also: "And when you stand up to pray, forgive whatever you have against anyone, that your Father in heaven may also forgive you your offenses" (*Mark* 11:25). Also, "And everyone who hears these my words and does not act upon them shall be likened to a foolish man who built his house on sand" (*Matt.* 7:26). Finally: "Therefore, all that you wish men to do to you, even so do you also to them" (*Matt.* 7:12).

In each utterance, you can clearly see the fact that man's free will makes the fulfillment of these commands possible. You will also notice upon closer examination that the motivating power behind the accomplishment of such noble deeds is love, a love which must first be *freely* given so that it can be expressed in following Christ's commands. Within each command there is a choice. Man can do one thing or the other. There is no force put upon man by God to follow His holy ways or to love Him.

God asks man: "Will you please do this because you love me?" And man uses free will to answer: "I will" or "I will not."

If man could not of himself answer, "I will," God could never ask: "Will you do this because you love me?" In that case, man could only say to God: "I will follow your ways *not* because I love you but because you have forced me to follow you as my Lord and Master. I have no choice but to follow you." So, herein you see the necessity of free will. It is absolutely needed not only to say to God that you love Him but as the *only way* that love can be expressed by means of fulfilling the commands of God.

This also explains why there has to be grace. It can almost be said that grace *allows* man to have the free will which allows him to tell God that he loves Him and His ways. Without grace, man could not possess nor even use free will to follow God's ways. Human nature, without grace, becomes merely natural nature. A man's natural nature leads him to natural fulfillment of human desires. Consequently, man would then seek to satisfy any and all natural desires or needs anyway he could.

But with grace, man rises above the natural and possesses supernatural desires and goals. So, if God had to give to man his free will, then God also had to give to man supernatural grace to protect that free will.

It is grace which makes even an infant in possession of free will. A baptized infant or child (or retarded person) cannot make an act of love for God nor choose His ways. But, on the other hand, he or she is not forced to follow God by a withdrawal of free will. Grace and free will, must of necessity go together. Because someone has no ability to put into use free will that does not mean that the person lacks this gift. When a person has not been able to put into action free will, it is grace which becomes the light that guides the person to salvation. As long as grace is present, God knows that free will could have been used by the person to follow and love Him and His ways.

Now someone could say: "Well, if an infant has grace and goes to heaven without putting into action free will, which could be misused, then would it not be best for all of us to die before we reach the age of reason?"

That, of course, would be ludicrous, to say the least. God created us for a purpose. We have a job to do for God. First of all men and women must mature, marry and reproduce other children of God if this is their state of life.

The first requirement of God for Adam and Eve, after the fall, was to bring forth sons and daughters. To have everyone die before they reached the age of reason would be to stop the human race.

Also, without free will, no one could gain any merits. Merits are the eternal rewards given for good deeds, prayers, etc. Only with free will can merits be made available to us because there has to be a free choice made to gain a merit. A free choice means that a person must choose the good over the bad, the virtue and not the sin. That is why no one can gain one single merit after death. Not in heaven, not in purgatory nor in hell can merits be gained. The time for gaining them has passed. Why? Because in heaven, hell or purgatory there is no choice between good or evil, virtue or sin. The fate of the soul has already been determined.

A soul in hell is punished for sins already committed. A soul in purgatory, likewise. A soul in heaven is rewarded for good deeds already done. No one can sin in hell or in purgatory. No one can merit in heaven because all three states of existence offer no choice. There is no temptation in hell or purgatory and no good deeds to be performed in heaven. There is only a punishment or a reward or a delay in the cleansing fires of purgatory.

Earth is the place to gain merits. However, how could anyone gain merits if there was no free will? Merits come from grace in action and free will is needed so that grace can act.

No one could ever climb THE LADDER OF PERFECTION to a closer union with God unless he or she has the free will to make such a choice. No one could merit a greater degree of holiness or heavenly reward unless he or she freely desires to seek such and to strive for an increase in grace. Unless we use our free choice to do a good deed, there can be no merit gained for such a deed done. A flower is not rewarded because it grows and looks beautiful. It merely does what it is supposed to do. It has no freedom to be something else. It has to be a flower. It has to grow and bloom. It cannot suddenly develop wings because it wants to fly like a bird. It cannot change and become something it is not. Such being the case, it cannot expect to be rewarded for being what it was created to be because it has no free will to make a choice and be something other than a flower.

On the other hand, man can expect a reward (or merit a reward) for a good deed done or a cross well-carried because he *has a choice*. He does not have to do the good deed nor carry a cross well. He has the freedom to make the choice and the ability to carry out what he has decided to do.

So, understand how free will is needed and used when you attempt to climb THE LADDER OF PERFECTION. Then you will also understand why so many crosses come your way as you struggle up each rung. As soon as you begin to use free will to desire virtue and holiness, you will automatically bump into crosses, conflicts and burdens because the opposites of virtue and holiness will be there to try to pull you away from the choice you made. But also remember that it is your ability to *choose* which makes the climb possible and meritorious. Without the opposites, the temptations, the evil desires, etc., there would be no reason to even begin the climb. You might then be at the top, but without merits. Also remember that the temptations, the sins, evil thoughts and so forth are within your own control. Someone once told me that the devil had control of his mind and there was nothing he could do about it. He said to me: "Somehow, some way the devil got into my brain."

I replied: "The devil did not get into your brain nor does he have control over your mind. You can very well control your own mind and you have the free will to do just that."

He said that was impossible because he was helpless, at the mercy of the devil. I replied: "It is possible with grace. Grace helps you rise above the sinful desires of human nature. Use grace and your free will to win your spiritual battles. Remember, you are not alone upon the battlefields. If the devil and his temptations are on one side of you, know that God and grace are on the other side. You can make a choice. It is up to you."

Chapter 10

AWARENESS

The whole process of spiritual advancement up THE LADDER OF PERFECTION consists of a long series of what I call awareness. To become aware of how much God loves you, how good He is to you, how many blessings He has bestowed upon you, how many weaknesses you possess and so forth, is to discover the next step up this ladder. All such awakenings or realizations form the nucleus of a good, active spiritual life. Awareness becomes the center post or part around which there revolves constant spiritual activity. Without such awareness, you could never know what has to be done to improve your spiritual life. Many sins and even virtues lie dormant, unnoticed, until an awareness of them brings them into view of the eyes of the soul and focuses the mind upon them.

For example: someone wrote to me and said that he had suddenly discovered that he had spiritual pride. He was quite upset because of his discovery. He never saw this weakness before; however, with the help of God's grace, he realized that this barrier did exist in His union with God. I wrote to him these following words: ". . . if spiritual pride has entered the picture, it is not that you did not have this pride before. This pride was with you all the time, but you never really noticed its presence. However, this enlightenment should cause you joy not anxiety, relief not worry. Suddenly, you are able to see your enemy whereas before this enemy was hidden and camouflaged. Now that it can be seen, something can be done to remove this thorn from your spiritual life."

Now, what exactly is spiritual awareness, how does one obtain it and what does one do with it once this form of self-knowledge becomes more and more evident in the quest for sanctity?

An explanation of spiritual awareness can be more readily understood when material awareness is brought into the picture. How often has someone explained something to you that went "over your head"? But later on, when certain events happened or more information was given, you suddenly remarked: "Ah, now I see! Now I understand!" Suddenly you had an awareness of the situation. You were enlightened, you came to realize what the situation was all about. You walked out of the darkness into the light and your mind, heart and eyes were opened to the truth of the event. You saw, you knew, you understood. That is becoming aware of something. Sometimes this awareness does not come. People all over the world often say: ". . .well, I knew nothing about it. I was not aware of the facts. If only I had known, I could have done something about it."

In the spiritual life, awareness acts in exactly the same way. In order for a person to advance towards closer union with God, the person must be fully and completely aware of what hinders this advancement or what causes it to surge forward. Without this knowledge and enlightenment and understanding, there can be no spiritual advancement. A person will spend a whole lifetime living a life of spiritual ignorance and inactivity unless he or she becomes aware of the fact that God expects much more than a prayer now and then or a short visit to a Church.

So, the very first thing which must be done if you want a closer union with God, is to understand what spiritual activity is all about and how this activity centers or revolves around spiritual awareness.

As with material-related awareness, spiritual awareness comes in various degrees. A person *does not* suddenly experience total awareness of union with God and then suddenly discovers that he or she is at the top of THE LADDER OF PERFECTION. Why? Because each step must be taken up the ladder one at a time and each step upward can be taken only after there is a complete awareness of why the ascent must continue. Many, many people begin the climb toward perfection, but never continue simply because somewhere along the way they lost this awareness, and saw no reason to continue the struggle. Others thought that they had reached the top of the ladder, yet they soon discovered that they had not because a serious fault or sin, which they had never been aware of before, raised its ugly head and shattered their complacency. Believe me when I say that there is no easy short cut up THE LADDER OF PERFECTION. It is simply impossible to fly up this ladder in a short time.

One thing which I objected to, when the Pentecostal or prayer group meetings became a fad during the late 60's and 70's, was the way the members started to literally "fly" up the ladder without proper preparation or guidance. Most claimed "instant" holiness or union with God for themselves yet they were not even sure what union with God was. Because they had been through some sort of a spiritual experience, they not only viewed this as the "top" or ultimate of spirituality, they went as far as to loudly declare that all who did not go through this same experience were far from union with God. As a result, many of these Catholics left the Church stating that they no longer had any need for such things as the Mass or the Eucharist or Confession. On the other hand, most people who did believe that they had flown up the ladder, often suffered a severe relapse when a hidden sin or fault suddenly surfaced and caused much havoc to a "perfect" union with God. Also, many of those who claimed "instant" union with God, after attending only one or two such meetings, lacked the knowledge which is a must if one is to be completely aware of what union with God is all about. Several of these people who went through an experience of "at last finding God" attempted to tell me that they were baptized and I was not.

All such problems could be avoided if a person, who honestly seeks a closer union with God, understands the spiritual process or workings of awareness.

For example: if a person, who did indeed experience a genuine spiritual awakening during a special prayer meeting understood what happened, that person would have known that suddenly he or she was aware of the fact that God loved him or her. The

love was always there, but the person had not been aware of
it. To become aware of God's love for you is just one step and
only one step up THE LADDER OF PERFECTION. To regard
this one awareness as the whole or as a complete union with
God is to make a very serious mistake. This first step toward
union with God becomes only the beginning of that union and
not the beginning and end all wrapped up in one neat package.
It simply is not that easy to reach a high degree of holiness or
sanctity. One of two or even three soul-shaking experiences do
not elevate the soul to perfect union with God.

Why? First of all, the Holy Spirit can reveal His presence
and His gifts to the soul only to the *degree that the* person prepares his soul for such; so that, this preparation will allow the
Spirit freedom to act and bestow upon the person His precious
gifts. This preparation is of upmost importance and it takes time:
a long time, often a whole lifetime.

How can this preparation be done? The answer: through
spiritual awareness and struggles. I place the awareness before
the battles because without this awareness, a person will not
know why the battles are necessary.

Now, how does a person cultivate spiritual awareness? As with
all aspects of the spiritual life, awareness comes through the
channels of grace. One cannot know God, His love, His ways,
etc. without the help of God's grace. That is why people, who
are careless about their own spiritual lives, who live away from
the sacraments and grace, always seem to think so highly of
themselves. Common talk among such a group or groups
revolves around their own conception of their own goodness. You
are apt to hear remarks from these people such as: "I'm a good
person. I don't do anything wrong, why do I have to go to Mass
or to Confession?" Such people have lost not only their sense
of the true values of life, but also their awareness of the true
condition of their own spiritual lives. As I said, awareness tells
a person what is wrong with or lacking in his or her spiritual
life as well as what God's love is all about. People who find
nothing wrong with their own personal relationship with God
have not as yet come to the awareness that there are many things

wrong with or out of place in this relationship. People who say they "never sin" or are "perfect" fail to realize that to "never sin" or to be "perfect" without first climbing THE LADDER OF PERFECTION is in itself a serious spiritual problem.

Now, let me go back to the very beginning of spiritual awareness to show how it is used to improve your own personal relationship with God. Say that you are not sure if you have or do not have spiritual awareness, then what happens? First of all, if you had this awareness you would know it without anyone telling you. For example: you, no doubt, have read a spiritual book or a booklet at one time or another. The first time you read it the words meant little or nothing at all to you and you could not apply them to improve your own spiritual life. But months or even a year later, you reread the book or booklet and suddenly you saw, in the words, meaning and depths which you did not see the first time you read them. You, no doubt, remarked in such a case: "These words are just for me. They were written with me in mind." Then you did apply them to your own daily spiritual program. What happened was that suddenly, when you read the words the second time, you became aware of their true meaning. Another example: you had a very bad habit for a long time. It was part of your human nature. You always said about this bad habit: "Well, that is the way I am and there is nothing I can do about it." Then you wanted to try and overcome this habit for you reasoned, correctly, that it interfered with your relationship with God. Suddenly the bad habit was not just "part of human nature," it was a sin which had to be cast aside. Another example: you had always been told that God loved you with a pure, infinite love; however, such love seemed far away and unreal. The fact is you always thought of God as "someone" way out in space, watching the whole world and not even noticing you. Then suddenly, one day after you received Holy Communion, this "someone" out in space became for you a true Father who loved you very dearly, so much so, that He made His love known to you in the depths of your heart. You were aware of God's love for you and His personal concern about you.

Now, where did all this awareness come from? What had happened between the time you were not aware of something like the examples I gave and the time when you were aware of this something? Did you do anything to bring about this awareness? Can you bring about such types of awareness in the future?

The answer to the last two questions is yes. Yes, you did do something to bring about this awareness. Yes, you can do something to bring about such types of awareness in the future. The fact is, what you do in the future concerning awareness determines your progress up THE LADDER OF PERFECTION.

What did you do? You opened the channels of grace and allowed this grace to bring to you spiritual awareness. How did you do that? Through prayer and the sacraments.

The more you pray, the more often you receive the sacraments, the more you increase grace within your soul. The more this grace is increased, the more you will become aware of what hinders or favors your union with God.

Chapter 11

PRIDE: THE DOWNFALL
OF THE SPIRITUAL LIFE

There is a saying in the spiritual life which goes something like this: many true mystics may not save their souls and are lost for all eternity. That sounds difficult to believe. A true mystic is a person who had received extraordinary gifts and graces from God. A true mystic loved God and served Him at one time. How then could such a person ever lose his or her soul? The answer is pride. Pride turns God's gifts and graces into "my" gifts and graces. The mystics, who may have lost their souls, allowed pride to tell them how great they were instead of allowing humility to tell them how great God is.

Now, if a true mystic can actually lose his or her soul, you might well wonder what chance do you have to, not only save your soul, but to actually climb THE LADDER OF PERFECTION to a close union with God. That depends on many things, especially the understanding and conquering of pride.

Most people fail to understand pride and what harm it does to their spiritual lives. Very few people will admit that a deep hidden pride prevents their spiritual advancement or destroys the spiritual merits of their good deeds. Pride, at its worst, is so much a part of a weak human nature that it alone motivates all the person's deeds and actions good and bad; yet at the same time, it disguises itself behind a mask of self-righteousness. At its best (if you can say that pride has a best side), pride gives to a person a feeling of security in his own powers making the person forget that what talents and graces and powers he does possess were given to him by God.

Pride always was and always will be the greatest enemy of the spiritual life. There is a saying that most sins stem from pride. That is true. Pride makes a person turn away from God, His ways, His teachings, His truths. This turning away is sin. Because of pride, great and small sins develop from the first tiny sins against faith to the greatest sins against the Commandments of God and of the Church.

Pride belongs in the group known as the seven capital sins. The fact is, it is listed as the first of the seven. The capital sins are the ones to which almost every other sin can be traced. They are: 1. Pride 2. Covetousness or desires for temporal goods. 3. Lust 4. Anger 5. Gluttony 6. Envy 7. Sloth (or laziness).

So before anyone can improve his or her spiritual life, pride, the first of the seven capital sins, has to be understood and conquered because pride becomes the foundation for numerous sins and faults which prevent or interfere with spiritual advancement.

First of all, when I speak of pride I am not speaking of the pride used in the expression "I am so proud of you." Being proud of someone, such as the parents' pride when their son or daughter graduates from college or is given a high honor, is not the sin of pride. Actually such a feeling or emotion is not pride at all. It is more a feeling of satisfaction, joy and happiness. When a parent says to his child: "I am so proud of you at this moment," the parent is really saying: "You have caused me feelings of great joy, happiness and satisfaction." It is no sin to have such feelings of joy and happiness when someone you love, receives an honor or does a job well. You can certainly feel happy and satisfied when someone you love achieves a certain goal or aim. It is no sin even when you, yourself, reach a certain goal and this accomplishment brings to you immense joy and satisfaction.

The sin of pride which prevents spiritual advancement has nothing to do with a sincere joy found when a certain goal is reached. Pride in itself is not filled with joy or happiness. It usually is the cause of a person's deepest personal misery and discontentment. A proud person is never a peaceful, happy person because pride keeps the person from a union with God who is the source of true joy, peace and happiness. A proud person, who has a high esteem of or a high regard for himself, has to battle constantly whoever or whatever reminds him that he is not really as great as he thinks he is. When someone says to such a person: "Oh, Joe, you made a mistake," Joe's instant reaction is one of battle as he quickly replies: "Who, me, make a mistake! Never! Someone else made the mistake, not me." And because a proud person will never admit that he has faults, he must constantly find other people or circumstances upon which he can place the blame for his own mistakes and wrongdoings.

One of the most difficult things for a human being to do is to see and admit his or her own faults and shortcomings. How perfect we imagine ourselves to be! How shocked we become when our mistakes are exposed! How easy it is for us to see the faults and mistakes of others and to exclaim: "I would never do such a thing!"

Where did such a pride come from in the first place? It came from the Garden of Eden when the first man and woman used pride to say to God: "I will not obey!" Pride then became part of the weaknesses of human nature which resulted from our first parents' fall from grace. Grace can be restored to the soul of man, however, the weaknesses of human nature remain. Two of these weaknesses, pride and self-love or selfishness, are so much a part of human nature that most people do not consider them weaknesses at all. They tend to think of them merely as part of themselves. They usually say: "Well, this is the way I am and there is nothing I can do about it."

But that is not true. There is a great deal which can be done about pride and selfishness and *must be done* if a person is to live a more active spiritual life.

What can be done to correct these weaknesses of human nature? The very first step to take is to view your own human pride through the eyes of God. Compare your inner self to God's pure, perfect self and not to other human beings. The main reason why people cannot see their own pride and other faults and weaknesses is that they are too quick to see the faults and weaknesses of others and to use their neighbor's faults and weaknesses as their standard of judgement or criterion. When a person does that, it is very easy to see oneself as being most righteous and even holy. More than one fallen-away Catholic has told me that he or she will not go to Church because only hypocrites go to Church. Such fallen-aways know "all about" the "sins" of these hypocrites and feel that they would "never do such terrible things." If such fallen-aways looked towards God instead of their neighbors, they would soon discover that they have no right to so judge their neighbors or to use their misdeeds, (if the neighbors do indeed commit all those sins) as an excuse to justify their own lack of faith and their own failure to fulfill their religious duties and obligations.

Christ very clearly said: "Do not judge that you may not be judged. For with what judgement you judge, you shall be judged; and with what measure you measured, it shall be measured to you. But why do you see the speck in your brother's eye and yet cannot consider the beam in your own eye?" (*Matt.* 7:1-4). Christ goes on to tell us who the real hypocrites are: "How can you say to your brother, 'Let me cast out the speck from your eye;' and behold, there is a beam in your own eye? You hypocrites! First cast out the beam from your own eye and then you will see clearly to cast out the speck from your brother's eye" (*Matt.* 7:5-6).

With these teachings of Christ's, a person can see the way to true union with God. He or she must start the quest for this union using God and His teachings (not a neighbor) as a base upon which will rest the self-judgement of what holiness and sanctity are all about and how to obtain such holiness.

However, before anyone can change the source of his own spiritual evaluation from his neighbor's "sins" to God's teaching, pride must be replaced by a true humility.

Only a humble person can see the perfection and greatness of God. Only a humble person can kneel before God and ask for His help in overcoming sins, weaknesses and faults; because, only when pride is cast aside will the door open to expose a person's sins, faults and weakness. Such exposure is a very necessary thing in one's quest for holiness and union with God.

Although, it is true that God dwells within the souls of all who are in the state of grace, it is also true that God gives to a person the realization of His presence *only to the degree of the person's attempts to bring about such a realization.* God does not lightly bestow the grace of understanding His presence upon everyone. Why? Well, for one reason, unless a person overcomes his sins, faults and weaknesses, the light of understanding cannot fill his soul because such sins, faults and weaknesses take the place where this light of understanding should be. In other words, as Saint Theresa tells us in her beautiful book, INTERIOR CAS-TLE, the Master or King lives deep within the soul. However, before a person can reach Him and share the fruits of His mag-nificent peace and joy the person must wade through dark, dan-gerous waters filled with all sorts of distractions. The more a soul is distracted away from the divine Guest dwelling therein the less the soul will understand who it is who dwells within its depths.

The greatest distraction is pride. Pride focuses the soul's atten-tion upon self and away from God who dwells within the soul. When the soul sees only itself, this soul cannot understand Divine Indwelling, and cannot have the union with God which God so desires to share with the person.

Pride also brings forth numerous feelings of self-pity, desires for material possessions, rebellion against God's laws, rebellion against the teachings of the Church and so forth. All such exam-ples of pride keep the person away from a precious union with God who may be deep within the soul but completely ignored and unrecognized. And if the Divine Guest remains ignored and unrecognized for a period of time, usually mortal sin comes to destroy the grace which is necessary for Divine Indwelling.

The strangest thing about pride is that even though it *silently* leads a person into all sorts of rebellion against God, His laws, His rules and His Church, it loudly reveals a great deal about the person who does the rebelling. It is said that when a severe critic of the Catholic religion (usually a fallen-away Catholic) loudly condemns Holy Mother Church or a Catholic teaching, the person reveals more about himself than the subject he is discussing. Such dissension has a way of focusing more attention upon the speaker, than upon the subject spoken of or written about. It is impossible to separate a person's inner conflicts from his outspoken attacks against Holy Mother Church. His attacks quickly reveal a problem which he tries to hide behind these attacks. Whenever I am confronted by a Catholic who severely criticizes the Catholic Church and her teachings, I will ask the person which rule or teaching he or she does not want to accept. The person usually is startled by such a question; however, I keep asking questions until the person admits that he or she does have a serious problem with one of the teachings or rules which he or she refuses to accept or believe.

Only pride leads a person into such a tragic situation. All such people make the very same serious mistake concerning themselves and the Church. They turn around and *blame the Church* for their own spiritual neglects and failures instead of blaming themselves; and then they allow a very deep pride to tell them that they are correct and the Church is wrong. Anyone who desires to climb THE LADDER OF PERFECTION cannot allow pride to force them to make this same mistake. To be "perfect as your heavenly Father is perfect" is to acquire a very deep humility to replace the pride which causes a person to rebell against God, His laws, His teachings and His Church.

Holy Scripture tells very clearly that such is exactly what God expects us to do: "Is it my will that a sinner should die, saith the Lord God, and not that he should be converted from his ways and live? But if the just man turns himself away from his justice, and does iniquity according to all the abominations which the wicked man uses to work, shall he live? All his justices which he has done shall not be remembered. In his sins which he has committed, in them he shall die. And you have said: 'the way of the Lord is not right.' Hear Ye, therefore, O, house of Israel! Is it my way that is not right; or are not rather your ways perverse? For when the just turns himself away from his justice and sins, he shall die therein" (*Ezechiel* 18:23-29).

Now read these words which explain the great difference between a proud and a humble person: "But if the wicked do penance for all his sins which he has committed, and keeps all my commandments, and does judgement and justice, living he shall live and shall not die (lose God's grace). I will not remember all his iniquities that he has done. In his justice which he has wrought, he shall live. And when the wicked turns himself away from his wickedness, which he has wrought and does judgement and justice, he shall save his soul and live. For I desire not the death of him who dies, says the Lord God. Return and live" (*Ezechiel* 18:21, 22 and 27-32).

Psalm 24 (25) tells us: "Good and upright is the Lord, thus He shows sinners the way, He guides the humble to justice, he teaches the humble his way. All the paths of the Lord are kindness and constancy toward those who keep his covenant and his decrees."

The ways, teachings and decrees of the Lord are taught to us by Holy Mother Church. Before a person can truthfully say, "I am doing the will of God," the person must ask: "What does God want me to do and to believe?" Holy Mother Church tells us and we must be humble enough to listen, to accept, to believe and to follow her teachings. Thus, humility is the beginning of the destruction of pride.

Chapter 12

WHAT IS THE WILL OF THE FATHER?

In the gospel of St. Matthew, Chapter 7, verse 21 to 23, Christ makes some very startling and astonishing statements. He declares: "Not everyone who says to me, 'Lord, Lord' shall enter the kingdom of heaven; but he who does the will of my Father in heaven shall enter the kingdom of heaven. Many will say to me in that day: 'Lord, Lord,' did we not prophesy in thy name and work many miracles in thy name? And then I will declare to them: I never knew you. Depart from me, you workers of iniquity."

Here Christ is teaching us a most profound truth. Many people who use His holy name, who seem to work for Him, and who even work miracles in His name may not be saved! Why is that so? Well, first of all, salvation is not won merely by sensational deeds, acts or even gifts; nor by the assumption that because one seemingly has a gift of this type, one is automatically saved. Also, salvation is not won by people who fail to live a Christian, a holy life as well as a sensational life. They failed to do the holy will of the Father in heaven.

Such a statement sounds a bit paradoxical; however, it is not. It may seem that to prophesy in Christ's name and to work many miracles in His name is doing the holy will of the Father in heaven, but that is not always true. Many false prophets do exist. Many people seem to have great gifts from God, yet they are not living a Christ-like, holy life. Many people truly want to be saved. They believe in heaven, hell and purgatory. They scream for help, calling "Lord, Lord" whenever they are in danger, especially if they are in danger of death. However, in spite

51

of that, they live a life far away from the Church, the sacraments and God's grace. Many people leave the Church and her spiritual protection to find "God's paths" and end up destroying the faith which teaches them how to enter God's kingdom of heaven. They refuse to do God's will.

To do God's will. What does it mean to do God's holy will? Well, read more of Saint Matthew's Gospel, Chapter 7, verse 24-27 and you will find the summary of what it means to do God's holy will: "Everyone therefore who hears these my words and acts upon them shall be likened to a wise man who built his house on rock...and everyone who hears these my words and does not act upon them, shall be likened to a foolish man who built his house on sand." We also find God's will for us in the teachings of Holy Mother Church.

In other words, doing the will of God is to follow the teachings of Christ and the teachings of the Church. Why also the Church? Because Christ gave us the Church to teach us what His truths are: "All power in heaven and on earth has been given to me. Go, therefore, and make disciples of all nations, baptizing them in the name of the Father, and of the Son and of the Holy Spirit, teaching them to observe all that I have commanded you; and behold, I am with you all days, even unto the consummation of the world" (*Matt.* 28:18-20). Whom is He talking to, whom does Christ say "go" to? The answer is found in these words: "I say to you, thou art Peter, and upon this rock, I will build my Church, and the gates of hell shall not prevail against it. And I will give thee the keys of the kingdom of heaven, and whatever thou shalt bind on earth, shall be bound in heaven, and whatever thou shalt lose on earth shall be loosed in heaven" (*Matt.* 16:19). "Go into the whole world and preach the gospel to every creature. He who believes and is baptized shall be saved, but he who does not believe shall be condemned" (*Mark* 16:15-16).

There are many people, Catholics included, who try to convince themselves and others that Christ did not mean to form an institutional religion called His Church. They claim that all He meant to do was to pass out the Bible and let everyone find their own way through its pages. But the very Bible itself proves how incorrect all these people are.

Christ made no mistake when He formed His Church with Peter as the head. The Bible, as we know it today, did not even exist when Christ formed His Church. How then could the masses of God's children know what God wanted them to do and to believe? Why did Christ not tell His sublime truths to these masses and leave it to each individual to decide for himself or herself what He meant by these truths? Why did He gather around Him only 12 men whom He taught and then formed into His Church and then commanded them to go forth and teach all others?

Why was Christ so careful to explain these truths of God only to the teachers, the leaders of His own Church?

The answer to all these questions can be found in these words: "Not everyone who says to me 'Lord, Lord' shall enter the kingdom of heaven: but he who does the will of my Father in heaven shall enter the kingdom of heaven" (*Matt.* 7:21).

Not everyone who calls Christ "Lord" and tries to follow Him, alone, through the complicated maze of daily living can find God's holy will for them along the way. Any Catholic who leaves the Church and tries to find God's holy will another way is making a very serious mistake. Such a Catholic is running away from God's holy will because it is God's will that a Catholic find the correct way or path to salvation with and through the sacramental union of a soul to Christ found only within the Church. The main reason why Christ established an institutional Church with a head or leader (we now call the Pope) is because the holy will of God for us, His children, revolves around a *sacramental* union with Him. The way to salvation is through the sacraments which give to the soul the graces necessary for salvation; as well as believing in and following Christ and knowing what the Bible is all about.

Christ makes that very clear in His teachings. How anyone can say that all he needs, as far as religion is concerned (especially a Catholic), is the Bible, is beyond my comprehension; when *in that same Bible*, there exists the fundamental reasons why there has to be an established Church and an established Priesthood! No wonder Christ stated: "Not everyone who says to me 'Lord, Lord' shall be saved," not even if the person appears to have special sensational gifts! The path to salvation is found in doing the holy will of God, and this will is found in the sacramental Church, not in having certain gifts or favors. To make that point clearer, I will add this comment: When a person is a candidate for sainthood, the Church looks, *not* to the special gifts the person may have had, but instead tries to determine if the person lived a holy life with and through a sacramental union with Christ. In other words, visions, gifts of healing and so forth are put aside as only one question is asked: "Was the person faithful to daily duties and religious responsibilities?" If the person was, then the Church knows that that person did the holy will of God. If the person was not, if the person showed signs of rebellion or disobedience to Church authority, then never could that person become a saint no matter what sensational gifts he or she possessed and used.

Now, what is this sacramental union with Christ that is so necessary to doing the holy will of God? Why do I stress the fact that we must have such a union with Christ in order to find and do the holy will of God? Because Christ, Himself, established, not only the sacraments, but His Church as well to protect and administer them for the benefit of souls as part of her mission.

It must be remembered that there are three broad fields covered by religion or doing the holy will of God. Number one is that there are truths of God which we must believe. But merely believing is not enough. So, number two is that we must act according to what we believe. Then we enter into the third broad field, which is to discover the helps which God gives to us as we go about doing what we believe. There within these three broad fields of religion you see the need for the sacramental Church which Christ established.

Christ tells us what we must believe and what we must do, according to these beliefs; and the help He gives us so that we can act according to what we believe is Holy Mother Church who makes available to us the *way* to *act* according to what we believe.

If, for example, Christ told us to be baptized, which He did, and to eat His flesh and drink His blood, which He also did, and if He left no ways or means for us to follow these commandments, how then could we act according to our beliefs? It would be impossible to do that without the Church.

So, as can be plainly seen it would be next to impossible for a Catholic to leave the Church and find God his or her own way having only the Bible as a guide: and no sacraments.

The main reason why a person would even consider doing such a dangerous thing is that such a person fails to understand the duties and obligations which are in the will of God which become clear and precise only when a sacramental union with Christ is well-established. For someone to attempt to seek such a union with Christ outside the established Church is absurd to say the least. That is like telling Christ that He did not know what He was doing or saying when He made Peter our first Pope and established His Church.

He did indeed know what He was doing and saying. His words are still as true and as real today as they were when He uttered them. He knew what He had to say and what He had to do, which was to establish His Church, so that His truths and sacraments would not be lost.

Just reading, in the Bible, what Christ says about the sacraments of Baptism, Confession and Holy Communion tells us that God's will for us is to be found in the truths and in the sacraments of Holy Mother Church. Our union with Christ must come through the sacraments; or else there is no union with Christ.

The first sacrament, Baptism, must come through the Church. Our Lord said to the first teachers or priests of His Church: "All power in heaven and on earth has been given to me. Go, therefore, and make disciples of all nations, baptizing them in the name of the Father and of the Son and of the Holy Spirit, teaching them to observe all that I have commanded you; and behold, I am with you all days, even unto the consummation of the world" (*Matt.* 28:18-20). About Confession: "Receive the Holy Spirit. Whose sins you shall forgive, they are forgiven them; and whose sins you shall retain, they are retained" (*John* 20:23). "Amen, I say to you, whatever you bind on earth, shall be bound also in heaven; and whatever you loose on earth shall be loosed in heaven" (*Matt.* 18:18).

About Holy Communion: "And while they (only the 12) were at supper, Jesus took bread and blessed and broke it and gave it to His disciples and said: 'Take and eat, this is my body.' And taking a cup, He gave thanks and gave it to them saying: 'All of you drink of this for this is my blood of the new covenant which is being shed for many unto the forgiveness of sins'" (*Matt.* 26:26-28). "Amen, amen I say to you, unless you eat the flesh of the Son of Man and drink His blood, you shall not have life in you. He who eats my flesh and drinks my blood has life everlasting and I will raise him up on the last day. He who eats my flesh and drinks my blood abides in me and I in him" (*John* 6:53-56).

"He who eats my flesh and drinks my blood abides in me and I in him." *That is* sacramental union with Christ! That is the holy will of God! And you find both, the sacramental union with Christ and God's holy will, within Holy Mother Church. For a Catholic, there is no other way to completely do the holy will of God.

If you study the Bible and know it by heart, if you say a thousand prayers in your own home or in an open field or even in your closet, if you compose numerous excuses—which sound so good—for not going to Church, all these and more would never give you a sacramental union with Christ: the union which He tells us we must have in order to "be perfect as my heavenly Father is perfect" (*Matt.* 5:48).

PART TWO

THE LIFE OF GRACE

Chapter 1

THE DISAPPEARING CONSCIENCE

In the 60's and 70's many people, especially the young, began to live what they called the "new morality." Actually the word morality should not have been used to describe this so-called "new morality." The word morality is associated with the words virtue and doing right. What the "new morality" really turned out to be was no morality at all. The concept behind this "new morality" was that nothing a person did was a sin anymore. The people who accepted and lived the "new morality" allowed their consciences to merely disappear. While their consciences were in the process of disappearing, such people allowed their attitudes towards sin and sinning to be shaped and molded by standards which were anything but Christian and Catholic. When the shaping and molding were completed, such a person turned to Holy Mother Church and loudly denounced her teachings concerning sin and sexual behavior. They told the Church that there was "nothing wrong" in such things as a man and woman living together without marriage. They said all sorts of sex acts, such as homosexual acts, were perfectly all right, that sexual activities among the unmarried were perfectly all right and that nothing was a sin anymore as long as a person wanted to do it and did not harm anyone else.

Of course such reasoning was wrong and in the early part of 1976 a document issued from the Vatican explained that the teachings of the Church regarding sexual behavior still were the norms for Catholics.

However, many people loudly shouted that they were right and the Church was wrong. How could such a sad situation develop?

How could a person's conscience disappear and reach the state where the person wanted to believe that there is no longer any sin?

Well, the first thing to remember is that living the life of a good, a holy Catholic is living against the standards of the world which always were and always will be hostile to the spirit and teachings of Christ. In other words, it is not easy to become a virtuous, spiritual person in a world which constantly projects into the lives of Christians very unchristian ideas and ways.

Truly, a Catholic is on a battlefield every day of his or her life. There is no letup of the temptations which the devil uses to destroy the Catholic's faith and high moral standards. The Church has faced this problem ever since Christ formed her. Saint Paul often had to remind the members of the early Church that their way of life had to exclude all and everything which was against the spirit and teachings of Christ. Even then, the very first Catholics had to battle the world, the flesh and the devil. They actually had to set themselves apart from the ways which tried to destroy their faith and their high moral standards.

This same battle is still going on. The world, the flesh and the devil have not changed, nor have they diminished in strength or in their power to capture careless souls. Catholics, who insist that there is no sin as far as they are concerned and who insist that the Church's teachings on sin and morality are wrong, allow their consciences to be destroyed and replaced by the world, the flesh and the devil. Such Catholics lack the spiritual strength to protect their own faith and their own high moral standards which were infused into their souls when they received God's magnificent gift of Baptism. In other words, they fail to live their faith as Christ wants them to live it. It is their failure, not the Church's!

Anyone who truly desires a closer union with God has to be well aware of the fact that the climb to perfection is an hourly battle against the world, the flesh and the devil. They must know that their consciences can disappear and be replaced by an attitude, which is most unCatholic, if they allow this to happen.

The key word in that statement is *allow*. No matter how strong the world, the flesh and the devil are, no matter how powerful temptation becomes, the person still has the freedom of choice. Virtue, high moral standards, holiness and a good conscience will never disappear if the person does not allow them to disappear.

How can this be done when, as I have just said, it is so difficult to keep Christian, Catholic ideas and morals? Grace is the answer to that. Remember that grace always was and always will be far more powerful than the strongest attacks of the devil's temptations.

The trouble is that most Catholics, even good, practicing Catholics, do not understand the power of God's grace. They do not even know what tremendous power they possess when their souls are filled with sanctifying grace. As a result, they fail to use this power or to rely upon it when storms and battles enter their spiritual lives.

When that happens they feel so "helpless" even abandoned by God, when in reality they have an amazing power which is theirs to use. God did not abandon them. On the contrary, He gave to them a weapon of tremendous might for them to use. However, many Catholics stand still on the battlefields of grace and temptation and do not even begin the battle to save their own virtues and morals because they neglect or ignore or fail to see the mighty weapon of grace which is theirs to use.

Chapter 2

WHAT ARE SINS,
FAULTS AND HUMAN WEAKNESSES?

It is always shocking and amazing (when one sincerely wishes to discover this), to find out how many faults and human weaknesses we really have. It is much nicer to see the faults of others. However, Christ said to us: "Why do you see the speck in your brother's eye and yet you cannot see nor consider the beam in your own eye?" (*Matt.* 7:3).

While, there is a great deal of comfort found in saying: "*I* don't do what *he* does. I am not that *bad*!" it is far more practical to look to oneself and to admit: "I do have my own faults, which can be corrected with the help of God's grace." Only then can the climb up THE LADDER OF PERFECTION begin.

There are many stages which one must pass as a closer union with God is accomplished. But, basically there are three major steps which are to be taken. Number one is the conquering of sins, especially mortal sins. Number two is the conquering of little (or venial) everyday sins. Number three is the conquering of human weaknesses and faults.

Surprising as it sounds, very few people know what sins, faults and human weaknesses are. Most people are inclined to think of sins as something big, such as: murder, adultery, robbing a bank or getting arrested for some other crime. Many people cannot see their own sins, even mortal sins, because they have lost the feelings of guilt for the sins which they do commit. They reason that they "don't sin" is because they don't feel guilty after the sin. Such sins have become part of their lives.

A most extraordinary development took place after Vatican

Council II concerning sin. In a very short time, the lines of people going to Communion increased and the lines of people going to Confession disappeared. One reason, of course, was that the average lay person finally learned that you do not have to go to Confession first before you go to Communion if you have no mortal sins to confess. A person could go to Communion as often as he wished as long as the soul was in the state of grace (no mortal sins committed).

While it was commendable to discover such a vast number of people who felt they no longer needed the confessional, it was sad to also discover that many of these people felt that it was impossible for them to commit a mortal sin, or any sin at all, for that matter. The attitude of "nothing I do is wrong" took the place of the feeling of guilt for sins committed. Far too many people lost the precious virtue of being able to look deeply into their own spiritual lives and to admit, by this prayer, that something was wrong: "I am sorry for my sins, I will repent." They preferred to say: "What did I do wrong? Nothing!"

But is this true? Are people so blameless? Are people so perfect that no matter what they do, they cannot sin? Of course not.

First of all, let me quote these words which are taken from the book: "The Catholic Religion" by Bishop Bernard D. Stewart, page 58: "Some are of the *opinion* that it is almost impossible to commit a mortal sin if you feel what you are doing is right: REPLY: Three things are required for mortal sin: A) gravity of matter B) sufficient knowledge of such gravity C) sufficient freedom in performing the action.

"The common teaching of the Church has not changed in this matter. The story of Adam and Eve, the story of Cain and Abel portray the magnitude of sin in its offense of God and its fearful consequences for man. The stories of Jonah and Noah tell how widespread is serious offense to God. The simple reading of so many of the Lenten Masses should convince us that mortal sins are not rare.

"There is a tendency not to use the word sin, to exclude it from the formation of children. Yet in the great prayers to be taught to all children such as Our Father, the Hail Mary there is mention of sin; the word sin is used repeatedly in the Canon of the Mass. Officially and liturgically the Church brings the word sin to children. . .educators and catechists should not ban it.

"If one 'feels' that what one is doing right this can be understood as lack of knowledge. But if one feels e.g. that adultery is all right and at the same time knows that the Church teaches it is quite wrong then one is putting one's private feeling against the clear teaching of the Church; and any instructed Catholic knows that one cannot do that.

"To say that it is practically impossible to commit a mortal sin is directly contrary to experience; anyone who knows what serious matter is knows also that he or she is quite capable of doing such a thing."

Secondly, let me explain the true malice of sin. What is the malice of sin? Well, I used to explain that to my C.C.D. Religious Instruction Class, in this manner:

I began by explaining to the youngsters that it would not be such a crime if one youngster suddenly slapped the face of another child his own age. There may be a little fight, but no real damage would be done. However, if this same child slapped the face of his mother, ah, then that is a different story! If this same child slapped the face of a teacher in school, down to the principal's office! Now if this same child ran up to the President of the United States and slapped him, look out! The F.B.I. would come forth to arrest this child. If this same child slapped the face of the Queen! The "Tower of London," that is where the child would be put! So, think about this. What if this same child ran up to God and slapped Him in the face? Then what? What kind of an insult would that be, to actually slap God in the face? Terrible! Unthinkable!

I ended this little lesson with these words: "You know, each time you sin, no matter how small the sin is, it is like going up to God and slapping Him in the face." And that is the malice of sin!

So good, so loving, so gentle, so merciful and forgiving is God, that each sin you commit no matter how small becomes an insult, to His goodness, His love, His gentleness, His mercy and His forgiveness. But more! Each sin you commit, no matter how small, is a turning-away from God and His goodness and His love. It becomes an act of rebellion against the holy will of God. It becomes a statement of "I will not obey!" "I will not serve!" "I will do what I want to do!"

So many people think lightly of their own sins because they never really learned what Christ said about sin. But read carefully these words from Holy Scripture: "Do not judge that you may not be judged. For with what judgement you judge, you shall be judged; and with what measure you measure, it shall be measured to you" (*Matt.* 7:1-2). And these words: "You have heard that it was said to the Ancients, you shall not commit adultery; but I say to you that anyone who so much as looks with lust at a woman has already committed adultery with her in his heart" (*Matt.* 5:27-28). And these words: "You have heard that it was said to the Ancients: 'You shall not kill; and that whoever shall kill shall be liable to judgment;' but I say to you that everyone who is angry with his brother shall be liable to judgment" (*Matt.* 5:21-22). And these words: "So if your right eye is an occasion of sin, pluck it out; rather that, then go to hell" (*Matt.* 5:29).

Here is Christ telling us that sin is a very serious matter and we cannot merely shrug our shoulders when the word sin is mentioned and say: "What do I do wrong? Nothing!"

Sin, even venial sin, is a very serious matter. And all sins prevent a person's spiritual growth. Never become so proud that you say to yourself that you do nothing "wrong." On the other hand, do not become filled with false humility (or scruples as this is often called) and think that everything you do is a sin. Just be realistic about sin.

The saints were. They never ceased calling themselves "sinners." They had good reason. It was not that they were great sinners, although some were before their conversion. The reason they called themselves "sinners" is that they compared themselves to the perfect God, the perfect Christ; and they saw the difference between His perfection and their imperfections.

The biggest mistake which people make about sin, is that they are always comparing themselves to *others* and not to God. They look at the wrongdoings of their fellow men and feel safe and secure because they, themselves, would not commit such sins or crimes. Even the worst of sinners will do this. They always look for someone who does far greater wrongs than they are capable of doing. Then they turn their thoughts inward and breathe a sigh of relief and declare: "Well, I'm not as bad as that! What do I do wrong? Nothing!"

It is interesting to note that many a husband, who is not faithfully fulfilling the duties and obligations of his married life, who may be drinking or gambling away the family's limited income, will turn to his innocent wife and accuse her of the most foul wrongdoings. To do so gives him a false sense of righteousness because he reasons: "She does worse things than I do so what I do isn't so bad!"

It is always a great comfort to see yourself as being above someone else who has reached a very low point in his or her relationship to God.

But is this the way to union with God? Of course not! Christ told us the way: "Be you perfect, as my Father in heaven is perfect."

Then see yourself and your own spiritual life as God sees them not as you imagine they are: all shiny and bright. Compare the brightness of your spiritual life with the immense brightness which shines forth from the Being of God; and be humble enough to admit that there is need for a great deal of improvement.

Once I worked in a printer's office as a bookkeeper. Very often, my employer would try to look for flaws in a printing job. When he wanted to make sure that the printed paper was as perfect as it could be, he would not trust his examination of this paper to an electric light. He would instead take the paper outside in the stronger sunlight and look for the imperfections. The electric light, no matter how strong, lacked the brilliance of the sunlight which clearly showed up every imperfection.

In much the same way, when you climb THE LADDER OF

PERFECTION to a closer union with God, you must constantly examine your relationship with God not from the frail misleading point of human association but from the brilliance of God's Being.

The closer you come to this brilliance, as you slowly, but surely advance upward, the more clearly you will see your own faults, weaknesses and imperfections in much the same way that sunlight reveals imperfections in a printed paper which electric light could never reveal.

Even when mortal sins are conquered (which is the first major step to take up THE LADDER), even when venial sins are brought under control, there still has to be the conquering of faults, weaknesses and finally imperfections.

Do not ignore these faults, weaknesses and imperfections. They also must be worked upon, day in and day out. A virtue must replace a sin or a fault, or else there is no advancement.

How can all this be done? The answer is grace. For every sin, for every fault, weakness or imperfection, there is a grace which can replace these with virtues. For example: if after all your mortal sins are done away with, you find such a fault as anger within your spiritual life, graces are there to replace that anger with gentleness or kindness.

Grace is the reason why Christ knew we could strive for perfection. He knew that we could never do that alone. So He provided grace which becomes our weapon or tool upon the spiritual battlefields. He also knew that with grace we can become what He told us to become. The saints proved that. With grace they rose above all human weaknesses and became what they desired to become and what God desired them to become.

Chapter 3

IN WHAT WAY DOES SIN HURT GOD?

Each and every sin, which is committed, in some way hurts God. Each and every sin carries with it a certain amount of malice towards God. What is the malice of sin? I tell people that every time you sin it is like slapping God in the face. That is the malice of sin.

However, can God, in His glory in heaven, actually be hurt in any way? Yes, He can. The proof of that statement can be seen by the way God reacted to the first sin ever committed. In the garden of Eden, our first parents so hurt God that He cast them out of the garden and took away from them His supernatural gift called grace. Also, God was so hurt, when the Israelites reverted backward into pagan habits, that He made them wander aimlessly in the desert for forty years. I will say here that people, who consider their sins as "nothing" or who think little of such sins because "God understands," should reflect seriously upon the fact that the price paid for the sins of Adam and Eve and the Israelites was a very high, severe price.

Even a small sin, what we call a venial sin such as a "little, white lie," calls down upon the sinner God's justice because of the hidden malice of that sin. God is indeed hurt by each and every sin.

However, in what way, form or manner is He hurt? In other words can God suffer because of our sins? If so, how can He suffer when His infinite glory and joy and happiness are complete and perfect? Perfect, complete joy and happiness allows no room for tears, suffering or pain. Yet the fact is that God does suffer greatly because of our sins; however, on the other hand, He does not because He cannot suffer in heaven. Such a statement sounds paradoxical, but in reality it is not.

First of all, to say that God cannot be hurt by sin or cannot suffer because of sin would be a great mistake. Christ, who is God, did indeed suffer because of our sins. Every sin no matter how small, which is even now—today this very moment—being committed, added in some way to the sufferings of Christ during His Passion and death. Because we are all sinners, we, ourselves, caused some pain to God during His crucifixion. We added to His enormous burden when He carried His cross and died upon it. When we understand this truth, then we can see that indeed our sins caused God very great suffering and pain.

We must not view the crucifixion as something which happened about 2000 years ago and does not concern us now. The crucifixion is not something belonging to a bygone era. It is a reality which finds its presence in each and everyone's daily life. It is here, now. It shall remain part of today's horizon as long as there is one sinner present on earth. Christ died upon that cross to save you and me. Christ suffered upon that cross for your sins and mine. A beautiful prayer which should be said daily is: "Thank you, dear Lord, for taking upon yourself the burdens of my sins and for suffering for me." Christ's crucifixion is renewed each time a sin is committed no matter how small that sin is. Christ, God, suffers anew His own Passion each time a sinner turns away from His love and grace and loudly declares: "I will not follow you, I will sin." Christ dies in agony, again and again, each time a person allows the grace of God to die within his soul when he commits a mortal sin. The suffering, dying Christ is always there each time a sin is committed because that sin was deeply embedded somewhere within His Passion.

Do not see sin, your sins, as affecting "no one." Many people constantly make excuses for their sins by saying: "Whom do I hurt by what I do? No one!" For example: an unmarried couple living together in sin tell themselves, and everyone else who will listen, that they do "nothing wrong" because they hurt "no one." That is very far from the truth. They hurt their own souls and they do hurt God. Somewhere within the torments of the crucifixion their sins were present. Such sins became part of the blows of the scourging or the piercing points of the crown of thorns because sin, all sin, in one way or another contributed to the pains and agony which brought about our personal salvation.

So, sin, our sins, do indeed hurt God, the God who suffered upon the cross and died because of our sins. However, that is not the only way sin can affect and hurt God.

Whenever there is a sin committed, venial or mortal, there is a rejection of one of God's own laws or rules. Something which God told us we should not do, we do. We disobey one of His laws, but more, we make a mockery of these laws. We are saying to God: "I don't care what your laws are, I will do what I want to. I will live my life the way I want to." Especially if the sin is mortal we not only make a mockery of God's own laws, but we totally reject God as the one who has the right to make these laws for us to obey. We place ourselves above God and try to be wiser than He. In reality, it then becomes the same sin which caused Adam and Eve to try to place themselves above God. Saint Augustine tells us: "He who sins wants to be a God himself, a little god maybe, but one who has no great God above him." When we do this, place ourselves above God through disobedience to His laws, we hurt God by hurting His *omnipotent right to be God:* the God who has the right to make laws which we must obey. This was precisely why Adam and Eve were banished from the Garden of Eden. Everyone speaks about their disobedience as the reason for this banishment but that was only one reason. The other was what Saint Augustine said when he wrote that "he who sins wants to be a god..." Not only does the sinner want to become a "god" with no "great God" above him but the sinner also wants to take away from God His right to be the "great God" and His right to make laws which lowly men must obey. When Adam and Eve disobeyed God, the sin of disobedience was only part of the overall picture of their banishment. By their sin they had actually tried to take away from God His heavenly throne and they attempted to tell Him that He had no right to make a law which He expected them to obey.

Needless to say, Adam and Eve were sadly mistaken. So are the ones who also disobey God's laws and try to tell Him that He has no right to make these laws or that His Church has no right to make laws. By and through such disobedience and rejection of God's laws and rights, we hurt God. We hurt His laws, we hurt His rights. However, when we hurt God in this way, by our sins, *we are the ones who end up suffering* the pain of this hurt.

Now see this way that sin hurts God. The actual pain or suffering from sin reverts backward to *the sinner!* God feels the pain of our disobedience to His laws and rules *in us!* As I said, there is no way that God can actually suffer what we call a physical pain or hurt. He is in His infinite glory where there is no suffering. However, there are many ways that His image and likeness can and does suffer because of sin. We are God's own image and likeness. The harm or hurt from our own disobedience soars upwards toward God; however, the pain from this hurt cannot find a place to rest so it returns to the sender: to the sinner. The sinner suffers the consequences of his own sins. Man is the loser, not God. Man will suffer for his own sins, not God. Man will be condemned for his own sins, not God.

Understand the way God and His image (us) are combined as one so that we can say that God is hurt by sins because we are hurt by sins. God's own image and likeness becomes a mirror which should reflect His goodness, love and grace. In other words, He can look into this mirror and see Himself, His love, His goodness, His grace. When sins are committed, the mirror becomes cloudy, hazy and distorted. When a mortal sin is committed, this mirror breaks and God can no longer see Himself in His own image and likeness in us. So God is hurt because the mirror or image of His own goodness, love and grace cannot give back to Him a pure, clear reflection of His own goodness, love and grace. But notice that it is the *mirror* or *image* of God which becomes cloudy, hazy, distorted or broken. It is the sinner who suffers from his own sins even though sins hurt God by hurting His reflection. As I said: sin punishes the sinner. Christ tells us: "Everyone who acknowledges me before men, I also will acknowledge before my Father who is in heaven; but whoever denies me before men, I also will deny before my Father who is in heaven" (*Matt.* 10:32-33).

It is very important to always remember that sin punishes the sinner. However, having sin hurt the sinner, who is God's own image and likeness, hurts God in the sense that He wants to give many good things to His children, to His own image and likeness, but sin prevents these gifts from reaching His children.

Now there must be a distinction made between what God wants to give, as good things, to a person and what the person may desire or think are these good things. Only then can you truly see the way sin hurts God by hurting the sinner who prevents God's reflection from being seen in his or her soul.

Certainly what some people consider to be good for themselves may not be good at all. A man who has a valid marriage but leaves his wife and children in order to live with his girlfriend may think that God has been good to him because he finds a happiness in his new life which never existed in his old one. However, just the opposite is true. The good things God had planned to give this person could be found only in his unhappy life; because even though his marriage brought him unhappiness, it also brought him grace.

The very first good gift which God wants to give all His children, after giving them the gift of life itself, is to give them the gift of sanctifying grace. This gift, first received in Baptism and restored, if lost, in the confessional, is the very gift of eternal salvation. Life and eternal salvation are the two greatest and most priceless gifts which God can bestow upon His children. The very first religious duty and obligation of all of us is to protect and cherish these two gifts. If that is done, then no calamity or catastrophe of life can cause us dismay. We know we will find eternal happiness.

However, among the roses of life, there are to be found many thorns. Among the disillusions of life's todays, there are to be found many avenues of escape. It is in the following of such detours when human and spiritual values switch around in such a way that what is not good for a man's soul seems to be very good to him. Then the battles with a conscience begin. If sin wins these battles and grace is destroyed, then also are the good things which God had planned to give to the person. For only through the channels of grace can man receive the wondrous spiritual gifts, including salvation, which God so desires to bestow.

Now, when this grace is lost, the way or means needed by God to give gifts to us, His beloved children, is closed. It is the closing of this passageway which not only hurts God, but hurts the sinner as well. God suffers a hypothetical hurt or injustice; however, the actual pain or loss generated by the mortal sin, which closed the passageway, reverts back directly to the sinner. As I said, sin punishes the sinner never God.

An example of what I mean is as follows: it is ludicrous for a person to say that she will "punish God" by no longer going to Mass and receiving the sacraments. God cannot be punished by a sinner. What actually happens is the person only punishes herself. By closing the channel of grace within her own soul, she has closed the way and means by which God wanted to give *to her* wondrous gifts which will last forever.

So in summary: we hurt God by not loving Him and by not becoming what He wants us to become; however, when we do not become what God wants us to become, when we do not return love for love, we only end up by hurting ourselves. The image and likeness of God then becomes the image and likeness of sin.

Chapter 4

WHAT IS A WELL-PLANNED SPIRITUAL PROGRAM FOR UNION WITH GOD?

Very few people daily climb THE LADDER OF PERFECTION. Even those who want to make God first in their daily lives fail to advance towards a closer union with God. Many people came to me to tell me that they want to love God more and do more for their own spiritual lives, but they do not know how. Other people told me that they have been going to Mass (often daily), they have prayed for years and yet: "nothing happens! I get nothing out of going to Mass or praying." Still others think that going to Mass every Sunday (or Sat. evening), saying a few prayers during the day, and making their Easter Duty is all that has to be done for God and for their souls.

All such people are making the same serious mistake. They do not have a well-planned daily spiritual program which could help them reach a closer union with God.

First of all, just exactly what is union with God! What does it mean to climb THE LADDER OF PERFECTION to a closer union with God?

The final phase of union with God is the eternal union with Him in His Heaven of Love; however, before we can reach that union, we must start the climb towards that union while on earth.

Some people misunderstand union with God and say that merely "finding Christ" is to be united with Him.

But this term "finding Christ" is most deceptive. During the 60's and the 70's, this term became most popular, the reason being, that numerous evangelists told millions of people that they had only to "find Christ" and be saved. They did not need any

Church. They did not need any sacraments. All they needed were a few well-chosen Bible passages and they would "find Christ" and that was all there was to religion. These T.V. evangelists were so convincing because they expressed tremendous joy as they told of their own experience of "finding Christ" in this manner without any Church or any sacraments, only with the Bible. As a result, hundreds of thousands of people left their Churches to join these do-it-yourself type of religions.

That may sound very good if you say that perhaps thousands of people turned to Christ who never would have. For them, that could have been a "saving experience." However, there was one very serious problem which resulted from this type of "finding Christ." Once Christ was "found," no one was told what to do with Him. Their religion was left hanging up in the air, based only upon one emotional encounter with Christ. Most of these hundreds of thousands of people soon discovered that merely finding Christ was not enough especially when the emotions of finding Him disappeared in a daily life of cares, sorrows and crosses.

The T.V. evangelists would stand before the audience or the viewers (sometimes in a stadium filled with thousands of people) and through a series of emotion-packed experiences (such as a "miracle" or two), they would capture the hearts of those who really wanted to do something for God, but did not know how. But when the lights of the T.V. camera went out, when the lights on stage went out, when the preacher or evangelist left, there existed a very deep void or empty space in a person's individual spiritual life. Their union with Christ did not carry over into their everyday, humdrum life. Often the "miraculous" conversion ended when the program ended, or when the stage show was over.

I often witnessed such religious exhibitions on T.V. When the evangelist shouted: "All who want to be saved rise and come forward," I would want to rise up and do some shouting of my own because it is not *that easy* to live a life of total union with God. There is a vast difference between true union with God and an emotional encounter with Christ.

Also, there is a vast difference between sacramental union with Christ and merely "finding" Him in the Bible. A person can read the Bible everyday for a thousand years, a person can know the Bible by heart and *still* never reach the union with Christ which comes from a sacramental union with Him; the type of union He told us we must have when He said: "Unless you eat the flesh of the Son of man and drink His blood, you shall not have life in you" (*John* 6:53).

The sacramental union with Christ! What is that? Well, for one thing it is living a Christian religion *as well as a* biblical religion. Why do I say that? Is not living a religion based solely on the Bible, without a Church and sacraments, living a Christian religion? Not always. One can live a biblical religion (based only on what one learns from the Bible) and still not live a Christian religion. How is that possible? Simply because Christ tells us to live a sacramental, biblical religion which is found only in the Church, and unless we do that we are not living a true Christian religion but only the religion we tell ourselves to live. The Catholic religion is the only religion which faithfully carries out the teachings or instructions of Christ from the moment He made Peter the head of His Church until His last words about Confession: "You are Peter and upon this rock, I will build my Church" (*Matt.* 16:18). "Receive the Holy Spirit, whose sins you shall forgive they are forgiven them; and whose sins you shall retain, they are retained" (*John* 20:22-23). The Catholic religion is a true sacramental, biblical religion as well as a biblical religion of encounter with Christ through the words of Holy Scripture.

Anyone who truly wants to reach a complete union with Christ must reach this complete union with Him in and through the sacraments; otherwise, he is not following the complete teachings of Christ.

Very often Catholics have been and are condemned or criticized because they do not know the Bible as others know it. The reason why is that *we know* we are living a sacramental religion *along with a biblical religion.* We do not have to know the Bible by heart. The most ignorant Catholic lay person, who cannot even read, can reach a close union with Christ through belief in the sacraments and use of them. That is also the reason why Catholics were not urged to study the Bible, although we were always allowed to read the Bible contrary to what others think. The Church gave us the sacramental religion of Christ in addition to a biblical religion. In other words, it is not enough just to know what is in the Bible. One has to live according to all the teachings of Christ. Only then can one live a true Christian religion as well as a true biblical religion. The sacraments are one of the main teachings of Christ in the Bible and we Catholics know that fact.

It is possible to save one's soul through a simple faith in the Bible and what it teaches. However, it is most dangerous to substitute the sacraments of the Church for the Bible. That is why the Catholic Church was a sacramental Church long before the Bible even existed as we know it today.

So, a well-planned spiritual program begins with the sacraments along with Bible study. The Bible study is important but not more important than the sacraments.

How anyone can read the Bible and not realize that religion has to be a sacramental union with Christ is beyond my comprehension, when the sacraments are so vividly clear within the pages of Holy Scripture. For example, Saint Paul tells us: "Therefore, beloved, flee from the worship of idols. I am speaking as to men of sense. The cup of blessing that we bless, is it not the sharing of the blood of Christ? And the bread that we break, is it not the partaking of the body of the Lord? Because the bread is one, we though many are one body, all of us who partake of the one bread" (*1 Cor.* 10:14-17). "For, I myself have received from the Lord what I also delivered to you." (Note here that Saint Paul speaks about the act of teaching the truths of God and also the act of giving the Sacrament of the Eucharist to the people) "that the Lord Jesus, on the night in which He was betrayed, took bread and giving thanks broke and said: 'This is my body which shall be given up for you; do this in remembrance of me.' And in like manner, also the cup, after supper, saying, 'This cup is the new covenant in my blood, do this as often as you drink it, in remembrance of me.' For as often as you shall eat this bread and drink this cup, you proclaim the death of the Lord, until He comes.' Therefore whoever eats this bread and drinks the cup of the Lord unworthily will be guilty of the body and blood of the Lord. But let a man prove himself, and so let him eat of that bread and drink of the cup" (*1 Cor.* 11:23-28).

Saint Paul understood what Christ meant when He said: "I am the living bread that has come down from heaven. If anyone eat of this bread, he shall live forever and the bread I will give is my flesh for the life of the world. Amen, Amen, I say to you, unless you eat the flesh of the Son of Man and drink His blood, you shall not have life in you" (*John* 6:51-54).

Union with Christ then, starts with the sacraments, the first being Baptism. A Catholic continues this union with Christ through the sacraments of Confirmation, Penance and the Eucharist.

To be in union with God is to be in union with the grace which flows from the sacraments. In other words, a soul in the state of grace is a soul in union with God. Any baptized Catholic, whose soul is in the state of grace is in union with God, for the person possesses the requirement of union with God which is grace, the grace received from the sacraments.

Many people say that all they need is the Bible, because the Bible is the Word of God. However, a person needs more than this Word of God in order to be in union with Him: the person needs grace.

The Word of God, the Bible tells us not only that we need grace but also tells us how to obtain this grace and grace enables us to be a true follower of Christ in union with Him.

A person can learn the Bible word for word and then become a preacher or teacher and teach the Bible word for word. Yet, unless this same person teaches the sacramental religion of Christ, found in the Church, that person does not teach a total Christian religion and he, himself, does not live a total Christian religion. He teaches and lives only a biblical religion which at its best is only half a religion, and at its worst may not be even a Christian religion, because it does not teach the Christian way of union with Christ through the sacraments.

The Jehovah's Witnesses are a good example of what I mean. They call themselves Christians, yet they are very good at Judaizing the Gospels and turning the pages of salvation history back to Judaism. For example, they base the non-existence of the soul (their own version of this teaching) on *Ezekiel* 18:4. They very cleverly weave their complex and confused doctrines around selected passages from the Old Testament, more so than from the new. Even their name Jehovah's Witnesses is taken from the Old Testament. The Hebrews called their God by a name which was written Y H W H. This became Jehovah. So the Witnesses, who claim to be Christian, witness only for Jehovah, a Jewish name for God.

So, you can see why it is so important to have a well-planned spiritual program which begins with the sacraments from which flow the grace so necessary for a union with God, and continues within the framework of the Church.

However, while the sacraments are the main source of grace, they are not the only source. Grace can be and must be increased. A person, who finds his or her spiritual life "standing still" or "going nowhere," will begin to climb THE LADDER to a *closer* union with God only when he or she has a daily program for spiritual advancement.

This daily program includes, as I said the sacraments, and also other things such as: prayer, penance, spiritual reading, Bible study, charity, mortification, good deeds, good works and so forth. And all of these things can be done in a daily life no matter how busy that life is.

Chapter 5

UNION WITH GOD BEGINS WITH THE CHURCH AND THE SACRAMENTS

One day a young man, aged 19 or 20, decided to "tell me off" because he knew that I defended the Catholic Church. I had never met him before, but he had heard about me. When I went to visit his ill mother, he thought he had found the perfect opportunity to tell me that his own homemade type of religion was far superior than the teachings and ways of Holy Mother Church. His approach to the subject of religion was rather direct and bold and caught me by surprise. His first statement was that he saw no reasons why he had to go to Mass. He claimed that he loved God, but he could pray to Him at home much better than in a Church. He resented being told that he had to go to Mass with other people (most of whom he considered hypocrites). He challenged me by saying firmly: "You cannot tell me that I do not love God because I won't go to Mass!"

I allowed him to speak for a while without an argument, then I said to him: "You really do not love God because if you did, you would want to go to Mass and receive Christ."

He, of course, resented that statement, and told me again that I had no right to tell him that he did not love God because he would not go to Mass. He went on to tell me that God is so good, so merciful that He understands! He told me that to love God is enough and to pray to Him at home is also enough religion.

I asked him: "Then how do you fulfill the first and the second commandments? How do you worship God as He deserves to be worshiped? What makes you feel that your personal prayers

to God are truly worshiping God as He deserves to be worshiped?" The young man did not answer.

I continued: "And what about the sacraments? You go to Mass
not only to worship God as He deserves to be worshiped, but
to receive the Eucharist. Christ said: "Unless you eat the flesh
of the Son of man and drink His blood, you have no life in
you" (*John* 6:53). Just to say you love God is not enough. You
must have the life of His grace within your soul. You receive
this life through the sacraments."

When the conversation ended, the young man had not "told
me off," but had listened. He was no longer sure that his homemade religion was the best one for him.

One day I received a letter from a woman who told me that
she would no longer read anything I wrote because I was "too
severe" in my way of thinking. She also had a very bad spiritual
problem, and what she had read in one of my articles had
reminded her that she was not living as a good Catholic should
live. She also was looking for a God who was filled with love
and understanding and who ignored her spiritual neglects.

Both of these examples of Catholics who refuse to accept the
Church's teachings show the way many people want to still love
God and pray, but only their own way with their own homemade
type of religions. However, it is not possible for a Catholic to
truly love God or to climb THE LADDER OF PERFECTION with
a homemade religion which excludes the Mass, the sacraments
and the teachings of the Church. Union with God begins with
the Church and the sacraments.

Why am I so sure of that fact? Well, for one reason: anyone
who wants to climb THE LADDER OF PERFECTION to closer
union with God must develop a very sincere, deep prayer life.
While it is possible, and even necessary, to include prayers said
at home within this prayer life, the very first prayer must be liturgical prayer. When that young man said to me that he could pray
at home and that was all he needed for his spiritual life, he put
a limitation on his own prayer life. All Catholics who say and do
the same thing forget that an active prayer life must include liturgical prayer, which includes the holy Mass and the Eucharist.

The young man, who said that prayers at home were all he needed, revealed very clearly his lack of knowledge about prayer. It can be safely stated that his prayer life consisted only of a few vocal prayers. But such vocal prayers can do more harm to a person's spiritual life than good. Christ warned us against certain types of vocal prayers by saying: "This people honors me with their lips, but their hearts are far from me; and in vain do they worship me" (*Matt.* 15:8-9). Catholics, who have substituted their own homemade type of prayer life for the liturgical prayer of the Mass, do not worship God as He deserves to be worshiped. In addition, such a Catholic is completely ignoring other types of prayer such as: mental prayer, meditation and contemplation, all of which should be part of an active prayer life.

Another reason why I am so sure that a person cannot possibly love God "with his whole heart and with his whole soul and with his whole mind" (*Matt.* 22:37), if he does not go to Mass and to the sacraments is what Christ said when speaking of His Church as the teacher of His truths: ". . .and if he refuses to hear them, appeal to the Church; but if he refuses to hear even the Church, let him be to thee as the heathen and the publican. Amen I say to you whatever you bind on earth shall be bound also in heaven; and whatever you loose on earth shall be loosed also in heaven" (*Matt.* 18:17-18). The Church tells us that we must go to Mass in order to worship God and also to receive the Sacrament of the Eucharist.

The Eucharist is the center or heart of all Catholic spiritual activity and worship. Why? Because the center or core of all Christian, Catholic life is Christ. If a person is to have religion, that person must make Christ the center of religion. And where is Christ found completely and perfectly giving Himself to us? The answer is in the Sacrament of the Eucharist. If a Catholic states that he does not need the Church or the sacraments, that Catholic has cut himself off or away from the living Christ in the Eucharist: and as I stated, Christ said: "Unless you eat the flesh of the Son of Man and drink His blood, you have no life in you" (*John* 6:53).

Christ also said, and these words should be taken very

seriously by fallen-away Catholics who claim they still love God but they do not need the Church and the sacraments: "Not everyone who says to me, 'Lord, Lord' shall enter the kingdom of heaven; but he who does the will of my father in heaven, shall enter the kingdom of heaven. Many will say to me, in that day, 'Lord, Lord'...but I will declare, 'I never knew you' " (*Matt.* 7:21-23).

If a Catholic, who was baptized into the faith, fails to live up to his or her spiritual commitment to the Church and to Christ through the Church then that person becomes a stranger to Christ.

Christ can no longer recognize the person as the baptized Catholic whom He had so lovingly accepted into His Church. Even if such a Catholic insists that he still loves God and prays, that person is praying and loving God as a fallen-away Catholic who has separated himself from the Church and the sacraments. He has lost his true identity.

One such Catholic, a young woman, said to me: "I used to be a Catholic, but now I am a Christian, not a Catholic, and all Christians love God. I don't have to be a Catholic to love and follow Christ. All I have to be is a Christian."

I smiled and said: "You are not a Christian who is no longer a Catholic. You are a baptized Catholic. When you were baptized, you became a Christian, but a Catholic Christian. What you are now is a fallen-away, Christian Catholic. You cannot discard your Catholic religion to become a Christian. What has happened is that you have lost your true identity as a Catholic when you walked away from your Catholic duties and the responsibilities to your Church and to Christ."

All Catholics who make up their own laws and rules concerning religion, who will not accept the teachings and rules of Holy Mother Church and who want to still "love" God in their own way can never be sure that they are not part of the group Lord referred to when he said: "Not everyone who says 'Lord, Lord' shall enter the kingdom of heaven 7:21-23).

Any Catholic who denounces the Church and

she "loves" God and can pray just as well at home can never be sure that his or her prayers are really what God demands prayers to be.

If the person does indeed think that Christ did not mean him when He said: "Not everyone who says to me, 'Lord, Lord' shall enter the kingdom of heaven," or if the person feels that his own poor prayers said in his own home are enough as far as true worship of God is concerned, then such a person has a deep hidden pride which prevents spiritual advancement. It is often difficult for the fallen-away Catholic to see that pride because he rather imagines that his own homemade type of religion is good enough for a merciful, understanding God. The person cannot imagine that there is much more he has to do in order to please God. The person becomes very self-satisfied as he oversimplifies Christ's true religion to suit his own ideas and needs. But such a person forgets one very important fact: Christ meant for His religion to be lived as well as to be believed!

At the same house where the young man who was going to "tell me off" lived, there was another fallen-away Catholic present. This man had found some sort of a false feeling of security just because he said he believed in Christ and found all he needed, as far as religion was concerned, in the Bible. I looked at him and said: "It is one thing to read the Bible and to say you believe in Christ: however, it is another thing to actually *do what the Bible and Christ tell you to do*. What you are speaking of is something like Martin Luther's "justification by faith alone" which was condemned by the Council of Trent. Justification by faith alone is the teaching that a soul can pass from a state of sin to one of sanctifying grace without any type of outward religious acts or works. That is not possible. Saint James tells us, in Holy Scripture: "You see, that by works a man is justified and not by faith alone. Faith without works is dead" (*St. James* 2:24-26).

The man's smile of satisfaction disappeared from his face and a puzzled look replaced it. He had no idea what his homemade biblical type of religion *told* him to do.

The fact is, all religions that use only the Bible and nothing else, whether invented by fallen-away Catholics or others, make the same mistake. They use the Bible as the total of religion, which it is not. They say that just having the Bible and believing the words of Christ are all that is needed as far as religion goes. Many times I have seen people who use and want only the Bible as their "Church" completely oversimplify the teachings of Christ. They forget that the Bible not only tells them to *believe* in Christ, but also tells them who Christ is and what He, Christ, wants them to *do*.

That fact was brought home very clearly to me when, years ago, this happened as I sought to improve my religious knowledge. For a time I, due to lack of religious knowledge, was confused about the Sacrament of The Eucharist. I had heard it said that some Protestant religions believed and taught that the Lord's Supper was only an imitation of the Last Supper. They received bread and wine only in memory of what Christ did at the Last Supper. I looked in the Bible and indeed it seemed that such a teaching was in Holy Scripture: "This is my body, which is being given for you; do this in remembrance of me" (*Luke* 22:19). Then one Sunday morning, a priest during his sermon on the Eucharist stated: " '...do this in memory of me,' our Lord said. Do what? Change bread and wine into the body and blood of Christ! That is what Christ told us to do: not just to eat bread and drink wine, but to actually do as He had done, to change the bread and wine into His body and blood." All my confusion disappeared. I knew that I not only had to believe that at the Last Supper Christ did actually change bread and wine into His body and blood, but I also had to, myself, receive this same body and blood by means of the Eucharist. I had to be united with Christ and not only believe His words, but to follow them as well.

Without exception, people who make up their own religion, especially fallen-away Catholics, do so for only one reason. They want God, they want religion; however, they want a religion which tells them that what they want to do and believe are approved by an understanding God. In other words, they attempt to tell God what He meant by His ways and truths instead of accepting the true ways and teachings of God. When they do that, they are sadly mistaken because Christ already told us what to believe and what to do in order to please God; and Christ left His Church to so teach these truths and to protect these truths. He said: "Go into the whole world and preach the gospel to every creature. He who believes and is baptized shall be saved; but he who does not believe shall be condemned" (*Mark* 16:15-16). He also said to Saint Peter: "And I say to you, you are Peter and upon this rock I will build my Church and the gates of hell shall not prevail against it. And I will give you the keys of the kingdom of heaven and whatever you shall bind on earth, shall be bound in heaven and whatever you shall loose on earth shall be loosed in heaven" (*Matt.* 16:18-19).

In these two biblical passages, it can be clearly seen that Christ not only formed an active Church, but a sacramental Church as well. He gathered all His people into a new kingdom on Earth, a new Church. Entrance into this kingdom was by means of the Sacrament of Baptism. Within this kingdom were those who protected and taught Christ's teachings. Saint Paul tells us: "He has rescued us from the power of darkness and transferred us into the kingdom of his beloved Son, in whom we have our redemption, the remission of our sins" (*Col.* 1:13-14).

This kingdom is still with us today. This Church Christ formed, with Peter as the head or first Pope, is that very same kingdom. And the same teachings of Christ and the same sacraments, which He gave His infant Church, are still with us today. No homemade religion can take the place of Christ's true Church. No personal biblical beliefs can change the fact that the Bible proves that Christ formed a sacramental Church and expected His followers to receive these sacraments through His Church.

Anyone who invents his or her own religion and decides to do only what he or she wants, in regards to religion, forgets the fact that Christ was very insistent that His ways and teachings were followed and not changed to suit individual needs. For example, He very clearly stated to His first Apostles: "Go, behold I send you forth as lambs in the midst of wolves. He who hears you, hears me; and he who rejects you, rejects me; and he who rejects me, rejects him who sent me" (*Luke* 10:3 and 16). By these words, Christ did not say that whatever people wanted to believe of His teachings, they can. He did not say that anyone can believe what they wanted to and He would understand. He clearly said: "...he who rejects you (the teachers) rejects me."

Christ never meant to have His teachings torn apart by an individual's homemade religion. He chose only a few teachers and sent them to the multitudes to teach His truths the way He wanted them taught. This same method of teaching the truths of God is still with us. We learn the truths of God by and through the Catholic Church. We find and follow Christ within the Church and her sacraments. We reach union with God through and with the grace found in Christ's Church and in the sacraments.

Chapter 6

GRACE, THE LIGHT OF PERFECTION

As I said in another chapter, Christ told us to be perfect. But how could anyone become perfect while still living a human life, filled with weaknesses and human faults and frailties? Some people are so overwhelmed by such faults and weaknesses that they make no attempt to overcome them. They merely shrug their shoulders and say: "Well, that is the way I am and there is nothing I can do about it!"

But is that true? Can something be done so that sins, faults and weaknesses can disappear, actually changing someone into a better person?

Yes, something can be done and that "something" is called grace.

However, even before grace comes into the picture, something else must be taken into consideration. Before a person can seek, ask for and use grace, he or she must discover within his or her spiritual life the *need for grace*. In other words, the person must come to the realization that something is wrong with his or her relationship with God, and then desire to correct that wrong.

One day a gentleman was speaking to me about his personal spiritual life. Before his conversation, he had been a rough and tough construction worker working with men who were equally rough and tough. They cared little about God or their souls. They used the worst possible kind of language and believed the worst kind of moral teachings. One day, after this man had been converted, after the realization of what his life had been, after his attempts to improve his own spiritual life, he looked at the ways and heard the remarks of his fellow workers and said to himself: "My God, did I act and speak like *that?*" He had to answer that he had indeed acted and he had spoken in the way which now seemed to him to be so deplorable. When he was "one of the crowd" in deeds, words and beliefs, he could not see how wrong they were. But suddenly he no longer wanted to be "one of the crowd." He wanted to become closer to God.

What changed him? What gave him the spiritual insight to see the difference between what he was and what he wanted to become? What made him realize that his whole life had to change if he were to have a meaningful relationship with his Redeemer?

The answer to all those questions is one word: grace.

He was, first of all, given the grace to see the wrongs in his life. He was given the grace to want to change his life. Then he was given the grace to change, and finally he was given the grace to compare his new life with his old. Grace, the illuminating light of grace, made all those things possible. Without grace, none of those things could have happened. Without the light of grace which reveals and purifies, that man no doubt would have stayed, as he was, living a life away from Christ, the sacraments and the pathway which leads to eternal salvation.

How did he receive such graces? Well, the very first graces could have been obtained through his own desires to correct the wrongs in his life, or they could have been obtained through the prayers of others: perhaps a nun in a faraway convent who prayed that someone might have the graces to repent.

But it is not enough just to receive grace. Grace must be used. Many graces go unused because the person ignores such gifts from God and refuses to use them by refusing to admit to himself that something is wrong with his spiritual relationship with God.

So the very first thing one must do, if grace is to be effective, is to admit to oneself that there is a great need for grace within his or her relationship with God. In other words, one must humble oneself and say: "I am a sinner, I need help, please help me."

This is not an easy thing to do. Oh, the pride of human beings! Truly, the greatest sin of all! It is said that pride is the beginning of most sins. But, on the other hand, humility is the beginning of all virtue.

If you do not have the humility to admit that something is wrong with your personal relationship with God, then never could you climb THE LADDER OF PERFECTION. You could not even begin the climb, because this LADDER OF PERFECTION must be planted deeply within the solid foundation of humility. This humility must be so penetrating that it exposes your own soul to your eyes so that you can clearly see the sad condition of your soul. That is how perfection begins: when the light of grace makes you see the defects in your personal relationship with God.

This is true even if your soul is not in the state of mortal sin. Many people fail to climb THE LADDER OF PERFECTION simply because they cannot see anything really amiss in their relationship with God. They tell themselves that they don't do any "bad" things, they go to Church, they go to Communion, so what is wrong?

A great deal is wrong, Their souls may not be in the state of mortal sin, but their souls are not growing in grace. They have stopped their climb to a closer union with God. They allow their souls to linger in the stagnant waters of inactivity, and by doing that they daily, even hourly, let pass by numerous spiritual treasures which could have been theirs. They also run the risk of easily slipping into mortal sin, not caring, because they are so indifferent about God, grace and their own spiritual relationship with God. They are the lukewarm ones who refuse to face that fact that they are not the type of person they could be. If someone told them they were selfish or that they were spiritually lazy or that they were not daily living their faith, they would be insulted. Yet, the truth is that they are not living their faith as they should be, as Christ demands that they should by saying: "Be perfect as my Father in heaven is perfect." They do not have the humility to say that they lack true holiness.

Holiness! So many people misunderstand holiness or sanctity. We have a goodly number of people who will not go to Mass or to Confession or to Communion because they reason that such things are only for hypocrites or sinners. Such people rather imagine that their personal "holiness" has placed them far above us poor sinners who do go to Mass and to the sacraments.

On the other hand, we have people who won't go to Mass or to the sacraments because they feel "too unworthy," too much of a sinner to go to Mass or to receive the sacraments.

Both these examples, one of pride, the other of false humility, are wrong and prevent a person from climbing THE LADDER OF PERFECTION. Both are far removed from what true humility really is.

The humility needed before one can climb THE LADDER is a very simple, a very pure, a very sincere type of humility which is acknowledged in these facts.

Learn how to take a good look at yourself, your weaknesses and your failings. Be very honest with this self-examination. Do not compare your "goodness" to the "bad" things done by people you know. Compare yourself and the state of your spiritual life to the infinite goodness and perfection of God. When you do that you will discover that you do need a great deal of grace to become the type of person God wants you to become.

This type of humility brings the grace which is needed to help the person conquer sins, faults and human weaknesses, and increase grace within his or her own soul so that he or she can become the type of person God wants the person to become: a person filled with goodness, holiness and grace. It is very important to keep this in mind. Say often: "I must become the type of person *God* wants me to become."

Chapter 7

WHAT IS GRACE?

As I said in previous chapters, religion was not meant to be emotional nor was it meant to be merely a condensed biblical type of religion. Nor was religion meant to be a sort of do-it-yourself brand of encounter with Christ. Religion was meant to be a solid way to salvation which was established by Christ for our benefit. Unfortunately, when religion is surrounded by the emotional and condensed biblical types of religion, its true nature and values become hidden behind a high, thick barrier of false teachings.

But, take away all the trimmings of false teachings, emotions and of the do-it-youself type of religion which surround the true teachings of Christ, and a beautiful picture of what religion really is all about emerges.

Within this picture you will discover that the true, main focal points are the Bible, the sacraments and grace. From the Bible comes the sacraments. From the sacraments come grace. The sacraments are vessels of grace.

But, what exactly is this grace which is so essential to salvation? First of all, it is a gift from God. It is not just any kind of a gift, it is a lifesaving gift of tremendous importance.

Life itself is a gift from God. That is the most important gift from God, life for the body. Equally as important is God's gift of life for the soul called grace. The fact is, grace rises above the human gift of life for the body because grace is a supernatural gift for the eternal soul. Without this supernatural gift, it is impossible to know and to understand Christ. Grace becomes then the pathway to God to salvation and to sanctity.

Grace is what enables a person to climb THE LADDER OF PERFECTION. One day a woman came to me and told me about a friend of hers who was a fallen-away Catholic. This friend was afraid to return to the sacraments because she felt she had no strength to live the life of a good Catholic. She feared that she would fall again. I was asked to write a little note to this woman to give her the courage to return to the sacraments.

I wrote: "I have been told that you do not have the courage and strength to return to the sacraments because you are so afraid that you will never be able to live a true Catholic spiritual life. Indeed you are correct! Alone, relying only upon your own human weaknesses, you could never do that. However, with the help of God's grace you can! It is grace, which is received from the sacraments, which gives you that supernatural strength and courage needed to follow Christ as a true child of the Church. Stop relying only upon yourself. Know that the grace of God will give you what you could never obtain from your own human weaknesses. Pray for this grace, return to the sacraments and know that you are not alone in your struggles for union with God." This woman returned to the sacraments because she realized that with the help of God's grace she could have the strength and the courage which she needed. Her fears left her.

Grace then becomes the center of a well-planned and well-balanced spiritual life.

One of the greatest faults of the condensed bibical religions in that they focus all attention upon knowledge—learning the Bible—and not upon grace. I personally know several people, who are not Catholics, who know the Bible quite well but who do not even know what grace and the sacraments are.

Another person, who was a fallen-away Catholic, studied the Bible day and night; however, she refused to return to the sacraments. When I asked her what grace was, she said she did not know. I asked her how she expected to understand what she read in the Bible if she lacked the grace necessary for such an understanding. She could not answer my question.

Lack of grace is also the reason why many, many people lose their faith. Faith is a gift from God given to a person through the Sacrament of Baptism. However, this faith can be lost, and often is, if this faith is not protected with grace. If a person stops practicing his or her religion, if a person no longer receives the Sacraments of Confession and the Eucharist, then this faith slowly but surely disappears.

Many people have come to me in tears lamenting the fact that a loved one no longer has faith and refuses to go to Mass. Such a person cries: "But, why? He used to be such a good Catholic, now what happened to his faith?" The answer is lack of grace, the grace which is needed to save a person's faith. When the person no longer seeks and uses grace, then it is very easy for faith to slip away.

So, the very first thing that a person must be sure of before he or she can start the climb up THE LADDER OF PERFECTION is to make sure that his or her soul is in the state of grace. What does that mean to have the soul in the state of grace? It means to be in union with God through grace. It means to have the soul shine brighter than the noonday sun because grace lights up the soul. It means that mortal sin has not destroyed this light of grace.

Grace then is the supernatural light of the soul which makes us one with God. We then resemble God. We then become true children of God. We then are in the image and likeness of God. It is this grace, this supernatural light within the soul, which makes us able to say that we are like God: His true children, heirs to His kingdom of heaven. When the soul is in the "state of grace," it is filled with this supernatural light which unites it with God. When the soul is not in the "state of grace," when mortal sin (and only mortal sin can do this) has destroyed this grace and this light, then the soul has lost its supernatural union with God. If the person dies in such a deplorable spiritual state, "not in the state of grace," then the soul will be condemned for all eternity.

Catholics, who attempt to "find" Christ with some sort of a "do-it-yourself" type of religion, not only ignore the facts concerning grace, *but can never be sure that they, themselves, possess this supernatural requirement* for their own personal salvation.

Biblical religions, which refuse to even acknowledge grace, also refuse to see the dangers which surround souls which may not be in the state of grace. Thus some of them may practice all sorts of vile, evil ways to "find" Christ which include wild songs, dances, and even sex or drugs. There is an expression among some such groups which goes something like this: "Let us get high on Christ." They may even believe that as long as they read the Bible as part of their religious practices, then any and all indecent actions, deeds and words are perfectly all right.

Such so-called "modern" teachings and practices are not as modern as some people think. They are reminiscent of long-dead, ancient heresies called Justification and Jansenism.

The heresy of Justification came into being during the Martin Luther era and was condemned by the Coucil of Trent (1545-63). Basically, this heresy (false teaching) revolved around man's inability to fight sin. It taught that man is passive, like a stone. After Adam's fall there was no longer any freedom of the human will and that nothing but faith is required to achieve justification and salvation. The heresy went on to teach that nothing, not even the Ten Commandments, had anything to do with salvation or living a Christian life. There was only one mortal sin, that of not believing. Once a person believed in Christ as only the Redeemer (not as a lawgiver who has to be obeyed) that alone assured salvation. The final conclusion of such a distorted teaching was that once a person is justified through faith alone in Christ, the Redeemer, he cannot sin nor fall from the one grace of belief. He is then automatically saved no matter what he does.

As I said, these teachings were condemned by the Council of Trent. So also were the teachings of Cornelis Jansen, bishop of Yores, Belgium (1585-1638), which said almost the same things. The errors of Jansenism as this heresy was known, were condemned by Popes Urban VIII, Innocent X and Clement XI, yet today you find echoes of these same false teachings rising up (especially in some biblical religions) to confuse great masses of people.

There is a strong tendency among these people to believe that nothing they do is a sin as long as they want to do it. This is called "doing your own thing." It includes Bible study, even belief in the Redeemer; however it *does not include* feelings of guilt for sins committed. "There is only one sin," we are being told by some biblical students, "and that is not believing in Christ, the Saviour!" What nonsense!

I received a letter from someone who had fallen into such a spiritual state. The letter and also a booklet, which I received, were filled with the worst possible pornographic, obscene materials and words. Yet I was told by the writer that such words were used in the book and her letter to tell people that nothing is a sin as long as you believe in Christ the Redeemer. Human beings are not capable of conquering sin, so it is all right to sin because Christ already saved us with His death upon the cross. She adopted some sort of a theory of total innocence relating to sin which took away all responsibility for sins committed.

Needless to say, that person was sadly mistaken. Merely to lose the feelings of guilt for sins committed does not make a person innocent of sin nor does it make the person incapable of committing serious sins. Morality and moral laws come from God, through the Church and her teachings. Such laws are for all people of all eras. God does not change His Commandments every century to suit the needs of certain generations or of certain individuals. If a person's conscience has been silenced through false teachings or lack of grace, it is the person's responsibility and duty to find out the truths of God's laws and to return to the practice of these truths. It is man who must change, not God and His moral truths and teachings. It is man who must learn how to use grace to overcome sin, human weaknesses and faults so that he can become more closely united with his God in holiness and love for His holy will.

Grace then, not only gives to the soul the supernatural light or requirement for salvation and union with God, it also gives to the person enlightenments about God, His truths, virtue and holiness. Grace not only places the soul in union with God, but also places the soul in a state of enlightenment about God whereby the person wants to know *whom it is he or she is in union with*. The greater and more abundant grace becomes within the soul, the greater becomes the person's capability to know and understand God, His ways, His laws and His teachings. So it is not enough just to have grace, a person must and should increase this grace. How? Through prayer and the sacraments.

Grace first enters the soul through the Sacrament of Baptism. That is the very first step to becoming a true child of God made in His image and likeness. That grace is called sanctifying grace.

Many people think that Baptism makes a person only one with the Church, a member of the Church. But there is much more to Baptism than that. Baptism brings to the soul the very first magnificent rays of supernatural light. The sunlight from the sky can fall upon an infant and bring to this child a feeling of warmth and bathe the child in light. But this warmth and light is only for the body if the child is not baptized. Baptism gives to the soul of this child a far more intense warmth and light than the sun could ever bring to the infant's body. The child's soul then has the supernatural light of grace making this child one with God. This light remains within the soul of the child until the first mortal sin is committed.

When that happens, when this child, having reached the age of reason, commits his or her first mortal sin, the light of sanctifying grace goes out and darkness descends upon the soul. The reason why serious sins are called mortal is that such sins destroy or kill the light of grace within the soul. Some people misunderstand this because they do not know about grace. They say that mortal sin kills the soul. They might even use biblical passages saying that the Bible says the "soul dies." That is not true. The soul is eternal. What dies is grace the supernatural light of the soul.

Mortal sin destroys the light of grace within the soul and plunges the soul into darkness. At that moment many disastrous things happen. The person loses his or her union with God. The person loses his or her right to merit from any good deeds or actions done. The person loses the right to receive the Holy

Eucharist. The person turns away from God and places himself or herself in darkness outside the company of God and the saints. The person makes himself or herself an outcast and drifts alone on stormy waters which could lead to eternal torment.

As long as the mortal sin remains, so does the darkness which has invaded the person's soul. All his or her good deeds and actions have no supernatural merits, because the condition for obtaining these merits has been destroyed. Very soon, if the person has no intentions of repentance, his or her faith will suffer. Without grace, there is no spiritual strength to fight temptations. As this strength fades, it will become easier and easier to commit more and even greater sins. The longer the soul remains in the state of mortal sin, the easier it is to silence a nagging conscience, and the more difficult it will become to return the soul into its former state of light and grace.

But, thank God, there is a way and a means to return the soul into the state of grace. There is the confessional, the Sacrament of Penance, and within this sacrament there can be found the sanctifying grace which mortal sin had destroyed. A valid confession restores sanctifying grace and once again the supernatural light of grace floods the soul to repair all the damage done by mortal sin: the soul becomes reunited with God. It now becomes an heir to the kingdom of heaven. Merits are restored and can now be gained in greater number. The soul becomes stronger and temptations weaker. The soul is returned to the company of God and the saints, and Holy Communion can be received bringing an increase of sanctifying grace.

After sanctifying grace has been restored, then actual grace enters the picture. Sanctifying grace is the *supernatural light* which makes a person one with God. Actual grace is a *spiritual help* which gives him or her added spiritual assistance to live a holy Christian life. Examples of actual graces are: a desire to learn more about our beautiful Catholic Religion, a desire to learn how to love God more, an inspiration which draws a person closer to Mary, the Mother of God, the ability to use ways and means to practice charity, a longing to receive the sacraments more *often,* acquiring a virtue such as patience, and so forth. Actual graces may come to us through words, deeds, actions, desires, longings and prayers. Or they may come from others whereby we are given an opportunity to know more about God, to love God more, to be a better Catholic and to live a holier spiritual life or to follow someone's examples of holiness.

Actual graces come upon us in a steady-never-ending stream of lights and inspirations which we receive from others, or from the Church, or through the sacraments, or through prayers or through spiritual reading.

However, it is not enough just to have these actual graces come to us in a never-ending stream, we must use *them!*

Unused graces, graces which are ignored or cast aside, can do us no good. If these graces are lost, they are lost forever never to return. Becoming holier, climbing THE LADDER OF PERFECTION is a "now" thing and it is a constant, daily, hourly challenge. There is no waiting for another day or another year to get started. It has to be a "now" a "today" sort of thing. Why? Because graces for spiritual improvement and advancement are not reserved for any special day or time of the year or for any special year. They come and go, like flashing lights in a dark night, every moment of every day and night. You must use them as they come. They cannot be put in storage to be used another day, another month or another year. Lost graces, lost merits are gone forever.

Also, as I already stated, a person without sanctifying grace is a person who has lost union with God and there is *no merit* in anything he or she does. Merit is the reward, which will last forever, which God reserves for all of us because of our good deeds and good works. But if the soul has not been in union with God through the channel of sanctifying grace, if the soul does not merit first of all heaven, how can this soul merit any rewards for good deeds which will last forever in heaven? The soul cannot gain any merits if the soul has cast itself away from the grace which is needed for salvation and merit.

Picture the plight of a man or woman who has lost sanctifying grace and exists outside the union with God. No matter what grand and noble deeds and actions such a person does, no matter how much applause and praise such a person receives from society for said grand and noble deeds, not one of these actions has any value in the eyes of God.

The person, as long as the soul remains in the state of mortal sin, lives totally alone away from God. Such a person can try, and can even succeed, to please the world and society with great acts of a true heroic nature. Such a person can secretly carry heavy crosses. Such a person can show goodness and concern for others; and yet, all is wasted all is in vain as far as God is concerned.

Nothing that this person does or suffers has any eternal merit! Such deeds and actions may have some sort of a human value. Surely the ones who are helped by this person have a right to be most grateful, yet the value is only that: human. There is no eternal value, nothing which can claim for itself an eternal reward.

You often hear people say that goodness is enough for them. They will tell you that they are good, they don't do bad things, they don't murder or steal, so why do they need God and the sacraments! They forget (or do not know) that human goodness alone becomes and stays only human goodness if the supernatural power of sanctifying grace does not put an eternal value upon goodness.

So, the very first step to union with God and climbing THE LADDER OF PERFECTION is to make sure that your soul is in the state of grace. Go to confession. That is the start. It is also the safe harbor or refuge as one tries to climb THE LADDER and finds that once in a while there is a slip or a miss. No matter how often you fall into mortal sin, the Sacrament of Penance can repair the damage and merits from past good deeds and actions can be restored.

Also, be sure to recognize and use all the actual graces which come your way. They are a must if you want to keep your soul in the state of grace (sanctifying grace). They are the spiritual weapons which you need so that you can advance to a closer union with God; and they make your soul a dwelling place for God.

Chapter 8

HOW TO USE GRACE

Once sanctifying grace makes your soul a dwelling place for God, this grace must be protected, increased and used. As I have already stated in another chapter, most people are content merely to have grace. They think that making a valid confession is all that has to be done for God and for their own souls. As a result they do not use grace as it should be used to bring the soul into a closer union with God.

How does a person use grace for the good of his or her own soul? First of all, remember there are basically two different kinds or types of grace: sanctifying grace and actual grace. Sanctifying grace brings light to a soul darkened by sin; thusly, it is received when a person is baptized and when a valid confession is made after a mortal sin had been committed. Actual graces are the momentary impulses or desires or inspirations which prompt a person to do something good for God, for others or for his or her own soul.

An understanding of these two different types of grace helps you use grace more efficiently. To elaborate a bit, I will add this information for your benefit. Remember that sanctifying grace is *increased* as well as used. Actual grace is the kind that comes and goes. It does not linger in the soul as does sanctifying grace. Once an actual grace comes to you, such as a thought to put an extra dollar in the poor box, and this inspiration is pushed aside or ignored, that grace is lost forever. It has been said that in purgatory there is a special punishment for misused or ignored graces such as the one I just mentioned. In other words, actual grace is a "now" sort of thing. Such graces come for a moment and if not used disappear as fast as they came. So the secret of using actual graces as they should be used is to follow through whenever you are inspired to do a good deed, say an extra prayer, go to Holy Communion more often, etc. Such thoughts or desires are not accidental. They have been given to you by God to bring you into a closer union with Him. You will be amazed to discover that the more you use these actual graces the more such graces will be given to you. God gives you graces in proportion to your desires and abilities to use them. The more you ignore and push aside actual graces, the less graces will be sent to you. If you form a habit of looking for and recognizing actual graces, and using them, you will receive numerous graces. You will also be able to (have the grace to) freely acknowledge the times when you did not respond to grace and let slip by an opportunity to gain a treasure for heaven by ignoring a precious grace from God.

Also, sanctifying and actual graces are needed in order to gain and use virtue. The first virtues you receive are infused into your soul when your soul is given sanctifying grace. Actual graces are bestowed upon you so these virtues can be used and protected and new virtues acquired. The inspirations to do good not only are given so that an opportunity to gain merits is presented, but also there exists in these same inspirations the opportunity to gain or increase a certain virtue. Notice how closely using actual graces and gaining or increasing virtues are connected. For example: if a grace is given to you to help a friend in need and you respond to that grace, the virtue of charity is also strengthened and increased. At the same time, actual graces increase because charity is one way to increase actual graces. More actual graces are bestowed upon you because you accepted the grace to do a charitable deed. Finally, you are entitled to an eternal reward for your good deed. That is the merit you gained.

In essence then, actual graces serve many important functions in your attempts to climb THE LADDER OF PERFECTION. The fact is, you cannot even begin this ascent unless you are given the actual graces which inspire you to desire a closer union with

God. While fulfilling these desires, actual graces will be bestowed upon you in the necessary amounts needed so that your climb can continue. So you can see how vital, to your spiritual growth, it is for you to be able to recognize actual graces *and to use them.*

In summary, when you receive and use actual graces, all the following happen. If you use an actual grace to see your neighbor's good points instead of his faults and use another actual grace to bear with his faults, and then use another actual grace to tell yourself that you also have faults (three actual graces used), you have taken three steps up THE LADDER OF PERFECTION. You have strengthened sanctifying grace so that there is less chance of losing it. You have strengthened the infused virtue of charity. You have gained merits which are the eternal rewards for doing good deeds, etc. and you have opened the way by which God can give you more actual graces to use. In addition, you have perhaps received a new virtue, one called self knowledge.

Now reverse all of which I have just said and you will see what you could have lost if these three graces had been cast aside, ignored or not recognized. So the secret of holiness is to recognize and use to full advantage all the graces which are bestowed upon you.

It is fairly easy to find out if you do or do not use grace as it should be used. You have only to take a good, honest look at yourself and ask: how many sins, faults or bad habits did I do away with last year or the year before? Chances are this answer is: none! You are still the same person you were last year and the year before and the year before that as far as virtue and holiness are concerned. Oh, you might have thought about giving up a certain pet sin or bad habit, you might have made an attempt to pray more or say the Rosary, you might have made an attempt to go to daily Mass or to fast now and then; but you never quite succeeded in carrying out all your good intentions. If you have seen no noticeable improvement in your personal spiritual life (except, perhaps, to receive grace back if lost through mortal sin) then you have not used grace as it should and can be used. Then you have also constantly misused actual graces, these graces that inspire you to overcome bad habits, sins and faults as well as to do good deeds.

What would a "noticeable improvement" in your spiritual life be? The very first improvement which would be noticeable would be a desire to want to do more for God and for your own spiritual life. Most people do not have such a desire. Even some people who say the Rosary everyday or go to Communion every morning do not have a desire to want to do more for God and for their own souls. They are content to have their spiritual lives stand still in stagnant waters. They may not commit serious sins; however, they go on year after year tied up in bad habits or faults or "little sins." This binding is so tight that these people do not even see the lack of virtue or graces in their own personal spiritual lives. They do not commit mortal sins, as I said, but they overlook such things as being very selfish, being uncharitable, telling little "white" lies, keeping things that don't belong to them, showing anger or impatience, wasting time instead of doing a good deed, etc. In other words, they do not care how lacking in virtue and holiness their own spiritual lives are.

Chapter 9

HOW ACTUAL GRACES ARE RECEIVED

Where do the actual graces, which are so necessary to live an active spiritual life, come from? How does a person increase this flow of graces to his or her soul?

As I said, the first and most important grace received is sanctifying grace. If this grace is lost through mortal sin, then the person will start receiving actual graces or inspirations which tell the person to return to confession as soon as possible. Where do such graces come from and how do these graces find this particular person? After the person goes to confession and sanctifying grace is restored, he or she will start to receive more actual graces so that sanctifying grace is protected, increased and virtues gained. Where do these actual graces come from?

I could simply end this chapter here and say, "only God knows" but that would be only a half-true statement. Many graces come to us from unidentified sources, however, many graces we can obtain for ourselves.

First of all, a person who has the misfortune to fall into mortal sin and a worse misfortune to have no desires to correct this serious situation, may suddenly, for no apparent reason, have an intense longing to go to confession. Where did this longing come from? Now, you can say: "No one knows, only God."

True. Perhaps an ill nun in a convent thousands of miles away from this sinner offered her sufferings so that a sinner could be saved. God took this offering and bestowed an actual grace upon one individual, the one who, for no apparent reason, suddenly had an intense longing to go to confession. The nun will never know, until after her death, which sinner received the grace which she had sent outward towards someone who was in dire need of such a grace. The sinner will never know, until he is in heaven, who obtained the grace of his conversion for him. See the way God sometimes makes our very salvation interdependent upon others, upon their sufferings and prayers and love?

In exactly the same way others, whom we may not even know, may be obtaining many graces for us through their prayers or sufferings. Or else someone we do know may be praying for our spiritual welfare and we may receive graces that way. We also receive many graces from our Church because priests, bishops and even the Pope pray for the spiritual well-being of their "children," us. Saints in heaven, our guardian angels, the Blessed Virgin, relatives who are in heaven or in purgatory, all may be obtaining for us innumerable graces which we need.

Actually there is a never-ending stream of graces which flow upon souls every moment of every day and night. However, ninety percent of the time most people do not even bother to find spiritual refreshment and nourishment from this source. Each and every grace within that stream must be accepted and used or else it will disappear and be lost forever. One of the secrets of sanctity is to realize exactly how much grace is made available for your personal use. For every temptation which comes your way, there are many graces ready for the battle which can be used to fight such a temptation.

One way to realize how much grace is available for you to use in your climb towards perfection is to add to the stream of graces which falls upon your soul. You do that by asking for graces by your own prayers and desires for these graces.

That statement no doubt surprises you. I know it surprised hundreds of people I have helped live a more active spiritual life. The standard answer to that statement is: "Who me, pray for myself? I never pray for myself? I always pray for others! How can I ask for graces for myself?" To make such a remark shows a great deal of lack of knowledge about living an active spiritual life and climbing THE LADDER OF PERFECTION. Why? Because everything you do in order to live a closer union with God brings to you added graces whether you know that fact or do not know it. You open new channels of grace each time you take a step up THE LADDER OF PERFECTION. Each time you use grace to help someone, to pray more, to fast, to do penance, to receive the sacraments more often, you open the way for more and greater graces to be given to you. To ignore such graces would be a very serious mistake. To say you don't want any such graces for yourself would be making another serious mistake. You must want and recognize these graces simply because you *desperately need them* if you are to reach a closer union with God. The fact is, you need these graces so desperately that you must not be satisfied with anything less than a multitude of graces which can help you reach your spiritual goals. You must do all in your power to desire and strive to obtain all the spiritual help you need upon the battlefields of life.

Why do I make such statements? Well, for one reason, grace is the weapon used to fight the devil and his temptations. Without grace, you cannot hope to win even a small spiritual battle. Without grace, you cannot obtain and increase supernatural virtues. Without grace, you cannot gain spiritual treasures (merits) which will last forever. Without grace, you cannot protect nor increase your own holiness. So grace becomes not only the necessary weapon which is needed to fight spiritual battles, it becomes your armor as well.

No soldier would ever go out on to the battlefields without first checking to see that his weapons were in proper working order. If he had to wear armor, he would make sure that it did not contain any weak spots. In other words, he would make sure that he was well-prepared for the battle. Grace is what prepares you for your personal spiritual battles. When seen in that light, then you can better understand why you must recognize these actual graces for what they are and desire them at all times, and possess as many graces as it is possible for you to possess. Never say that you do not want or that you do not need or that you will not pray for graces. Instead see and know how much grace you really need and do not be too bashful to pray for the graces you need. That is the way you ask God or our Lady to help you fight the devil and his temptations: and you can be sure that your prayers for grace will be answered. God does not consider you selfish if you pray for this spiritual help. The opposite is true. Do not forget that Christ taught us to pray to Our Father in heaven for our daily bread. As important as food for our bodies is, food (or grace) for our souls is far more important.

Now, exactly how do you do that: pray for the graces which you know you will need to help you live an active spiritual life? That may seem to be a difficult task at first, but it will become much easier as your spiritual life shows improvement.

The secret of praying for the graces you need is to look at your own spiritual life and see what it lacks in the way of virtue; while at the same time, you look for and notice your human weaknesses. In other words, take an honest look at all your sins (venial as well as mortal) weaknesses and faults and realize that only with the help of God's grace can you overcome them. While it is true that often you receive graces which surprise you, such as a grand feeling of closeness to God after leaving the confessional, at least be sensible enough to *ask* for the graces you know you desperately need in order to fight the temptations which could lead you into sin and the venial sins which could lead you into mortal sin.

As I said, at first you may find a great deal of difficulty trying to decide what graces you need so that you can take the next step up THE LADDER OF PERFECTION. The reason why this task becomes difficult can be viewed as being sort of amusing. It is that few people see themselves as being in need of the spiritual help which graces bring. In other words, most people cannot find anything wrong with their spiritual lives and they see no reason to pray for the graces which they need in order to improve their relationship with God. That fact was made clear to me when one day a friend of mine called to tell me that her sister-in-law was in the hospital. This woman had been away from the sacraments. At the hospital she had asked the priest to bring her Holy Communion; however, she insisted that she would not go to confession because she insisted that she had never done anything wrong. Of course such an attitude was deplorable to say the least and was very much lacking in humility. Her proper attitude should have been not only to go to confession, but to pray for the grace of true sorrow for all her sins even if such sins had not been mortal. We have only to examine the lives of the saints and to see their reaction to their own faults and failings to understand what our reaction should be.

They may not have been great sinners, but they understood the true malice of even a slight fault or failing and they constantly prayed for the graces to overcome such weaknesses of their human nature.

If you honestly viewed your thoughts, words and deeds, you can indeed find many areas which need spiritual improvement. For example: many people become angry for no reason at all or show great impatience when confronted with a slight inconvenience. Other people love to gossip or say unkind things about their friends and relatives. Still others find it easy to steal little things such as stamps at the office where they work. All such faults or venial sins may not make a person a great sinner, but they do hinder the person's spiritual advancement. Unless such faults (and a "million" others like these) are seen *and corrected* with the help of God's grace, there can be no spiritual advancement!

One of the secrets of spiritual advancement is to pray constantly for the graces which you need so that you can see and correct the many failings in your spiritual life especially the so-called "hidden" faults and failings. These are the ones which have become so embedded in your personality that you do not even notice them, and which might shock you if someone mentioned them to you. I am reminded of a little story which brings out the point I am trying to make very well.

A friend of mine, who was (at that time) an executive, had a secretary who made several serious mistakes. She could not see them. One day she said to her employer: "If I ever do something wrong then please be sure and tell me." He explained: "Well, one day she did do something very wrong and I told her but after I did, she would not speak to me for a couple of weeks!" If this young lady had been trying to climb THE LADDER OF PERFECTION at that time she would have welcomed the opportunity which revealed her fault so that she could have prayed for the grace needed to correct it.

A truly remarkable thing happens when you do start to search for and to correct your faults and failings with the help of God's graces. The more faults and failings you correct, the more will take their place! For example, if you correct a fault of talking about someone in an unkind way, you may discover that in place of that fault you now have another which you never had before! Such a situation may become a barrier to your spiritual advancement unless you know the following information.

The fault or sin or weakness which took the place of the one you corrected was not really new at all. It is just that you never noticed it before. A direct result of using grace to overcome faults, failings, etc., is that you are more able to recognize your shortcomings. The more faults you correct, the more clearly will you see what remains which has to be corrected. Grace (and using grace) acts like a mirror in which become visible your faults and weaknesses. This is not a *bad* thing which should discourage you but a *good* thing because this is the way to advance up THE LADDER OF PERFECTION. Why? Because only when you are *aware* of your own faults, weaknesses and sins, only then can you pray for the graces which you need so that they can be corrected by replacing them with virtue.

The whole process of reaching a closer union with God is to become aware of your own failings, sins, faults, weaknesses, etc. and to replace them with virtue. Virtue is what holiness is all about. A truly virtuous person is a holy person. But this desired state of love for and union with God cannot be reached without grace.

So, in addition to the graces which God sends to you from sources which you do not know, never neglect to pray for the graces which you know you need as you daily battle the world, the flesh and the devil.

One last word: as you search to find your own faults and failings which prevent your spiritual advancement, *do not* become scrupulous. Do not think that "everything" you do or say or think is wrong. Just honestly search to find the faults which prevent your spiritual advancement and pray for the graces so that you will find them, correct them, and replace them with virtues.

Chapter 10

HOW TO INCREASE SANCTIFYING GRACE

By the time you reach this chapter, you should know that there are two basic types of grace: sanctifying grace and actual grace. Sanctifying grace when received stays with the soul until mortal sin destroys it. Then it can be recovered in the confessional. Actual grace or graces are the ones which come and go: the inspirations, thoughts, words, etc. which help you protect sanctifying grace and live an active spiritual life or return to confession if a mortal sin has been committed.

Now you must learn how to increase sanctifying grace: the grace which stays within the soul and remains until a mortal sin destroys it.

First of all you must know when you *do have* or *do not have* sanctifying grace. It is very important to be able, at all times, to say: "Yes. My soul is in the state of grace. It has sanctifying grace." Unless you can make such a precise, definite statement, you will not do anything to increase this grace.

Many people feel it is an act of pride to say that their souls do indeed have sanctifying grace. So they hesitate and make a statement such as: "Oh, I hope my soul is in the state of grace because I know it has to be so that I can go to heaven; but I am not sure I will go to heaven. I hope I do." Such spiritual insecurity must be remedied before a person can attempt to reach a closer union with God. Union with God must start with Divine Indwelling, God living in the soul. Divine Indwelling cannot take place unless the soul is in the state of grace, unless the soul has sanctifying grace. So, you must not only desire grace for your soul, you must not only desire Divine Indwelling, you must be certain that your soul is indeed in the state of grace. This is not an act of pride, it is your duty and responsibility as a Catholic. Christ wants you to save your soul. He wants your soul in the state of grace. You must be sure it is in the state of grace at all times.

How can you be sure? Begin by thinking of the mortal sins which you may have committed. A mortal sin is a deliberate serious offense against God. You must know that the offense is serious. You must have made sufficient reflection upon the matter and then do the deed with your full consent. Did you confess all your mortal sins? Did you hide away? If you did, you did not make a valid confession. Did you make a sincere act of repentance or sorrow at your last valid confession? Did you make a firm purpose of amendment? If you did make an honest, valid confession and did not hide any mortal sins, if you received absolution, then your soul was in the state of grace when you left the confessional. If you have not committed a mortal sin since your last valid confession (or if you have never committed a mortal sin) then you should know, without any doubts, that your soul is in the state of grace. If you are not sure and cannot be sure in your own mind, then go to confession, explain your doubts to the priest, and he will help you. Do not allow your past, *confessed mortal sins* to fill you with doubts and fears. A valid confession does restore sanctifying grace if it had been lost through mortal sin. If, by chance, you remember a mortal sin which you forgot to confess, then return to the confessional and explain to the priest what happened. He will put your mind at ease.

When there are no mortal sins upon your soul, your soul is in the state of grace. You possess sanctifying grace and God dwells within your whole being. Now increase the light or quality of that grace.

How and why? I will answer the last question first: why bother to increase sanctifying grace? Isn't just having your soul in the state of grace enough? Yes, it is enough if you want to settle for the least union with God. But if you want a closer, a more precious union with God, you must strive to increase the quality of grace. Grace, as taught by the Church, is given whole and complete. However, grace can be increased by and through our cooperation and participation in the life of grace through an increase in virtuous acts and deeds. The more your soul is purified, by such an increase and destruction of self-love, the more alert it becomes to the action of God within your soul and to the presence of God within your soul.

Your awareness of Divine Indwelling will increase *only to the quality* of sanctifying grace which your soul possesses. While God extends to you infinite love and mercy at all times, He cannot explode upon your soul the full awareness of His presence until your soul becomes ready for this intimate union with Him. Only an increase of sanctifying grace makes your soul ready for this realization, because without such an increase, you would not even know what the awareness of His presence is. You would not be capable of understanding it.

Also, increasing the quality of sanctifying grace allows you to do more of the work which God created you to do. God does not create a person merely to be the object of His love and grace, the recipient of His gifts. God does not expect a person to stand still, in this world, not responding to His love and grace. God created man and woman and gave them the supernatural gift of grace so that, by and through grace, they can freely work with God and for God. When you increase sanctifying grace in your own soul, you are more capable of doing God's work as He desires you to do it.

God's work for you or His will for you consists, basically, of two parts: what you do for your own soul and spiritual life and what you do for others. The first component involves carrying out your daily duties in your own state of life, while at the same time, living in close union with God. The second is helping others by the virtue of charity, while at the same time, living in close union with God. Christ summarized these two obligations when He said: "The first commandment is this, that you should love the Lord, your God, with your whole heart and with your whole soul and with your whole mind. And the second is like the first, you shall love your neighbor as yourself" (*Matt.* 22:37).

You could not even begin to fulfill these two commandments

if your soul does not have sanctifying grace. Grace, being supernatural, is what is needed to raise a person above purely natural, materialistic matter and motivations. Confusion, about correct, holy principles of life and religion, is always the trademark of those who attempt to live a life away from Christ, His Church, the sacraments and grace. That is why such people constantly attempt to rationalize away their wrongdoings and sins. Sanctifying grace leads a person into the type of life which God wants him to live; because, along with this grace, there comes the weapons needed to fight the temptations which would turn a person away from the goal of perfection which God wills all men and women to reach. Grace, sanctifying grace, not only unites them to God and God to them but brings to the soul the infused virtues which are absolutely necessary if a person is to love God with his or her whole being and love others as God does. Without such virtues as faith, hope, charity, love for God and others, Christian prudence, fortitude, spiritual knowledge and insight (as well as understanding), human life could not be seen as a journey towards everlasting, eternal joy in heaven with God. Without grace and the virtues which this grace brings, life becomes merely an endless, often futile, attempt to fulfill natural desires and ambitions.

So, by increasing the quality of sanctifying grace within your own soul, you increase your capability to more completely fulfill God's commandments and to reach the goals of perfection which He desires you to reach. This increase in grace increases the virtues which are a must if you are to become the type of a person and to live the type of a life God wants you to.

In addition, sanctifying grace must not only be present, at all times, cherished and protected but must also be *increased;* because, once the heavenly goal is finally reached, the measure or reward of your eternal happiness will be determined by the *quality* of sanctifying grace which is within your soul when you die. You see, this determination depends upon how well you knew and understood God while on earth and how much love you possessed for Him before your death.

You cannot know God in any other way except with, by and

through sanctifying grace. A person whose soul is in mortal sin can read about God and can know that He exists, but such a person could not truly understand God and His ways without grace. Grace is the only way which leads a soul into the virtues of wisdom and understanding which give to the person a clear knowledge of who God is and what God wants him to do with his life. And grace enables the person to see God face-to-face after death. That is why a person, whose soul is in the state of mortal sin at death, could never enter heaven. The element, grace, which is necessary in order to see God face-to-face is missing. Without this grace, the person, if he or she were allowed to stay in heaven, would be totally unable to understand who God is and would not have the capacity for a personal union with God. He would also be unable to love God or to even understand what loving God means.

Grace is thus required to enter heaven; however, there are many different degrees or levels of happiness in heaven. Not everyone receives the same eternal rewards. God's greatest reward are for those who knew, understood and loved Him the most while on earth. In order to know, love and understand God to a greater degree, you must increase sanctifying grace. Only by such an increase will you be able to, at the same time, increase the virtues (which come with this grace) of wisdom, knowledge and understanding which are needed if a person is to love and know God more intimately and obtain a greater increase of eternal happiness. That is what Christ meant when He said: ". . .but lay up for yourselves treasures in heaven. . ." (*Matt.* 6:20). These eternal treasures are your rewards or measure of happiness which you have gained while on earth. The more union with God you obtained on earth, the more treasures will be yours in heaven. The only way to this greater degree of union with God on earth, which results in greater eternal happiness, is by an increase in the quality of sanctifying grace. As I said at the beginning of this chapter, why settle for the least union with God and the least degree of eternal happiness when it is within your reach or power to obtain a very great increase of union with God and eternal happiness by an increase in the grace within your own soul.

Now you see that there are many reasons why sanctifying grace must and should be increased especially if you desire a closer union with God. But just how is that done, increase sanctifying grace?

There are two main sources of divine grace: prayer and the sacraments. Once we have sanctifying grace, it is basically by these two means that this grace is increased in our souls. If we lose this grace, as I said, the Sacrament of Penance restores this lost grace.

There are, of course, various types of prayers, which I shall explain in another chapter, but the greatest prayer of all is the Mass. Within the Mass is the Sacrament of Holy Eucharist. These two combined: the Mass and the Sacrament of Holy Eucharist become for you a truly limitless source of grace. As often as you receive the Sacraments of Confession and Holy Eucharist, as often as you go to Mass, then, constantly, the sanctifying grace within your soul increases as one responds to this grace. If we do not respond many graces at Mass or when the Sacraments of Confession and Holy Communion are received are wasted and the actual increase of sanctifying grace could be very slight. So the secret is to make use of all the actual graces which can be yours when you pray and when you receive the sacraments so that sanctifying grace and your union with God can increase tremendously.

In addition, sanctifying grace increases by and through good works which gain the merits which determine the degree or measure of your eternal happiness.

Sanctifying grace when first received, although complete in itself, is but a tiny seed that needs to be cultivated. That means that we grow in this grace and increase the quality through living a life of grace, ever striving to become more Christ-like in words, deeds and actions. That means that there should be, daily, a desire to acquire and use virtues for the love of God so as to make all deeds, words and actions worthy of an eternal reward.

Saint James tells us: "What good is it, my brothers, if someone says he has faith, but does not have works?" (*James* 2:14) And: "So also, faith of itself, if it does not have works, is dead" (*James* 2:17).

Chapter 11

THE POWER OF GOD'S GRACE

When I first started to write this book, I called it THE POWER OF GOD'S GRACE. Later I changed the title to COME CLIMB THE LADDER...AND REJOICE. The reason, why I gave this book the first title, was I wanted to convey to my readers the knowledge that God's grace has unbelievable powers. I wanted to make them completely aware of this fantastic power which is within their reach to possess and use. As powerful as the light and fire of the sun are, as powerful as the wind of a wild storm is, as powerful as earthquakes and tornados are, as powerful as a violent blizzard is, none of these forces can possess the wondrous, awesome power of God's grace! Why? Because storms, earthquakes, blizzards and the fire of the noonday sun affect the world we live in. Grace saves souls.

Christ said: "For what does it profit a man if he gains the whole world but suffers the loss of his own soul? Or what will a man give in exchange for his soul?" (*Mark* 8:36-37).

A man's whole world can fall apart and be destroyed by the violent forces of nature, but if he possesses God's grace within his soul, he has retained his most valuable possession for he has the way to eternal happiness. An earthquake can shake the forest and open the ground beneath the trees; but grace can unite a soul with its creator and open the gates of heaven.

Grace is an illuminating light so immense, so brilliant that in all reality it dazzles human comprehension. A person can meditate for a whole lifetime upon the subject of the power of God's grace and still never fathom the endless depths of this gift from God to us, His children. A person can say a thousand times a day that Mary, the Mother of God, was filled with grace and still never really understand what "filled with grace" means. Why? Because, grace is a supernatural gift from God, totally unlike any natural gift given by Him to humans. That being the case, grace has supernatural powers. What does it mean when I say that grace has supernatural powers?

Well, before I explain what the supernatural powers of grace are, let me explain what could be called great natural powers.

Let us suppose that a person possesses many magnificent, unusual powers. For example, say that a man knows all scientific data and facts and figures. Say that a person can speak every language which was ever spoken by man. All who win the gold medals at Olympic games have powers and abilities which they alone possess. You may very well marvel at such displays of power. You may even desire such for yourself. However, even if you did possess all of these powers at once, you would still possess nothing compared to the supernatural powers of grace! Why not? Because no matter how much power, of a human type, which a person possesses, he could still *lose his soul!* Human abilities and powers of themselves could never save a soul. The most brilliant and talented person on earth could not save his soul without grace; however, with grace an ignorant scrubwoman can not only save her soul, but sanctify it as well. But more! With grace, such a person actually has God dwelling within her soul. God shares His very life with a person whose soul is in the state of grace and when a person dies in the state of grace, that person has the supernatural power to actually see God face-to-face, as He really is, for all eternity! No human talent, ability or power could prepare the soul for what is called the "Light of Glory" or the ability to see God face-to-face for all eternity. A person can glory in his own abilities, powers and talents, but if he or she does not possess the supernatural powers of sanctifying grace, all talents and abilities and human powers mean nothing! If the person dies without this grace, he or she has lost everything for all eternity! On the other hand, a person who has nothing while on earth, who is poor, hungry and who lacks the bare necessities of life, can gain everything for all eternity if his or her soul is in the state of grace at the moment of death. One of the supernatural powers of grace is its ability to *last for all eternity*. All human, material powers, talents and abilities end with death. If you have ever stood next to a lifeless corpse which lies ready to be buried, you may have been deeply affected by the sight before your eyes. The person's abilities and powers have ceased to exist. No longer can this person display and use material, natural powers. But if this person died in the state of grace, he or she possessed a supernatural power to love God for all eternity, to share His heavenly home and to sing praises to Him forever. In other words, grace gives to a person something very precious which will last for all eternity, long after natural, material powers and abilities have ceased to exist.

Grace does more, much more, so much that human comprehension could never fully understand this magnificent gift from God to us, His children. It has the power to turn holy words, actions and deeds into treasures which will last forever. These treasures are called merits. Merits are the value which God places upon our good works and deeds. Merits will determine our eternal reward.

Good works and good deeds are always deserving of a reward; however, not all good deeds and good works are deserving of an *eternal reward*. Christ tells us: "Therefore, when you give alms, do not sound the trumpet before you as the hypocrites do in order that they may be honored by men. Amen, I say to you, they have received their reward" (*Matt.* 6:2). Without the supernatural powers of grace, good deeds and good works, even grand or noble works, obtain for the person only a natural reward. They have no supernatural value, a value which will last forever, if they are not done with and through the supernatural powers of grace. A person, whose soul is in the state of mortal sin, cannot merit or expect any eternal reward from God because God and His grace did not take part in the good deeds and works done by this person. In other words, in the eyes of God, such good deeds and good works have no value because the element of this value is missing: the element called grace.

Having sanctifying grace is like putting your name on the

payroll of heaven or writing your name in the book of eternal life. If your name does not appear on these records, if mortal sin erased your name from these records, you cannot expect a reward for your labors and good works. A man can walk into a factory, stand by a man who is working there and start to do exactly the same work. However, he will never be paid for this work even if he does a super job simply because he was never hired in the first place. His name was never put on the payroll. He can cry out and scream that he deserves payment for his labors, but all will be in vain. He cannot receive one cent of pay. In like manner, without sanctifying grace, a person cannot obtain the supernatural rewards found in heaven for his labors on earth.

Now add to these good works and deeds all other things in life which could be deserving of an eternal reward: carrying crosses of sorrow and pain, all sorts of personal sufferings, even prayers said, kindness, personal goodness, etc. All become wasted, without any eternal merit, if the person had done these things while his or her soul was in the state of mortal sin. Why? Because mortal sin and the lack of sanctifying grace made them without merit. "Dead Works" the Church calls them. Dead, because the supernatural life of God's grace was not present to bring to them the deserving eternal reward. If the person dies in the state of mortal sin, all his earthly good deeds and noble works die with him. He has lost everything for all eternity and must suffer an existence without merits or any kind of a reward.

So see the magnificent supernatural power of grace which brings an eternal life to all good deeds and works, sufferings, prayers, virtues, morals, goodness, and so forth. Grace takes human deeds, good works, and so forth, and rises them above and beyond a mere human value giving to them a supernatural value. Long after human value and rewards have faded into a nothingness, supernatural value and rewards will shine brightly as an eternal light which will never end nor grow dim: if this value was obtained by and through grace.

There are more supernatural powers in God's grace. There is the power given to us to help us fight temptations, overcome sins and live a virtuous life. Without the supernatural help of grace, we could never even hope to conquer the world, the flesh and the devil. Alone, without grace, we are helpless. It is a known fact that once a person commits his or her first mortal sin, it becomes easier and easier for other mortal sins to become part of such a life. Why? Because the spiritual strength needed to fight temptations and overcome sins is missing. As I stated, living a virtuous, holy life is not only difficult, it becomes almost impossible in a world which has been programed to sin, evil and corruption. A person needs great help, a supernatural help to live a good, Christ-like type of life. This help lies within the supernatural powers of God's grace. Because these powers do exist in God's grace, Christ felt that He had a right to tell us to be as perfect as His heavenly Father is. The supernatural powers of grace are what turned the greatest sinners into the greatest saints.

Grace also gives you the power to actually help God save souls. Think of how marvelous you would feel if you actually had the power to save lives! How would you feel if you could walk into a hospital where 1000 people, men, women and children, lay dying and if you could save each and every life by saying: "You are cured"! What joy would fill your heart and soul! However, such cures would be only temporal and would end when the person finally died. They would affect only the body. But what if you could actually help God cure a sick, dying soul? What if you could actually help to save a soul, a soul which will live in glory, peace, joy and happiness forever? Well that is possible because with the supernatural powers of grace, you can do just that.

There is a story told about a lowly servant who worked for a powerful, wealthy man of great social and political influence. He held thousands of people under his control. His very word was law to them. But he lacked the greatest power of all: God's grace. He lived his life without God, the sacraments and grace. Then, he was upon his deathbed. Suddenly, he realized what a waste his adult life had been because he had lived it without God. He called for a priest and reunited himself with God through the sacraments. When he did, the lowly servant walked up to his bed and slowly said: "Dear, master, I shall now tell you my most precious secret. I have been your servant for twenty-five years and during that time, I was constantly sad because of your lack of grace and religion. So, I have, for these twenty-five years prayed for your conversion. I have gone to daily Mass and received the Holy Eucharist just so that you might one day return to the practice of your religion. Today that miracle happened. Now, I, myself, can die in peace. My mission has been accomplished."

The grace possessed by the lowly servant was far more powerful than the combined power and influence of the Master. With that grace, the servant helped to save a soul.

There you can see the greatest power of grace; not only to save your own soul but the power one has to actually help God save a soul of a sinner!

So, fully realize what supernatural powers you can possess with grace, the powers which bring salvation, virtues and eternal merits, which generate a light strong enough and bright enough to last for all eternity. Imagine, if you can, the unbelievable power which surges through high tension wires over hundreds of miles from the generating plant to each individual light bulb in hundreds of thousands of homes. But such power is as nothing compared to the power of grace which can surge forth from your own soul and reach out and touch eternity. If your soul is in the state of grace, it becomes a spiritual generating plant producing wave after wave of light bright enough to illuminate the pathway of your entire life so that you will never become a bewildered, lost, lonely soul unable to see the footprints of Christ which lead to your home with Him and His Father. All this and much more, grace brings to you. There is no end to the miracles which can happen in your own soul, in your union with God and in helping the souls of others when you understand and use the supernatural powers of God's grace.

The most marvelous part of grace and its powers is that this grace is yours for the asking. It is not given to nor reserved for only a few chosen souls. The grace which was lost in the

Garden of Eden and then restored on the hill of Calvary belongs to each and every one of us. It is freely given to each soul at Baptism and can be restored, in the confessional, if mortal sin destroys that grace. Realize that grace is a treasure to be cherished. It is your path to salvation. Remember that you will never have a more important job in life to do than the one of saving your own soul through the supernatural powers of God's grace.

Chapter 12

HOW GRACE REVEALS ITSELF

If people could actually see grace, how they would long for it if they did not possess this treasure and how they would cherish grace if they did have it. Grace in itself cannot be seen by human eyes but that does not mean that it is completely invisible. There is a beautiful story told about Mary, the Mother of God. They say that when Mary walked the earth, no one could look into her eyes, except Christ. There was something deep within her gaze which they could not understand. There existed, within the eyes of Mary, a penetrating mysterious something which no one could comprehend because no one knew what "full of grace" really was or meant. As I said, this is only a story; however, it is plausible because grace has a way of revealing itself within the eyes of a person. Mary, who had grace from the moment of her conception, surely must have had a look in her eyes which no one else had, except Christ, and which no one on earth could understand.

There is another story told which is also about eyes and grace. A renowned sinner boasted to all who would listen that he was going to confront a humble priest and "tell him off." The priest has said something which the sinner did not like. Gathering a crowd around him, the man went to the door of the Church and knocked loudly, daring the good priest to "come out from his hiding place." The priest had not been hiding, but praying. He was not afraid to open the door to meet his foe. When he did, he looked deeply into the eyes of his enemy and said softly: "What is it, my son?" The sinner became speechless as he tried to look away but he could not. "What is it, my son?" Father asked again. The sinner slowly stammered: "I...I...don't know" was the reply. Then suddenly the sinner clasped his hands over his eyes and ran away. Later when his followers asked him why he had acted in such a cowardly way, the man replied: "I don't know what happened, but when Father looked at me, it seemed as if I was looking right through him into the eyes of God!"

The grace, within the priest's soul, had revealed its presence through the look or expression in his eyes. The sinner had indeed looked "through the priest" and had seen a touch of something supernatural. In that way, grace had become visible to him. The sinner did not know what he had seen (in the same way that people, who tried to look into the eyes of Mary, knew not what was there); however, he knew that he had witnessed something which was far beyond the limitations of his own human comprehension.

There are other ways that the presence of grace can be seen. Grace can become visible by and through its use. When sanctifying grace is acquired (through Baptism or Confession after a mortal sin had been committed) the reflection of this grace can be seen within the daily life habits of someone who knows how to use this grace in his or her daily life. Grace shows forth in the person's words, deeds, actions and even in his or her physical appearance. It is not too difficult to see the difference between a humble, kind, gentle, holy person and someone who is nasty, mean and belligerent. The expressions on the faces of these two diverse types of people are as different as day and night. The lack of grace becomes equally as easy to detect as the presence of grace.

But, how exactly does a person know if the reflection of grace is seen in all he does, think or say?

Well, let us start with sanctifying grace. Say that your soul has been returned to grace, after a mortal sin had been committed, by a good confession. Your soul now has grace. It is filled with brilliant light. God is dwelling deep within your soul. However, this does not automatically make you a living saint, nor does it automatically change all your attitudes, personality, actions, words and deeds into holy, perfect ways without a fault or defect. Just having sanctifying grace does not fly you on wings of love to the top of THE LADDER OF PERFECTION.

You are still you. You are still a human being filled with faults and weaknesses. You are still back (often very quickly) into old sins and bad habits. You may not even, as yet, have the ability to realize that God's grace floods your inner being with a magnificent light. Why? Because having grace is one thing, using grace is another.

Many people are content merely to have grace. This is not bad or wrong. Everyone needs grace for salvation. A person who goes to confession, after a mortal sin is committed, wants grace returned to his or her soul. A soul in the state of grace has a beauty all its own. There is no need for anything else. Even if the person never uses grace to improve his or her union with God, sanctifying grace makes the person truly God's child worthy of heaven. However, if the person does not use grace to overcome faults and weaknesses, many actions and attitudes will not change from bad to good. Venial sins, bad habits and numerous faults will be where virtues, holiness and love for God should be. Sanctifying grace will not be increased.

Grace then is not only the gift for a soul free of mortal darkness, but grace becomes the person's most powerful weapon on the spiritual battlefields where temptations are fought and virtues acquired. Having grace is one thing, having virtue is another thing. That nasty, mean, belligerent person I spoke about could make a valid confession and receive sanctifying grace; however sanctifying grace does not change the person into a virtuous person overnight. Virtues are obtained only when grace is used upon spiritual battlefields. Virtue then becomes the reflection of grace within the soul, and in order to live a virtuous life, there has to be a daily program of self-improvement as well as keeping your soul in the state of grace.

The presence of grace within a soul must reveal itself through a person's quest for virtue and holiness or else grace is not being used as it should be used. This quest for virtue and holiness is what climbing THE LADDER OF PERFECTION to closer union with God is all about. Only after virtues and holiness are sought after and acquired, only then does grace show it is present.

Chapter 13

WHAT IS VIRTUE?

Before a person can have virtue reflect God's grace within his soul, that person must understand what true Christian virtue is. The dictionary tells us that virtue is goodness and moral excellence; however, Christian, Catholic virtue is far more than goodness and moral excellence.

A person whose soul is not in the state of grace can have a certain amount of goodness and moral excellence; however, his words, deeds and actions would not reflect grace because grace does not exist in his soul. Such goodness and moral excellence would be only what is known as natural virtue.

There is a vast difference between mere natural virtue and Christian, Catholic virtue which reflects grace within a soul. Natural virtue makes a person a good person whose goodness affects only the natural world he lives in. The virtue which reflects grace within a soul, makes the person Christ-like because Christ (God) dwells within that soul. Divine Indwelling turns virtue into supernatural virtue and gives the person the power and desires to do certain actions or deeds which are supernaturally good because such deeds and actions bring a supernatural or eternal reward.

Natural virtues come through a person's own efforts to overcome a sin or bad habit for purely natural reasons. For example: a person may be a faithless husband and father but gives up a secret love affair simply because he loves his wife and family more and does not want to break up his home. Or a man may stop telling lies when he discovers that people are beginning to doubt everything he says.

On the other hand, true Christian virtues come when grace enters the soul and when grace is used for a spiritual self-improvement goal of union with Christ.

The virtues which come when grace first enters the soul in Baptism are called infused virtues. Such virtues cannot be obtained without grace. The three main or most important virtues which are infused into the soul at Baptism are called: faith, hope and charity (or love). Faith is the ability to know and believe all the truths of God, hope is the ability to have great hope in God and His promises of everlasting joy, and charity is the ability to love God and to love our neighbors. Along with these three virtues there are four more, called the cardinal virtues, which are infused into the soul at Baptism. They are: prudence, justice, fortitude and temperance.

These seven virtues which are gifts to us from God along with sanctifying grace start a person walking along the paths of Christian virtue. Notice that I said, only start. I said that because while these virtues are supernatural, they can remain inactive if grace is not used as it should be used and increased as it should be increased.

After sanctifying grace is received into the soul (through Baptism or Confession after a mortal sin has been committed), this grace and the virtues given to the soul should form the foundation for a solid, active spiritual life. Unfortunately, most people fail to build upon this foundation. They do not grow in virtue nor do they increase sanctifying grace. Most of the time this lack of spiritual growth is due mainly to lack of knowledge about virtue and grace or to pride.

People who say, "I know all about my religion" after attending only a few religious instruction classes, also make this same type of a mistake with virtue and grace. They tell themselves that they are a good person and "never sin" simply because they do not commit such acts as murder or adultery or stealing.

We are all sinners and we all lack certain virtues. Lack of virtue is always replaced by a sin, fault, weakness or bad habit. If you want to find out what virtues you lack, then take an honest look at your sins (venial as well as mortal), faults, weaknesses and bad habits. The opposite of these are virtues which you do not have but should have.

For example: if you doubt or do not want to believe a teaching of God or of the Church, that is a fault or sin against faith and weakens the virtue of faith. This weakness, unless corrected by strengthening faith, could lead to total destruction of this virtue and disappearance of sanctifying grace through not going to Mass and receiving the sacraments. Many people who say they "never sin" commit numerous sins by saying they not only do not need confession, but they do not even need the Church or God and His laws.

Another example: if you always show anger during the simplest disagreement, then you lack the virtue of patience. If you always look for and talk about your neighbor's faults then you lack the virtue of charity. If you always want everything your own way, then you are filled with a selfishness which destroys the virtue of generosity and thoughtfulness.

To grow in virtue means to take your faults, weaknesses and sins and one by one overcome them with the help of God's grace, and to replace them with a virtue.

If you are honest with yourself, it will not be too difficult to discover your own faults, weaknesses and sins. But you would have no desires to correct them if you did not use grace. So increasing virtue means not only to use grace, but to increase grace as well. It is this combination of increasing grace as you increase virtue which carries you up THE LADDER OF PERFECTION. Once you discover the way grace increases virtue and virtue increases grace you will be able to daily, even hourly, keep your spiritual life active and alive, ever advancing forward and upwards to a closer union with God.

Chapter 14

WHY WE MUST GO TO CONFESSION AND DO PENANCE

When a sin is committed two things happen to the spiritual life. Guilt presents itself and the person is to be blamed for wrongdoing. There is an offense against God. In addition, there is also a debt due to God, something a person now owes to God.

While many people admit that they did offend God, they completely forget about the debt due to God for the offense or sin. Other people, who will not even admit their guilt, will care less about this debt due to God.

The two, guilt and debt, are entirely different. They are not one and the same thing. So we must have two separate ways to repair the damage done to our souls by sin.

The first way is confession which removes the guilt of sin. The second way is penance which takes away the debt due to sin.

Although confession is often called the Sacrament of Penance, confession and penance are not the same thing. Within the Sacrament of Penance, two very different and distinct actions take place. The first action is the forgiveness of sins. The priest forgives the sins through the power of absolution. This removes the guilt. The second action is the priest calling the person to do penance: "For your penance say five "Our Fathers" and ten "Hail Marys." This penance helps to remove the debt after the sins are forgiven.

Because there is so much confusion about the Sacrament of Penance, most people think that going to confession is all that one has to do about sin. That is not true. More often than not, the penance which the priest gives out in confession is only a beginning of the penance which is actually needed so that the debt due to God for sins committed can be abolished as well as the guilt.

Many people, who go to confession, or the Sacrament of Reconciliation as it is now called, want to believe that all they have to do about sin is to tell God they are sorry. They forget about the debt due to God for sins committed; so the average Catholic does not even know why the priest gives a penance after the confession and absolution.

Speaking of sorrow for sin, when a confession is made, it must be noted that this sorrow alone is not enough to make a good confession.

Sorrow for sin is the beginning of confession; however, in order to make the confession valid, other dispositions regarding sin must be present. Even the sorrow itself must have certain qualities in order to make this sorrow genuine. You cannot merely tell God that you are sorry for sin as if this sorrow had no meaning. Many people tell others that they are sorry for something yet deep down they do not really feel this sorrow. They may have made the statement: "I'm sorry," just to be polite or to avoid an argument. In the spiritual life, sorrow for sin is called contrition. If this contrition is not real or genuine, a confession cannot be valid.

In addition, in order to make a good confession, a person must not only have a sincere, genuine sorrow for the sins he or she committed, but the sinner must also have a firm purpose of amendment. Also, there must be a desire for penance because it is the penance which helps to pay the debt due to God for sins committed.

It would be folly to say that you are sorry for your sins but you have no intentions of giving them up. It would also be folly to say that you have no need for penance.

A good confession, with the desire to avoid sin in the future and the desire for penance, is the start of the climb up THE LADDER OF PERFECTION. It can be readily seen that there would be no spiritual advancement if the person refuses to see his or her sins and refuses to go to confession.

After Vatican Council II, it became very evident that many Catholics felt they no longer needed to go to confession or to do penance. They simply refused to believe that they were capable of committing a sin. Others began a do-it-yourself sort of confession, saying: "Well, I told God I was sorry, why should I go to confession?"

Of course, such Catholics were sadly mistaken. Confessing one's sins and wrongdoings is a very, very serious matter. You cannot do this with little or no meaning; nor can you do it in a do-it-yourself sort of way deciding for yourself that the Church is all wrong about the Sacrament of Reconciliation. You cannot make up your own rules about confession and then go ahead with these ideas saying to yourself that you know more about sin and confession than the Church does.

You must remember that God while being merciful and forgiving is also just. A just God cannot be indifferent to nor can He overlook a person's sins or moral evils. He will quickly forgive a sinner when the person expresses true sorrow for sin; however, if the person is indifferent to his own sins, that does not mean that God has this same attitude.

Someone once told me this little story. She said that her young, teenage son was all excited about the so-called "new morality" and he now felt free to do anything he wanted to. She turned to him and quickly replied: "There is no such thing as a "free" life of sin and corruption. There is a price to pay and some day God will come to collect the bill owed." Words of wisdom!

It is true that a person has a free will that God will not interfere with. However, while the sinner is "freely" committing one sin after another he is making for himself a bill owed to God which some day has to be paid one way or another. So many people like to think that God is weak and timid and does not have the power to step in so that evil can be destroyed. They rather imagine that God can do "nothing" about sin, evil and corruption. So they feel very much secure in a life of evil and corruption. However, that is far from true. There will come a day of payment and then the sinner sees and knows the power of God.

There is a timeworn story about the sinner who stands up and shouts: "If there is a God, then strike me dead at this moment," and is not struck dead. This is supposed to show a weak, spineless God or a God who does not exist. But what it shows is that God has not as yet come for the payment which is due Him. He gives the sinner more time to make amends and payment before it is too late, before the eternal payment of hell opens to receive a sinner who has chosen his own place therein or before the person finds himself in purgatory.

Make no mistake about it, sin is very real and very much a part of life on earth and confession must be accepted and must be done correctly or else the payment which is owed God on the day of death will be most severe.

Fortunately, there is a way to make payment before death. First, the person can go to confession to receive absolution. Then there is penance. Penance should not only be done once in a while, but every day. Prayers can be said or small acts of penance can be done, such as doing a job one is not required to do but which one accepts and does as a penance. These acts of penance reduce the debt owed to God for sins committed. And if this debt is not paid in full, it will be paid in purgatory.

Many people refuse to believe in purgatory. They like to think it does not exist because God is "too merciful" to send anyone to that horrible place. But remember that God is also just. And purgatory is not that "horrible place to which God *sends* souls." Purgatory is where people *want* to go if, after death, they realize that they did not do enough penance on earth to pay the debt due to God for their own sins.

Purgatory, then, is nothing more than the place where souls can do the penance for their sins which they did not do on earth.

Chapter 15

WHAT IS LOVE?

There is a saying which goes something like this: "Love Makes The World Go Round." Every person on earth has heard the word love or uses it in daily speech; however, very, very few people actually know the true meaning of the word love. So we find, within human conversations, such expressions as: "I just love this new car" or "I would love to go with you, but I cannot" or "I really do love you...but..." or "My dog loves to go walking with me," etc., etc. In addition, we have cults or groups which claim to be so filled with love for all humanity, but at the same time, they tell everyone who is not a member of the group that God hates them and they cannot be saved.

There is no other word in existence which is as used or as abused as much as the word love. Most people use the word very lightly such as the examples I have just given. To say that one loves a car or a hat or an object is surely an abuse of the word love; simply because, a material object cannot return the love which the person claims he or she has for it. However, the greatest abuse of the word is when love is mistaken for sex and used as an excuse to gratify uncontrollable, illicit passions.

So, the first step to take in trying to understand love is to take the word and place it in different categories. A person will never be able to control or stop the worldwide abuse of the word love, but a person can at least know the difference between true, pure love and the many other types of love which surround us.

The first and most widespread abuse of and use of the word love is to call illicit sex between two persons love. The word is, in such cases, used only as a tool to try and justify the sin. Just saying that a person is "in love" does not give that person the right to engage in premarital sex, adultery or homosexual acts. Any love that leads to sin is hardly love at all. Why? Because the first use of pure love has to be love for God and His grace within a person's soul. Whatever love harms or destroys God's grace within a soul has to be no love at all or merely a very poor substitute for love.

The second widespread abuse of the word love is to attach it to anything and everything from a car to a new T.V. game. The trouble with this type of love is that it quickly disappears when a new or better object is desired or obtained. So one day a person will "just love" a new dress until another new dress is bought or obtained. A person will simply "love" her new home until her friend buys a better more expensive home, and so forth. This type of love is hardly love at all, what the person means when she tells the world that she "just loves" something is that she likes it very much; but, will no longer like it if it becomes old or useless or broken or out-of-date or if her friend has a bigger, more expensive object.

The third abuse of the word love is to "love everyone" and not really mean it. As a known writer, once in awhile I receive a very vicious, searing letter from someone who does not agree with what I wrote. Usually the person has what is commonly called "Christian love." After "telling me off," the person will end the letter with words like: "I do love you in Christ." Such a stated love is a farce. So also is the following example of so-called "Christian love." Someone I knew was bitterly denouncing Catholics because we, as he said, do not love the black people. In glowing words, this person expressed his personal love for black people. It sounded as if his love for all the blacks put ours to shame until I suggested that if he had such love for black people, why not have a poor, black person, who lived in the ghetto, come to live with him? The person quickly changed the subject. That type of love is "all talk" used to make a person filled with self-righteousness and as such is not very meaningful.

Then there is the love which people say they have for God

which is even a greater farce. I have often heard people say, "Sure I love God, but I do not have to pray or go to Mass" or "You cannot tell me that I do not love God because I do not go to Church" or "What do you mean I do not love God? I love Him, but in my 'own way.' " Such people do not really love God. They only use the word love to convince themselves that they are right and the Church is wrong. It is a grand "cover" which allows them to live a life away from their personal religious duties and obligations to this God whom they claim they love.

Now, if all these examples of love, which are not really love at all, come forth to reveal what love is not, then what is love?

Well, first of all, love is an infused virtue given to a person when he or she is baptized. When the baptism occurs, then three virtues are given to the person: faith, hope and charity, which is love. So the first thing to understand about pure, holy love is that it is a virtue given through grace and protected by grace. That being the case, this virtue of love has to be cherished and used *only as God intended* it to be used. Why? Because this pure, holy love becomes a *reflection* of God's own love and can only be used to *love what God loves*. To use love in any way contrary to the laws, ways and teachings of God, is to distort love, abuse love and turn it into something which, although it may be called love, is very far from being love.

The very first object of one's pure love and affection has to be God Himself, and the second has to be other people, through the virtue of holy charity. Christ Himself told us that: "You shall love the Lord your God with your whole heart, and with your whole soul and with your whole mind and with your whole strength"...the second is..."You shall love your neighbor as yourself..." (*Mark* 12:29-31). This commandment puts love in proper order. It tells us our responsibilities when we use our love. God, then, has clearly told us what love is and how to use it *as He wants us to use it.* Love has nothing to do with meaningless expressions of one's love or with sinful sexual acts. Love belongs to God, who is the "God of Love" and is given to us so that we can return this love to its source.

How can we do that, return this God-given love to its source? The most obvious answer is to do what God wants us to do as a sign of our love for Him. In other words, to do God's holy will. What is God's holy will for us? The very first "will of God" for us is to love Him with our whole minds, souls, hearts and strength.

That is where the greatest failure of pure, holy love abounds. So we have millions of people who say, "I love God, but I don't have to pray or go to Church." And we have hundreds of thousands of fallen-away Catholics who shout: "I do love God! But no one is going to tell me that I have to go to confession and Mass!" Every fallen-away Catholic I have ever met has told me that he or she loves God. But what kind of love is that? It is not the pure love which must be returned, as an act of love-for-love, to God. It is but a shadow of that love. A person who claims he or she loves God and at the same time refuses to fulfill religious duties and obligations is only fooling himself or herself. When a person says to me: "I love God! You can't tell me that I don't love Him just because I don't go to confession or Mass!" I respond: "No! You do not love God! If you truly loved Him, you would *want* to go to the sacraments. You would *want* to go and say: *"This* is how much I love you, dearest God! I want to do your holy will!"

Having God's gift of pure love is a very serious obligation. This love must be used only as God intended it to be used. It cannot be used for purposes or desires other than what God intended. It cannot be misused or abused. If it is, it becomes no love at all, just a false imitation of the real thing. Once love is distorted or abused it ceases to exist. There is no such thing as a "bad" love such as sexual, sinful love. Love of itself cannot be bad because the source of pure love is infinitely good. God, being the foundation or source of pure love cannot bestow upon His children a "bad" love, one which becomes sinful and filled with greed or selfishness. His children may still call it love, but real love no longer exists once it is removed from the light and grace of its origin or beginning.

The second "will of God" for us is to love others as we love ourselves. This self-love is as misunderstood as the word love itself is misunderstood. To love one's neighbor as one loves oneself does not mean to participate in any sinful act which arises from self-love. So if greed, selfishness, hate, jealousy, etc. are part of self-love then one can hardly love one's neighbor as one loves himself or herself.

To love one's neighbor as one loves oneself is to be very much in love with goodness, virtue, grace and God. A pure, holy self-love is composed of loving in oneself *all that God loves* in oneself. It is to have a legitimate concern for one's interests which revolve around daily life needs and especially spiritual needs. First of all, each person must be concerned with his or her own salvation and to follow the teachings of God and of the Church which lead to salvation. That includes living a life of grace, acquiring and polishing virtues, praying, striving daily to reach a closer union with God, and to love the members of one's family. Also, one has the duty and responsibility to care for his own material needs and the material and spiritual needs of his family as best as he or she can.

Once these two basic, essential needs are cared for, the spiritual and the material, a person can look outward to his neighbor's basic spiritual and material needs. Then, because of the person's understanding of his own spiritual and material needs, he can best see where this self-understanding can best serve his neighbor. If the person truly loves his own life of grace, virtue, and love for God and family then that person can express this self-love in acts of pure love and charity. It is this outward expression of one's own love for grace, virtue, God and his neighbor which fulfills the commandment of God's to love our neighbor as we love ourselves.

Finally, there can develop a very serious abuse of pure, holy love by simply *not* using it. As I said, God gives this wondrous gift of love to all His children. If a person never uses this gift as God intended it to be used, then it will vanish in the same way that pure love vanishes when it is distorted.

If a person never loves God, goodness, virtue or his neighbor as God intended him to, then love disappears from lack of use.

So we have millions of people who never love anyone simply because they never used the virtue of love. They are usually the people who constantly complain, stating that no one loves them. Yet, how can they be loved when they themselves never loved anyone? Love's power is seen when it renews and increases itself with daily use. Truly, the more love a person gives, the more love he receives. There is no depth to this beautiful, precious virtue of love. If it is directed towards its source first, then expanded outward to embrace oneself, loved ones, family, friends and neighbors, this love can only become more abundant and useful.

Chapter 16

A CLOSER LOOK AT THE SAINTS

In this chapter, I would like to explain the way it is possible to live a very holy, even saintly life without actually doing the wondrous deeds which some saints accomplished. I call this chapter "A Closer Look At The Saints," because I would like to help you understand and know the saints in a way which perhaps you have never seen them before.

Far too often, when the saints are presented to us, we are made to see the grandeur of their noble deeds. We are too familiar with their visions, their penances and the unbelievable accomplishments which writers love to mention in their stories of the saints. Such accounts do inspire us. They show us the greatness of God's gifts to His beloved children. However, most people are lead to believe that it is almost impossible to imitate the saints simply because God never gave them the blessings, gifts and missions which He gave to the saints.

Yet, if we but take a closer look at the saints, we will discover that the very things which made them holy *are available to all of us!*

First of all, you must separate in your minds, holiness from deeds or missions. Just because a saint did something which is considered great, that does not mean that the person automatically became holy just because of the deed or accomplishment.

Many people, who perhaps are living sinful lives, can also do great noble deeds. They can win medals for bravery, but that does not mean that such a person possesses the virtues and sanctity of the saints.

So there is a great difference between holiness, works and

what the saints accomplished for God; and it is something within the realm of this difference which we will now explore.

When we do, we will discover a very great hope knowing that we can indeed follow the very footsteps of the saints to a wonderful close union with God.

How can we take a closer look at the saints? First of all, realize that even if they were blessed with visions of all sorts, even if they accomplished extraordinary missions during their lifetimes, they *did not* live a life of constant visions or successful missions. They often had many failures, discouragements and sufferings along the way. They often faced days of loneliness. At times they thought sure that God had abandoned them. They knew how to cry, how to become upset and often they thought they had accomplished nothing worthwhile. They also made their share of mistakes. They fought, fell and rose again upon the spiritual battlefields. Sometimes they did not even know what God wanted them to do and they did not have the slightest idea how to accomplish whatever it was God wanted them to accomplish. They became discouraged, sad, frustrated and many of them even tried to run away from the job God wanted them to do.

There you see the other side of sainthood and if you are beginning to think that they were very much like yourself, then you are beginning to understand what I am trying to explain to you.

The saints were human beings with all sorts of human weaknesses. The halos they had were not upon their heads at birth. Halos have to be won upon the battlefields. It is encouraging for us to know that halos not only have to be won, but the battlefields are the very same ones which we find ourselves upon.

For example, Saint Teresa of Avila and Saint John of the Cross are two of our greatest saints. We marvel at their deeds, especially their writings on the mystical life which are considered to be among the greatest ever written. In addition, St. Teresa had many marvelous visions. Still, if you read the lives of these two great mystics you can find that in between their outbursts of greatness, there lay hidden many purely human emotions and situations not unlike our own.

Often St. Teresa was filled with moments of discouragement,

even depression. For years she could not even accept the role in life which God wanted her to fulfill. When she did attempt to follow God's will for her, she met with much opposition. When she was ordered to write an account of her inner union with God, all her favors and even her prayer life were condemned. That threw her into a state of total confusion and despair. Once when she went into a certain city to open a new convent, the bishop, whom she had thought was on her side, forbade her to do that. She sat alone in her room, crying for days, not knowing what to do next. Towards the end of her life, at one point, she refused to go to another city to open a new convent because she felt so useless telling herself that she had accomplished nothing worthwhile in her whole life.

At another time in her life, the brothers who had helped her reform the Carmelite order and who were living the life of the reformed order in their own monastery, were all arrested and put in jail because they were called rebels. One of these brothers was Saint John of the Cross. Then there is the famous story about St. Teresa which goes like this. One day she was on her way to open another reformed convent in another city. This convent had cost her many tears and anxious moments. But she was finally on her way to making that dream come true.

On the way, during the cold winter, she had to wade through the rushing waters of a very ice-cold stream.

She took her sandals off and stepped into the waters. As she did, she said to the Lord: "After so much suffering, this too?"

She heard Him reply: "My daughter, this is how I treat my friends."

She immediately replied: "That is why you have so few, my Lord."

Saint Teresa and Saint John of the Cross were not the only saints who had to suffer through ordinary days of pain, darkness and even heartache.

After St. Francis of Assisi spent years creating his order just the way he wanted it, he returned from a long journey to find that some of his brothers had taken charge and changed the rules; and he was in fact pushed out of his own order.

When St. Bernadette was in a convent after she had seen the visions of our Lady of Lourdes, she was ordered never to speak about her visions. Yet the other nuns found great joy talking about the latest news from Lourdes. Bernadette was ordered not to enter the room when such conversations were taking place.

Saint Margaret Mary, who saw the splendor of God's own Sacred Heart, was so little admired by some of the nuns in her convent, that they threw holy water on her because they thought she was possessed by the devil. Often visions make the saint's life more difficult.

Also, were such wondrous visions and mystical favors really a source of great joys and consolations to the saints who received them? Could these saints merely return time and time again to them to find encouragement, hope and comfort?

How often have you thought that you could perhaps carry your crosses better if only you could see our Lady or our Lord in a glorious vision. Ah! It would seem that the saints had a great advantage which was not given to the average lay person. But did they really have that advantage? The answer is no! Why? Because a saint was called to suffer and often the very visions they saw were the cause of their greatest sufferings.

How can that be true! Well, for one reason, often the visions told them to do something which they did not want to do.

And listen to these words written by St. Teresa of Avila about the wonderful visions which she was blessed with: "When my trials and distress were so great and caused me such deep depression, I would forget all the favors that the Lord had bestowed upon me. Nothing would remain with me but the mere recollection of them, like the memory of a dream, and this was a great distress for me...and I would be tormented by a thousand doubts and fears. I felt so evil that I began to think that all the evils and heresies that had arisen were due to my sins." (Autobiography by Msgr. John S. Kennedy, page 279).

Other favored souls tell about the sufferings which filled their hearts and souls because they were praised by Christ and Mary and felt so unworthy of such praises. So, as I said, more often than not, the mystical favors received by the saints from God *added* to their sufferings and made their lives more difficult to live.

For example: many saints who were nuns or brothers felt that their visions set them apart from the other nuns or brothers. They felt "different" and this fact bothered them tremendously. They, themselves, wanted nothing to do with visions, even if such favors were most wondrous to behold. When Saint Margaret Mary saw our Lord and His Sacred Heart, she was dragged almost like a criminal to her superior to explain what happened.

Contrary as to what most people want to believe, visionaries are not welcomed in religious communities.

St. Margaret Mary wrote: "When I was taken before Mother Superior, I felt like a criminal and filled with so much shame. She then mortified and humiliated me with all her might. She treated, with scorn, everything I had said to her."

I could tell many more stories about the lives of saints when the glow of their great accomplishments is moved aside so that we can take a closer look at the saints.

For example: there are saints who have died believing they were total failures. There are saints who had many family problems. St. Teresa had a brother who was mentally ill and this brother caused her much worry. Saint Thomas More's family took the king's side against him and tried to convince him that he was wrong. Many saints had to face severe financial problems. One saint who was a queen was forced to take her children to live in poverty after the death of her husband. Saint Elizabeth Seton's family and friends disowned her after she became a Catholic and left her in poverty to raise her children after the death of her husband. Another saint who was cripple and blind was totally abandoned by the parents whom she dearly loved.

So, you see, when the lives of the saints are stripped of the grandeur of their incredible deeds and blessings from God, it can be seen that such lives were not much different from those of ordinary lay people like us. However, there was a difference between the lives of the saints and the lives or ordinary people. And it is this difference which makes us capable of actually imitating the saints' holiness and sanctity. What is that difference? Well, it is not so much that they had duties and responsibilities to perform or to accomplish. We also have our own daily and religious duties and obligations. Maybe they had different types of duties or missions that we do not have; however, we, nevertheless, have the very same obligation to faithfully carry out God's will for *us* in the way that saints had to carry out God's will for *them*. So it is not that they had something to do for God and we do not. That is not the difference between them and us.

The difference is *the way* they followed God's will for them and the way we follow God's will for us. In other words, it is not *what* we do in our daily lives, but the *way* we do it that counts. And it is this *way*, which the saints used to carry out God's will for them, and *not* what they did, that we can imitate in order to find our own holiness.

What was that way? First of all, we must realize what greatness means in the lives of the saints. When a saint is to be canonized, Holy Mother Church actually sets aside all the person's incredible, fantastic accomplishments. Such things may dazzle us, but they do not dazzle Church authorities. The authorities are not so much interested in such things as visions, healings, stigmatized hands and feet, as they are in finding out if the person faithfully fulfilled his or her daily and religious duties and obligations. Did the person, who had extraordinary missions, blessings and favors from God, also sanctify and save his or her own soul by and through the daily use of the ordinary means of sanctification? What are these ordinary means? They are exactly the very same means of sanctification which we all have: prayer, the sacraments, the Holy Mass, the Eucharist, charity, penance, spiritual reading and obedience. In other words, it is not what or how much you do for God which counts, it is the *way* you do what He wants you to do. It was not what the saints did which mattered as much as the *way* they did what God wanted them to do, and the way they used grace and virtue as they traveled along the roads God wanted them to follow.

Now, please do not misunderstand me. I am not downgrading mystical favors or visions. I, myself, love to read about such things in the lives of the saints. I love Padre Pio and the fact that he was stigmatized with Christ's wounds.

What I am saying is that visions and such mystical favors *do not make a person a saint.* There were over 300 known and true stigmatics, who have ever lived, but only a few, 8 or 10, have ever been canonized or will ever be canonized.

What then was it that won for the saints their halos? It was virtue and their personal response to grace.

That fact is a very good thing for us to know because that means that a plain, ordinary person, lay person or religious, can indeed follow the very same paths which saints followed without leaving their state of life. That means that all of us can sanctify our souls in the very same way that saints sanctified their souls. Why? Because sanctification and holiness do not come from great deeds, extraordinary missions or even visions, but from grace; and grace is available to all.

So, if you have in mind the goal to become a holier person, to reach a more complete union with God—and I sincerely hope that all of you have such a goal in mind—do not look for special mystical blessings, such as visions. You do not need them. Do not look outward to great mission fields and long to go there to work for God. Look only for grace and virtue. Grace and virtue are what really makes a person a saint.

To give you an example of what I have just said, let me quote from a list of some of the questions asked when St. Therese of Lisieux's cause was brought forth to be examined by Church authorities. Now, here was a person whom many people said could never be a saint. She died young having accomplished no great mission for God. She had no extra special talents or gifts. She had no visions or divine messages. What she did have was grace and virtues. That was what made her a saint.

Listen to some of the questions which witnesses for her cause had to answer so that it could be determined if Therese was a true saint.

1. How did she cope with the difficulties of her state of life?
2. How did she show or express her love for God?
3. Did she respect and obey her superiors?

4. Did she always tell the truth?
5. Did she submit to divine revelation, to Holy Mother Church and to the authority of the Pope with a very deep trust and love?
6. What kind of trust did she have in God?
7. Did she have a horror of sin?
8. Did she have a love for her neighbor?
9. Did she care about the spiritual welfare of others?
10. How did she react if treated harshly? (Doc. canonization process)

All such questions and many more like them had nothing to do with missions or favors and blessings from God. What the questions were referring to were grace and virtues.

We have available to us the very same grace which gave the saints their heroic virtues. Grace can do the same for us. We have the ordinary means of sanctification which they used: prayer, the sacraments, Holy Mass, penance, accepting crosses, spiritual reading, obedience and charity. The way we imitate the saints is to use grace and acquire virtues.

When the saints found themselves at the bottom, they used grace and virtue to rise from where they had fallen. When saints found themselves at the top, they used grace and virtue to thank God for His love and goodness. When saints found only failure as a reward for all their efforts, they used grace and virtue to love and accept God's holy will.

Look at the incredible variety of saints which we have: kings, queens, lay people, nuns, priests, brothers, sisters, married men and women; unmarried men and women, children, teachers, doctors, housewives and husbands. Why such a variety? Because God is telling us that anyone who correctly and faithfully responds to grace, no matter what state of life one is in, can become a saint.

It is grace which is the key to sainthood; and we can all receive grace. All saints used grace to win their halos.

Finally, I would like to say something I have said many times: sanctity, holiness and saintly halos are as near to you as your parish church wherein you find the sacraments and grace.

Chapter 17

ACCOMPLISHING GREAT DEEDS
FOR THE LORD

One day a group of my friends were explaining to me about a book they all had read. The book told the story of a great saint who had accomplished fantastic deeds for the Lord, many of which caused her great personal sufferings. Each member of the group felt a cringe of fear when she talked about the saint's mission; yet at the same time, there was an inner longing to go out to follow the saint's examples and do what she had done.

I began to explain about grace and the way the saint used it to carry out God's holy will for her. Then I added: "But you people also have grace. You can do great things for God. You have a mission all your own, in your everyday state of life. You also do God's holy will."

They were surprised and replied: "What can we do for God that is big and important? We are nobodies. We are not chosen as someone special with a great job to do for God."

They forgot that they had the demanding task of saving their own souls. That is big and important to God.

Very often a person is tempted to give up the climb towards a closer union with God simply because he believes that it is impossible to change his way of life in order to accomplish great deeds for the Lord. For example: a man is forced to work eight to ten hours a day to support his family. When he arrives at home, tired, hungry and often in a bad mood, family duties and problems take up the rest of his time until he drops into bed exhausted. He can forsee no drastic change in his daily routine for the next 20 years. He may want to work for God in faraway missions, but he knows that is impossible. He loves his family. He wants to be with them, supporting them, helping them, taking upon his shoulders their problems. What more can he do for God except to fulfill the minimum requirements of his religious duties and obligations? Nothing, he thinks.

I have met many people like that, men and women, who feel trapped by a life of daily work and family problems; yet at the same time, who want to do so much for God. They usually are filled with discouragement, even depression, because they know their dreams will never come true. Many of them have completely stopped personal spiritual advancement simply because they feel they cannot do important works for God in their state of life.

The primary mistake which all of them make, about working or doing great things for God, is to imagine that the only way they can reach their goals is to change or leave their present lives. They believe that only in another state of life would they be able to accomplish high ideals.

This situation becomes a very serious spritual problem for many people who sincerely wish that they could do much more for God than they are doing. They believe they are actually living a life that is divided: one part for their daily duties and the other for God. When the daily duties take up the time necessary for God's work, they usually think that it is impossible to do anything for God, so they do not even try. Then they begin to feel that they are living only half a life and the half which consists of work, family duties and responsibilities does not satisfy them. They feel something is missing, something which they long for but cannot possess.

The secret to the solution of this problem lies within the correct knowledge and the person's own attitudes towards his life. Instead of changing a life, the person, with the correct knowledge, can change his way of thinking. The correct understanding and attitudes can bring into the picture wondrous acts or deeds which a person can do for God, for his own soul and for the souls of others *without* changing one single iota of a daily routine. The person's daily life can become a vast mission field of spiritual activity. What is more encouraging, the person does not have to put this activity on public display. Most of it can be done within the silence of an individual's personal spiritual life.

The first thing to know is that there is actually no division within the life of someone who has grace and wants to do more for God. There is not one part for daily duties and the other part for God. The whole daily life becomes one for God and with God when grace is present. How can that be? Because when a soul is in the state of grace, merits can be gained by the person simply by faithfully fulfilling his or her daily duties and responsibilities. So the opportunities to gain great spiritual treasures (the merits which will last forever) are always present. You gain merits when you shop, work, cook, clean the house, and so forth, if your soul is in the state of grace, simply because you are doing what God *wants* you to do, in your state of life. That is doing great deeds for the Lord.

God, very seldom, chooses a person to go out into the world to work exclusively for Him. On the other hand, He has chosen billions of people to live a plain, ordinary life filled with certain duties. If He did so, it is only because He knows that these billions of people can save and sanctify their souls within that state of life. They can do great deeds for Him without wandering away from daily obligations. The fact is, these daily obligations become the source of doing great deeds for God. Why do I say that? Because, very often, it is a great accomplishment just to keep your spiritual life in order as you struggle to carry all the burdens found in daily life.

There are many people who cannot carry a simple daily cross, yet who long for a great mission from God, one which will be filled with tremendous sufferings such as to be marked with the wounds of Christ. I know a few of these people. They seem to think that the only way they can work for the Lord is to be given some special gift. I said to one such person: "But how could you ask for and bear such sufferings when you cannot carry the crosses of your daily life?"

I added: "Carrying such crosses is a big job, you know. Why

add to that weight? Take only what the good Lord wants to send you. You will soon discover that what you do get will require far more courage to accept than that special gift that you want. And accepting such crosses is doing something greater for God than if you were marked with His wounds in such a way that others will see and notice you."

The person was stunned by my answer, for he thought it was rather an admirable thing to do: desiring to share Christ's agony in such a way. He asked: "How can you say such a thing to me?"

I replied: "Well, for one thing, it is always easier to carry a cross when the world sees you, admires you and thinks you are a living saint. Pride quickly can enter into that picture and diminish or even destroy all the merits from that type of suffering. But try carrying a cross with much love for God's holy will when you are alone in a dark room with tears streaming down your cheeks. At such a time, can you turn your face upward to God, smile and say: 'Dearest Lord, I don't mind this suffering. I so love you and your holy will.' If you can do that, then you are doing something really great for the Lord. Then you are acting like saints act. Then you are loving like saints love. Then you are pleasing God and becoming closer to Him."

There is a story told about a certain holy nun who followed her order's rule except for one item which seemed to her to be unimportant. Nevertheless, one day she just happened to mention it to her confessor. The rule called for all nuns to cover their feet when they were in bed. This nun thought that was a silly rule and not worth obeying, so she confessed that since childhood she had never slept with her feet covered and she wasn't going to start now. Then, one day many months later, this same nun asked her confessor to assign to her a special penance because she felt she needed this extra suffering to become closer to God. The wise confessor answered: "I can think of no better or greater penance for you to do then to follow the rule and keep your feet covered when you go to bed."

There is another story about a saint, who did have a tremendous mission to do for God. But she absolutely hated cheese. The fact is, when she became a nun, she asked to be allowed to always refuse that food if served to her. Then one day, a new superior noticed that the young nun never ate cheese. So, as a penance, she ordered the nun to eat the cheese knowing that there could be no greater penance for the saint. As recorded, this woman, filled with magnificent virtues and graces, plus extra gifts from God, found that the lowly act of eating cheese caused her more sufferings and became a greater task for her to do for the Lord than her God-given mission. Who knows how many merits she gained from that one act of obedience compared to what was gained from fulfilling her God-given mission? Here then are wonderful examples to follow in those two stories. See the way little, unimportant items in your daily life can become the foundation for doing great deeds for the Lord.

Remember that climbing the ladder to a closer union with God consists of very basic endeavors such as: to carry crosses well, to overcome sins, faults and weaknesses, to develop a pure, deep love for God and His holy will, etc.

If you were to analyze these steps which have to be taken, you would discover that all of them exist within a plain, ordinary life. Nowhere does it state that you have to be assigned a great mission for God in order to climb towards a closer union with Him. As I said, sometimes just fulfilling daily duties and responsibilities becomes an awesome, overwhelming task. A person should start the trek towards perfection within the will of God found in his or her daily life and not look elsewhere to another state of life.

Remember that God gives to each and everyone of us a very special mission or job to do for Him right in our daily lives. If a person does not do this job, to the best of his abilities, then *no one on earth can do it.*

See the importance of your daily life. Know that your plain ordinary tasks, duties and responsibilities are very important to God. If you are a teacher, doctor, lawyer, housewife, factory worker, office worker or what have you, you are pleasing to God and doing something "really great" for Him when you faithfully fulfill the duties and responsibilities of your state of life. Make that accomplishment the handrail as you climb THE LADDER

OF PERFECTION. Do not think that you could do more for God if only you were somewhere else doing a different type of job.

I have sad memories of several people I know who tried to run away from their daily duties and responsibilities because they wanted to "work for God." They even went as far as to break up their homes because they thought that "working for God" meant giving up family obligations. One man even ended up in jail because he refused to pay support money after his legal separation. He wrote and told me what "great" things he was doing for the Lord in jail. I wrote back and told him it would be far greater if he had fulfilled the duties and obligations of his marriage.

There is a saying in the spiritual life which goes something like this: duty before devotion. That means that the duties of your daily life such as your work, taking care of your family, painting your home, fixing your car, cooking, shopping, playing with your children are far more meritorious than spending all day in Church. If you were neglecting and leaving undone the daily tasks required in your state of life, in that case, spending all day in Church would not gain for you many merits.

Now, to put aside all thoughts of changing one's state of life, the first lesson to be learned is to realize that one's struggle for perfection is an inner struggle far more than an outer one. An outer or visible condition for spiritual improvement would consist of drastic changes in one's daily life, such as to give up daily duties and responsibilities. That type of a change is not required if sanctifying grace is already present in one's state of life. If it is not, such as could happen when a couple lives together without marriage, then the very first rule would be to change a life so that grace can be returned to the soul.

If, as I said, sanctifying grace is already present in your soul, there is no need to daydream about faraway places or a different state of life wherein one can better serve the Lord and become closer to Him. Remember that it is in fulfilling the obligations of your state of life where holiness lies. It is well to know that when a saint is to be canonized, the question which becomes number one is not how many miracles were present in such a life, but did the person faithfully fulfill the daily duties of his or her state of life?

If you take the time to really think about this obligation of fulfilling one's daily duties and responsibilities, you will come to the conclusion that often it does take a bit of heroic virtue to do just that. Also, remember that if you spend your time daydreaming about all the things you could do for God if. . .then you end up missing opportunity after opportunity to do things for Him *now*. If you do that, you will not see the chances to become closer to Him as you struggle to keep your daily life on an even keel.

One day a young man came to see me, filled with depression because he had missed the chance to become a priest. Now, with a wife and children, he became more and more discouraged and actually planned to leave his family to "work for the Lord." I asked him how much he was doing for God now within his state of life. He replied: "Nothing!"

I said: "Oh! Think again. You are working to support your family. You have helped to bring new souls into the world. Don't you think that is something?"

All the while he daydreamed for the life of a priest, he overlooked all the opportunities within his own state of life to use and acquire more virtue and to live a more active spiritual life and to help others reach a closer union with God by his example.

If a person does indeed do just that, to live a more active spiritual life, to gain and use virtue and grace every day, to help others, to fulfill religious duties, then the person is actually doing great deeds for the Lord. Why? Because the person will be saving and sanctifying his own soul, and there is no greater job than that which a person is given by God to do. Even if the person had gone to far off lands and had worked day and night "for the Lord," what good would all such noble deeds be if, in the final judgment, the person's soul was lost! Outward signs of holiness are no sure guarantee that grace is within the soul. Before anyone can start doing great deeds for the Lord there has to be the presence of sanctifying grace. For only the power of this grace allows the person to actually work for God.

If this grace is not there, then the deeds and works become only a useless outward sign of the person's own desires and not a true mission from God. As long as sanctifying grace is present, then you can do great deeds for the Lord in your own state of life.

What are some of these great deeds? Well, at first glance, they may not seem to be "great" at all. But with grace present, they do become wondrous accomplishments done with and for God.

For example, if you make sure that you do not miss Mass on Sundays and Holy Days, that is a great accomplishment. Why? Because there are numerous other things to do which could prevent you from fulfilling this religious duty. If you choose to go to Mass, you have chosen God first. You have fulfilled the first commandment. You have done something which brings you great spiritual rewards. You have indeed done a great act for God. If you go to work every day to support your family, that is a great deed done for God. Why? Because you could be selfish and lazy and not go. You could stay home because you were not in the mood to go to work. It is God's will for you that you work to support your family. So each time you drag yourself to work, you are doing a great deed for the Lord because you are doing His holy will. Who would do this job if you did not? No one! So your daily work becomes a source of spiritual enrichment because it is done, not only for your family, but for God as well.

If you speak a kind, encouraging word or lend a helping hand to a friend in need, you have done a great deed for God? Why? Because you could have been nasty or refused to help someone. When you do help, you use and polish the precious virtue of brotherly love, and it is God's will that you do just that.

There are numerous other ways to do great things for the Lord in your plain, ordinary state of life. You can do a secret penance to help save a soul. What a great deed that is! to actually help God save a soul! Wonderful! To cooperate with grace and overcome your faults and weaknesses. All that requires a great deal of effort on your part and so becomes great deeds done for the Lord. Remember that no matter what great deeds the saints did for humanity, they *still* had to use grace to overcome their personal faults and weaknesses. When you do this very same thing, you are placed in the category of the saints.

There are other numerous great deeds you can daily do for God, your own soul and the souls of others: praying is one of them. Just to tell God you love Him or to thank Him is a great deed done for the Lord. Why? Because there are millions of people who never once tell God, their Father, that they love Him nor do they ever, not once, thank Him.

The list of "great deeds done for the Lord" goes on and on. Just remember that all of them can be done in your plain daily life. And even if you did go to faraway places to do great things for the Lord, you would *still* have to do what I just mentioned: go to Mass, pray, overcome faults and weaknesses, save your own soul, help others and fulfill the duties and tasks of your daily life.

So, do not look away from your state of life to find a place to work and battle for the Lord. You already have the place. It is up to you to use grace to bring into that place all that is needed to save and sanctify your own soul. That is enough "work for the Lord" to last a lifetime.

PART THREE

GOD DRAWS THE SOUL
TO CLOSER UNION WITH HIM

Chapter 1

GOD DRAWS THE SOUL

Everything I have written to this point tells you why it is so important to live an active spiritual life in close union with God. Now, exactly how do you come into a program for spiritual advancement?

The answer to that question is conversion. No one can embark upon a spiritual journey into a closer union with God, without a change in one's relationship to God. No matter how slight the change is or how drastic, the grace of conversion must touch the person's soul. There has to be some sort of a spiritual awakening. There has to be an awareness of the malice of sin and of the value of grace. The Holy Spirit has to touch the soul with a special grace, and the soul has to respond to that grace.

When a person thinks about the word conversion, he or she usually thinks about someone who changes his religion; for example, a Protestant becoming a Catholic. However, conversion also comes when a person decides to use the graces which touch his or her soul to become a holier person closer to God's heart of love.

The ways used by the Holy Spirit to reach deep within the person's being to call it into a more active spiritual life are far too numerous to mention here. For example, a person can walk past a Church and suddenly feel an overpowering desire to enter and to pray, or to go to confession or to go to Mass. Graces such as these can be used or ignored. If the person uses them, his whole attitude towards God, religion and himself could change completely into a more pious one, even if he already thinks of himself as being a religious person. Saints' lives always revealed this type of conversion even if the person was never a great sinner. All of them had what they called their "conversion."

When we read the lives of the saints, stories are often told about the conversion of such and such a saint. We become a bit confused and amazed when we also read that this person was a "living saint" before his or her "conversion." We wonder, how could a saintly, holy person have a conversion? That question is relatively easy to answer. What is meant by the saint's "conversion" is that the person was drawn into a desire to become even more saintly and to reach a closer union with God.

In exactly the same way, millions of ordinary Catholics could respond to actual graces and enter into a more active spiritual life. The sad part of it all is that most do not. It is rather unbelievable to discover that millions of actual graces go unused and are merely cast aside by Catholics who could use them to enter into a very close union with God, but do not.

Often this fact can be clearly seen with the majority of elderly Catholics who had been faithful and practicing Catholics all of their lives. However, they remained within a very low level of spirituality. They never ventured beyond the Mass-Rosary-vocal-prayer stage. They never bothered to correct their most glaring faults. They never once read a good Catholic spiritual book; nor did they try to acquire a virtue which they did not possess. They never studied their religion after Confirmation classes ended. A "million" times during such a lifetime, without any doubts about it, the Holy Spirit had showered these people with actual graces, yet they did not respond to these graces. What a shame to think that these people never allowed God to draw them into a closer union with Him.

However, in spite of the fact that so many people reject or misuse His graces, God never ceases to send them to His children. The golden stream of graces from heaven never dries up. It is there for you and for me. Fortunately, God has infinite patience. He also knows that some people do allow Him to draw them nearer to His Heart.

For those who have had the wondrous delights of a spiritual

awakening, there is nothing more beautiful to experience. That is especially true when someone has had a miraculous conversion from a life of evil and sin into a life of grace. Of all the miracles sent to earth by God or the saints or our Lady, nothing is more precious than to watch grace recapture a sinful soul.

Then one can see the wondrous mercy and love of God for an individual soul in a way which could never be seen otherwise. The Almighty, All-powerful, Infinite God reaches down to one single soul and He touches this soul with the magic of His love and grace.

So elated is the person after this happening that he or she wants to "tell the whole world" about it so everyone can share this new-found happiness. Often, during this period of exuberance, the person finds prayer, penance, the Mass, and the sacraments absolutely delightful filled with all sorts of consolations. God allows the soul to taste all the sweetness of the fruits of its new union with Him. He gently cradles the soul in His arms as would a mother who holds her newborn child.

But children grow up, so do souls. They cannot remain safely cradled in the arms of God, hidden away from the realities of an adult world. God has use of souls who allow Him to draw them closer to His Heart. They have many lessons to learn. There are more steps to climb towards perfection. There is much work to be done for God and for the souls of others.

All too soon, the person discovers that actually living the life of conversion is far different than being converted from a life of the darkness of spiritual neglect into the sunshine of grace.

God is very anxious to test the results of the person's spiritual awakening. The testing starts when the joys, consolations and exuberance begin to fade. That usually happens when life reverts backwards into a dull series of daily duties, obligations and crosses. The heart and soul have been elevated into the "seventh heaven" of glory but the natural, human life remains.

Many spiritual awakenings and conversions cannot survive the cold blasts of reality when the door of the world is reopened and the soul must venture outward. The person desires only the joys and consolations, and refuses to accept the crosses. When the storms of life arise to rock the boat, the captain deserts the foundering vessel.

It is well to remember that the spiritual life is one of many "ups" and "downs." Only then can a person walk through sunshine into darkness and back into the sunshine. The call of Christ to the soul, the miracles of grace, the days of dryness and darkness are all part of the climbing THE LADDER OF PERFECTION.

If a person is to succeed in his or her quest for holiness, there has to be a well-planned spiritual program. And there has to be a tremendous will and determination to go on and not to give up. Only then can grace lead the soul to the heights of that LADDER OF PERFECTION.

Chapter 2

THE DIVINITY OF CHRIST

In order to get a clearer idea of what union with God is, you must realize that union with Christ is union with God. This is very important because many people, especially most of the evangelists who teach only a religion based on the Bible, without sacraments, go to Christ and "find" Him so that He can *lead them* to God, instead of recognizing Christ as God. Their big mistake is to present to their followers merely a human being—a perfect teacher, yes—but still only a human being. When that is done, when the divinity of Christ is denied or cast aside or not recognized, great spiritual voids immediately are produced and left unfulfilled in a person's relationship to or union with God.

These religions tell you that you do not need the Church nor the sacraments because, all you need, to find Christ, is the Word of God, the Bible. Within this Word of God, they say you will find Christ, and because that is all that is needed to "find" Christ then the Bible is all that is needed for any sort or type or brand of religious practice.

However! What these teachers of such a religious encounter with Christ fail to understand is that you do not "find" Christ within the Word of God as you would find, say, Abraham or Moses. The Word of God is not the way to "find" a purely human Christ; because, the Word of God is Christ! There is a vast difference between looking in the Word of God for Christ and to recognize that the Word of God is the divine Christ!

Saint John clearly tells us this in the very first sentence of his gospel: "In the beginning was the Word and the Word was with God; and the Word was God. And the Word was made flesh and dwelt among us. And we saw His glory—glory as of the only begotten of the Father—full of grace and of truth" (*John* 1:1-14).

Most religions, which cast aside the divinity of Christ, try to change that passage to read: ". . .and the word was a god." (Note the small "g"). However that change brings about more problems than it solves. For example, what is "a god"? Does Christ merely speak for God as His human representative, or does Christ merely reflect the light of God? If so, then all the prophets, who spoke in God's name as His messengers or representatives and all the people who reflect, through grace, God's own light become "gods." In that case, Saint John would have singled out only Christ and declared: the "Word was a god." But Saint John did not say that. He said: "The Word was God," and he knew what it was he said.

In another part of the gospel of Saint John (Chapter 4:22) Christ is speaking to the Samaritan woman from whom He had asked a drink of water. In one of His replies, during the conversation, Christ remarked: "Woman, you worship what you do not know, we (the Jewish people) worship what we know!"

Now the questions are: if you take the Bible, after leaving the Church and the sacraments, in your attempts to "find" Christ, whom do you seek: a human Christ whose story is told in the pages of the Word of God, or do you seek to find the very Word who is God? When you find a god to worship, do you know who it is you worship? Do you recognize your God as being Christ? If you find, within the Word of God your Christ, do you know what this Christ expects of you? Have you merely found a "friend," a "brother" who will walk by your side and approve all your actions and deeds no matter what you do?

So, ask yourself who it is you seek to find when you search for Christ. Are you looking for a teacher, a healer, a friend, a companion or do you really seek to find your God, your Savior, your divine Redeemer? If you do, if you truly want to be united with your God, your Savior, your divine Redeemer, then you must find much more than merely the Bible, you must find the very Word who is God and you must seek a sacramental union with the divine Word, Christ.

You see, it is possible to know about a Christ in the Bible. It is even possible to love Him and to believe in Him. However, a biblical Christ without a sacramental Christ is only a fuzzy, uncomprehensible outline of who Christ really is, and what He is.

To "find" Christ with the Bible alone as your guide, without the Church and the sacraments, is to find only a human Christ and not a divine Christ as well. That is why you discover such expressions among cults and religions as "Jesus Christ Super Star"; and why there is a purely human familiarity with Christ which destroys the whole purpose of His redemption which was to save souls. When this type of a personal relationship is established with Christ, then He often becomes merely another human being who is far more interested in a material life than in a spiritual life and who allows all sorts of sins such as adultery.

Do not misunderstand me, some people may never reach the capability of discovering the divine Savior before their own death. They may have found Christ only upon their deathbeds. That is not what I am asking about. It is indeed possible to save your soul in one last minute of an expression of faith in Christ and love for Him.

What I am saying is that if you search for Christ, you must find the complete Christ, the Christ of whom John said: ". . .and the Word was God."

Even the expression "Christ is our brother," which came forth within the Catholic Church, in the 60's and 70's is misleading. As a result, some Catholics began to feel that the Holy Eucharist was merely a "meal" shared with us with our "brother" Christ.

One day I saw a huge poster of the head and face of Christ (when these sort of posters were the "in" thing). At the bottom of the picture were huge letters which said: "With love, from Christ." Here was another example of the way some religions present to their followers only a human Christ completely detached from the divinity which is also His.

One of the most misleading statements about Christ, which most evangelists stress, is to call Christ the "great healer," then go into long details about illnesses of the body which the "great healer" cured. I have seen T.V. programs when, for one hour, the preachers did nothing but stress the healing power of "Christ The Healer."

One afternoon I sat through a Christian-unity meeting of different faiths and listened to a woman who spoke for one and a half hours about her cure (which turned out to be an incomplete cure). She spoke in glowing terms about the faith she had in the "Healer" Christ. Her praise of Christ the "Healer" was endless; yet her Christ was a healer of sick bodies only. Not once did she speak of Christ as the one who healed souls far more often than He healed bodies. Her whole relationship to Christ, which she projected outward to us, the audience, was one of "I demand you to cure my body, you Christ, the healer." In her testimony, she made us see a Christ, not as divine, but as one who stood by her side waiting for her pleads to cure her body. Not once did she say that she found union with Christ through grace. She attempted to find her union with Him only through the progressive healing of her sick body. When this is done, then the divine mission of the divine Christ, who said: "Take up your cross and follow me," is lost; for His mission was to redeem the souls of His beloved children and He, as God, remains far more interested in the salvation and sanctification of eternal souls than He is in the healings of sick bodies. In other words, His mission is not so much to heal bodies as it is to heal souls. He does, of course, heal bodies; however, He heals souls even when bodies remain gripped in the illnesses of mortal diseases. To say that Christ is the great healer only of bodies is to present for viewing only a human Christ and only an outline of who this healer really is. To say that Christ is the divine healer of bodies and souls as He hourly fulfills His divine mission of salvation, which began at the Redemption, is to present a full, a complete Christ.

We Catholics, in this respect, who stay within the sacramental

Church and find our union with Christ in her sacraments, have a great advantage over such incomplete biblical forms of religion because we know who it is we worship.

We understand and teach Christ as He was and as He is. We know Christ, our Savior, our Redeemer, our God. We do not have to guess about Christ nor about what He said. We know Him and we know exactly what He said, what He taught and what He meant.

We know that when He gave us the sacraments, we would use them to reach our union with our God, with Christ. We know He is the second person of the Trinity. We know that where Christ is, so also is God the Father and God the Holy Spirit. We know that within the sacramental structure of our church, God lives and works as surely as He lived and worked when He walked this earth as the divine Redeemer. We know that when He told the first Pope, Peter and the first apostle: ". . .and behold, I am with you all days, even unto the consummation of the world," (*Matt.* 28:20). Christ meant just that. He would not only leave His teachings, His ways, His light, His examples, but He Himself, Christ, God would be here with us for all days.

And so, we know that when we worship God, we worship Christ. We know that when we receive the Eucharist, we receive the body and blood of God, the Redeemer, who died upon that cross.

Christ said many times that He was true God as well as true man. For example: He said so plainly that the Holy Spirit, the Father and He, Christ were One and the Same: "But when He the Spirit of truth has come, He will teach you all the truth. For He will not speak on his own authority. . .He will glorify me because He will receive of what is mine and declare it to you" (*John* 16:12-15).

In *John* 10, there is one of the most important proofs that Christ is God. He was speaking to a group of people who became more and more angry by what they heard from His lips: "My sheep hear my voice and I know them and they follow me. And I give them everlasting life; and they shall never perish, neither shall anyone snatch them out of my hand. What my Father has given me is greater than all; and no one is able to snatch anything out of the hand of my Father. I and the Father are one" (*John* 10:25-30).

After hearing such words, the angry Jews took up stones in order to stone Christ to death. Christ saw what they planned to do and asked: "Many good works have I shown you from my Father. For which of these works do you stone me?" The Jews answered: "Not for a good work do we stone you, but for blasphemy, and because you, being a man, make yourself God." Jesus quickly answered: "If I do not perform the works of my Father, do not believe me. But if I do perform them and if you are not willing to believe me, believe the works that you may know and believe that the Father is in me and I in the Father."

"They sought therefore to seize him; and he went forth out of their hands" (*John* 10:31-38).

Many religions which deny the divinity of Christ say or teach that when Christ said the "Father and I are one," Christ did not mean that He was God; He only meant that He was one with the Father in thought, ever doing the will of the Father. However, Holy Scripture does not say that. The words plainly state that Christ said He was God! That was why the Jews wanted to stone Him.

Those who will deny the divinity of Christ stop at the words, "the Father and I are one"; yet if they continued to read the whole chapter (*John* 10) they would plainly see that Christ and the Jews knew that He was saying that He was God.

Again in *John* 17:22, Christ tells us that He and the Father are one, that He, Christ is truly God: "And the glory that you have given me, I have given to them, that they may be one, even as we are one."

Saint Paul knew that Christ meant it when He said He was God. In his writings, Saint Paul makes this very clear: "Have this mind in you which was also in Christ Jesus, who though He was by nature God, did not consider being equal to God, a thing to be clung to, but emptied Himself, taking the nature of a slave and being made like unto man, and appearing in the form of man, He humbled Himself being obedient to death, even death on a cross. Therefore God also has exalted Him and has bestowed upon Him the name that is above every name so that at the name of Jesus, every knee should bend of those in heaven, on earth and under the earth" (*Phil.* 2:5-11).

And no one can deny the fact that Christ made Himself equal to God and the same as God when He declared: "Go therefore and make disciples of all nations, baptizing them in the name of the Father and of the Son and of the Holy Spirit" (*Matt.* 28:19).

We Catholics are most thankful because Holy Mother Church has given to us the complete Christ: true man and true God! We know, because of that, union with Christ is union with God. We also understand this union as Christ understood and explained it: ". . .and the glory that you have given me, I have given to them, that they may be one, even as we are one; I in them and you in me; that they may be perfected in unity and that the world may know that you have sent me, and that you have loved them even as you have loved me. Father! I will that where I am, they also, whom you have given me may be with me in order that they may behold my glory which you have given me" (*John* 17:22-24).

We Catholics are not like Philip who said to Christ: "Lord show us the Father and it is enough for us." Jesus said to him: "Have I been so long a time with you and you have not known me? Philip, he who sees me sees also the Father. How can you say, "Show us the Father?" Do you not believe that I am in the Father and the Father in me?" (*John* 14:8-10). We know Christ. We know whom it is we seek union with.

Are you like Philip? You who have cast aside the Church and the sacraments and have searched the "Word of God" to find Christ? Have you gone up to Christ and said: "Lord show us the Father and it is enough for us?" If you have done this, then you will indeed hear the same answer from Christ, the one which He gave to Philip: "Have I been so long a time with you and you have not known me?"

If you seek to find Christ, if you seek a union with God, then you will find this union within the Church which presents to you a whole, a complete Christ, and the ways and means which lead to a closer union of perfection with your God, Christ, through the sacraments.

Union with God is union with Christ.

Chapter 3

DIVINE INDWELLING: HE IS WITH YOU RECOGNIZE HIM

There is an expression in the spiritual life which is called: Divine Indwelling. Most lay people never heard these words; yet, if their souls are in the state of grace, Divine Indwelling exists within each of these souls.

What is Divine Indwelling? It is a very special gift from Christ wherein He makes His home in a soul which has sanctifying grace. How do we know there is such a thing as Divine Indwelling? Because Christ told us, with these words found in *John* 14:23: "If anyone loves me, he will keep my word, and my Father will love him, and we shall come to him and make our home with him." Christ said that the Father and the Son (and the Holy Spirit who is also God) will actually dwell within the souls of all who are one with Christ and His teachings.

This teaching of Divine Indwelling is a basic, central truth of the Catholic Religion, and has been a truth of faith since the days of the infant Church. St. Paul tells us: "Do you not know that you are the temple of God and that the Spirit of God dwells in you? If anyone destroys the temple of God, him will God destroy; for holy is the temple of God and this temple you are" (*1 Cor.* 3:16-17).

Divine Indwelling begins at the moment of Baptism when the grace and light of God flood the soul. It is this grace and light which constructs the home, within the soul, wherein God dwells. If a person commits a mortal sin, this dwelling place is destroyed and will remain destroyed until grace and light return to the soul by way of a valid confession. When that happens, Divine Indwelling takes place again.

What are the results of this awesome gift to us from God called Divine Indwelling? Why would God allow us to share His very life with Him in such a way? Saint Peter explains or answers such questions in this way: "For indeed His divine power has granted us all things pertaining to life and piety through the knowledge of Him who has called us by His own glory and power. . .through which He has granted us the very great and precious promises that through them you may become partakers of the divine nature (Divine Indwelling) having escaped from the corruption of that lust which is in the world. Do you, accordingly on your part, strive dilegently to supply your faith with virtue and your virtue with knowledge? Do you try to supply your knowledge with self-control, your self-control with patience, your patience with piety, your piety with fraternal love, your fraternal love with charity? For if you do this, you will not fall into sin at any time. Indeed, in this way, will be amply provided for you the entrance into the everlasting kingdom of our Lord and Savior Jesus Christ" (*2 St. Peter* 1:3-11).

So, the indwelling of God becomes for us the way to virtue, spiritual knowledge and holiness. We then, as St. Peter tells us, are true: ". . .partakers of the divine nature. . ." which enables us to acquire a holiness like unto God's own holiness filled with virtue. Or, to put it another way: to become the living image of God. Without grace and Divine Indwelling, it would be impossible for anyone to acquire virtue and union with God. This indwelling, then, paves the way for us to become true children of God, heirs to the kingdom of heaven.

Sanctifying grace (the first requirement for Divine Indwelling) and the indwelling, or the living of God within a soul, then brings a person's spirituality into a new supernatural level of existence. On a purely human level, one without this grace and indwelling, man becomes merely an ordinary creation and his deeds are done only upon a level of human necessity and motives which are devoid of eternal merits or rewards. In other words, with grace and Divine Indwelling a person not only can save his soul, but sanctify it and gain eternal rewards as well. Thus, God allows us poor human creatures, to have a foretaste of heaven through Divine Indwelling; because, heaven is to be with God and to share His ways, nature and treasures. While still alive on earth, we can in this way: ". . .put on a new man which has been created according to God in justice and holiness. . ." (*Eph.* 4:24).

Now, knowing all these magnificent facts about Divine Indwelling, a person can better understand that ladder which leads to perfection. Also, such knowledge can bring tremendous joy to the hearts of those who come to know that God actually dwells within their souls when such souls have sanctifying grace. However, the average lay person cannot find this joy nor the next step up the ladder until or unless the person can recognize and understand this God who dwells within. Most people do not even recognize the God who dwells within them, let alone know how He came and why He is there.

So the next step to take concerning Divine Indwelling, after the soul receives or returns to sanctifying grace, is to *recognize* the God who dwells within and to become aware of His divine presence.

In the Gospel of St. Luke, Chapter 24, Verses 13-15, there is a story about two men who did not recognize Jesus, whom they walked with: ". . .and it came to pass, while they were conversing and arguing together, that Jesus Himself also drew near and went along with them. But their eyes were held and they did not recognize Him." The story continues explaining how Jesus asked the men what they were talking about and one of them related what had happened to Jesus of Nazareth concerning His crucifixion and death. They added: ". . .so some of our company went to the tomb, and found it even as the woman had said, but Him they did not see." Jesus answered: "O foolish ones and slow of heart to believe in all. . ." Then he explained: ". . .beginning with Moses and all the Prophets" what was in the Scriptures and the ". . .things referring to Himself." Finally, the three of them stopped to rest and to eat in a village along the way. Then Christ took bread and blessed and broke it and handed it to the men. "...and their eyes were opened and they recognized Him and He vanished from their sight."

Imagine how sorry these two men felt when they realized that Christ had been so close to them for the whole day—and they had not recognized Him!

This same type of tragedy happens constantly to people who do not recognize the God who dwells within them. That is the main reason why they slip so easily into the state of mortal sin. Sanctifying grace means nothing to them mainly because they do not recognize the God who lives within the dwelling of grace which exists in their souls. Sometimes, they might catch a glimpse of Him for a second before He vanishes from their sight; however, at the moment of mortal sin, they did not care enough for Christ to keep built for Him His abode within their souls. They then became like Phillip who said to Christ: "Lord, show us the Father" and Christ replied: "Have I been so long a time with you and you have not known me?" (*John* 14:8-10).

How do you get to "know Christ" the God who dwells within the grace in your soul? How can you recognize Him? To start, learn the lesson which Christ placed in that story about the two men who did not recognize Him. Just before He vanished from their sight, they did recognize Him. How and when? It was when He: "...took the bread, blessed it, broke it and handed it to them." They recognized Him through the Holy Eucharist.

That was not just a mere coincidence. Christ never did anything by chance. Everything He did and said was part of a divine plan of salvation. Christ, alive and present in the Eucharist, is the same God whose life we share through the mystery of Divine Indwelling. That does not mean that God is divided into different natures or forms, for that is not true. In viewing the presence of Christ in the Eucharist and also in us, remember one very important fact. Do not think of Christ, in the Eucharist, as Christ *giving* Himself *to us*. In other words, Christ *does not* become one with us, we become *one with Him*. This explains how there can be millions of hosts containing the body and blood of Christ taken by millions of different people. If Christ gave Himself to all these individuals then He would have to do, what some non-Catholics think we believe He does, create millions of "Christs" one for each person. Such is not true. What happens is that, through His presence in the Blessed Sacrament, Christ unites us to Himself. In that way, we become one with Christ. There is only one Christ, but millions of God's children who all become "one with Christ" through the Eucharist. That is what St. Paul meant when he wrote: ". . .the partaking of the body of the Lord? Because the bread *is one*, we, though *many*, are one body, all of us who partake of the *one bread*" (*1 Cor.* 10:17). In other words, no matter how many millions or even billions of hosts there are or have been, there is only one body and blood of Christ. They are all only *one Christ*. When millions of people receive these hosts, they receive the one Christ and they become *united to the one Christ* through this type of contact with Him in the Eucharist.

Holy Mother Church beautifully teaches this mystery of the Eucharist and how we are united with Christ in this way with her truths about the Mystical Body of Christ.

Theologians teach that Christ's presence in the Eucharist is a very real, alive presence which allows us to meet Him and to be united to Him "person-to-person" so as to form one body with Him. Once a person, whose soul is in the state of grace, meets Christ in the Eucharist there is a very wondrous union of the person not only with Christ but also with all who are united with Christ into one body. That is why it is very important not to think of the Eucharist as only a "meal" shared with our "brothers and sisters." Some Catholics have such a mistaken notion or idea about whom we meet in this way and are united to Him to form one body called the Mystical Body of Christ.

This body becomes the Church. Christ is the Church and the Church is Christ with all who are part of His Mystical Body. Christ referred to this Mystical Body with these words: "I am the vine, you are the branches" (*John* 15:5). We, the branches, become one with Christ the vine. To put it another way, Christ is the head of this Mystical Body, we the parts. Within this body is the soul, the Holy Spirit who brings all together into one union. St. Paul tells us: "For by one Spirit, we were all baptized into one body. . ." (*1 Cor.* 12:13). He also said: ". . .we are to grow up in every way into Him who is the head. . .from whom the whole body. . .grows and builds itself in love" (*Eph.* 4:15-16). Through the miracle of Christ's presence in the Eucharist, we can all become one with Christ to form the Mystical Body of Christ.

We also are part of the Communion of Saints which consists of the others in the Mystical Body. These others have likewise experienced this special union with Christ by and through Divine Indwelling and meeting Christ in the Eucharist. Souls who were baptized and have the Holy Spirit dwelling within them are part of the Communion of Saints which is part of the Mystical Body. Here again you can see the oneness of Christ and how we are united to Him and become one with Him. The Communion of Saints has three parts or branches. We, who are still on earth are the first branch known as the Church militant. The members of the Communion of Saints, who may be in purgatory are called the Church suffering. The ones who are in heaven are called the Church triumphant.

In order to better understand Christ's presence in the Eucharist and how you are united to him when you receive, imagine the following. Picture yourself, with millions of people, standing in an open field with Christ present in the center of this vast throng of people. Suddenly, Christ calls all together as one with Him. Each and every person sees Christ and walks toward Him. As all walk toward Christ, who is the center of the throng, all become as one with Christ, all become one unit. When we receive Christ in the Eucharist, we are on that open field walking toward Christ with millions of other people who become one union or unit: one Mystical Body of Christ.

Now, why is the Eucharist so important when one already has Christ within the soul through Divine Indwelling? There are many reasons why a person still needs the union with Christ in the Eucharist, even when the Trinity already exists in the soul through God's indwelling made possible by sanctifying grace. The fact is, it is by means of the indwelling of God within the soul which creates the way to union with Christ in the Eucharist.

A person must first of all have sanctifying grace and Divine Indwelling before he or she can receive or meet Christ in the Eucharist. (A person whose soul is in the state of mortal sin cannot receive Holy Communion.)

Now, before you become confused about why you still must receive the Eucharist, even when the Trinity dwells within your soul through grace, understand the following facts. There are three different basic stages of union with God involving His presence within your soul. The first stage is called the ordinary union: God dwelling in the soul through sanctifying grace. The second stage is meeting your God, Christ, in the Eucharist in a way, not possible, through Divine Indwelling alone. The third stage is the complete, perfect most desirable union with God when you are able to see His beatific vision in heaven. This is called the beatific union with God.

You can see by these three different stages of union with God, that this union is the same indwelling, the same God, but meeting Him in three different ways.

While it may be possible to have grace, the first stage of union with God, and heaven the last stage, without the middle stage, the Eucharist, there would be, in that case no Church or even no need for the Church.

It is most interesting to note that when a cult or a religion is formed without sacraments or a Church, the people involved try to find their union with God only through the first and last stages of this union. However, by doing away with Christ's Church, they have done away with His Mystical Body. It may be possible for them to find a union with God through the first stage of grace and it may be possible for them to find their complete union with God in heaven; however, by doing away with the Church and the Eucharist, they fail to follow the will of Christ who wanted His Church as the depository for His sacraments, and to use the Eucharist for the formation of His Mystical Body. Being united with Christ, or rather meeting God anew, in the Eucharsit allows us to become a living, active member of His Mystical Body called the Church.

Did Christ really want us to meet Him in the Eucharist and

to become part of His Mystical Body? Of course He did. He established His Church with Peter as the first Pope and when He sent Peter and the others out to preach, He said: "He who hears you hears me, and he who rejects you rejects me" (*Luke* 10:16). Here you can see that Christ as the head of the Mystical Body makes all in that Body, His Church, one with Him. When Saint Paul was persecuting the first members of Christ's Church, Christ caused a great miracle to happen to Paul and He asked Paul: "Why do you persecute Me?. . .I am Jesus, whom you are persecuting" (*Acts* 9:4-5). Paul was not actually fighting Christ, but the members of His Church. Yet, see the way Christ referred to Himself as being persecuted. Paul was not only harming individual Christians, but Christ's Mystical Body as well.

As for the Eucharist, Christ did indeed want all who are in His Church to meet Him in this very special way. He said: "I am the living bread which came down from Heaven; if anyone eats of this bread, he will live forever and the bread which I shall give for the life of the world is my flesh" (*John* 6:48-52). Then He spoke about the Mystical Body once more with these words: "Abide in Me and I in you. As the branch cannot bear fruit by itself, unless it abides in the vine, neither can you unless you abide in Me" (*John* 15:4).

It is also well to remember, when discussing Divine Indwelling and Christ's presence in the Eucharist, that at the Last Supper, Christ was present with the Apostles: yet, He wanted a closer union with them and gave to each one His own body and blood: "Take, this is my body. . .this is my blood. . ." (*Mark* 14:22-24).

In like manner, although Christ is with us through Divine Indwelling, still He desires an even closer stage or level of union which we obtain when we receive Holy Communion. In addition to receiving the Eucharist so that we can become part of the Mystical Body of Christ, there are many other reasons why we must receive if we are to live a holy spiritual life.

When we meet Christ in the Eucharist, the first benefit, after we become active members of the Mystical Body, is an *increase* in the grace which already forms the dwelling for God within our souls. It is very important to know that this grace can be increased and even must be increased. Why does this grace have to be increased? Because only with sanctifying grace can we understand *who* it is that dwells in our souls; and the more grace we have, the greater will be our understanding.

The "grace-presence" of God within the soul, as indwelling is sometimes called, is an awesome, mind-befuddling encounter if taken at its full value. A mere, weak human being could never handle such an experience unless he or she has the necessary grace to do so; and this same human being could never have the insight to come to a realization of the truth of Divine Indwelling unless and until the person has enough grace to be able to accept and relate to the comprehension and meaning of this event.

Even though God does indeed dwell within a person's soul when the soul is in the state of grace, most people are totally unaware of this fact. Also, most people who receive the Eucharist do not fully understand what the presence of Christ in the Eucharist really means. That is the main reason why they fail to advance up THE LADDER OF PERFECTION to a closer union with God; which includes a greater awareness of who it really is who dwells within the soul and the Eucharist.

Let me explain it this way. In becoming aware of Christ's presence in the soul and in the Eucharist, think about this awareness in degrees. There can be different degrees of someone's presence and also of another's reaction to that presence. Imagine that a very famous person suddenly enters a room where there are many people. If this person is not recognized, she will be totally ignored. Pretend that you were in that crowd and later you found out that the person was actually the Queen of England! How sorry you would be to think that you had not recognized and had ignored her. If only you had known who she really was, how differently you would have reacted to her presence.

I am reminded of what happened to a friend of mine at the Eucharistic Congress which was held in 1976. One day there was an enormous crowd in front of the Civic Center. My friend was next to the street trying to get through the crowd. Suddenly a car drove up and someone got out of the car. She was so close to my friend that he could have touched her; however, still trying to get through the mass of humanity, he had his back to her. Suddenly the crowd shouted "Princess Grace, Princess Grace!" My friend realized that she had been so close to him, but when he found out who she was, she had become lost in the throng. He never forgot how close he had been to her, but he did not even see her. How sorry he was!

This same situation exists concerning Divine Indwelling and the presence of Christ in the Eucharist. Most people are not aware of what this really means and they can spend a whole lifetime turning their backs to the presence of God simply because they do not recognize Him in His indwelling and Eucharistic stages. They never bothered to turn around to see God; even though His presence was with them all the time.

How can we do that, how can we "turn around" and face and recognize Divine Indwelling and the presence of Christ in the Eucharist? The answer is to increase sanctifying grace within the soul. Only with this increase can awareness and realization come.

When sanctifying grace comes to the soul and also Divine Indwelling, God, the Trinity, is there. However, His presence is not announced with choirs of angels singing or trumpets sounding. God enters His dwelling place in the soul as a silent, quiet guest. If He suddenly exploded His almighty might and power upon the intellect of a weak human being, such force would without a doubt bring death instead of joy to the individual. So the awareness of His presence must come through an increase in the quality of sanctifying grace. Only then can there be degrees of understanding and awareness which will enable the person to reach a closer union with God in the soul.

Now understand the way meeting Christ in the Eucharist brings an increase in the grace needed to recognize the God who dwells within the soul. How is that so? Because the sacraments *increase* sanctifying grace! The grace received, when one is baptized or when one makes a valid confession after mortal sins are committed, is the complete grace necessary for Divine

Indwelling, but only an increase in the quality of that grace can give to the person the awarness necessary to recognize his or her divine guest. God reveals Himself to a soul *only to the degree* which it is prepared for this recognition. How does one prepare for God to reveal more and more of His presence? Once again the answer is sanctifying grace, or rather an increase in this grace. Where does this increase come from? The answer: mainly from prayer and the sacraments. What is the greatest prayer and sacrament? The answer is the Mass and the Eucharist. A person cannot be baptized over and over, hundreds of times, in order to increase sanctifying grace; however, a person can increase this grace by receiving the Sacraments of Penance and the Eucharist hundreds of times, but more so the Eucharist.

The Eucharist then becomes *not* just a passive "reminder" of the Last Supper, as so many Christians, even some Catholics, make it out to be. Christ is actually present in the Eucharist and He is present for a very definite purpose and reason. The Eucharist *is* Christ, alive, and ready to meet us, His children on a one-to-one or person-to-person relationship to bring into a clear view or realization His presence in our souls. It is through the Eucharist where we find the grace to "turn around" and face the God who dwells within our souls; for then we can recognize the Christ in the Eucharist and the Christ in our souls as being one and the same God. Then we can enter into a higher degree of understanding this same God whom we will see face-to-face in heaven for all eternity.

That is why it is so important *never* to receive Holy Communion when the soul is in the state of mortal sin. Many people do just that and tell themselves it is "perfectly all right." But it is not "all right." It is a grave sin to do so. It is also a hypocrisy. How could anyone meet Christ in the Eucharist and attempt to understand and love Him when the base for such understanding and love, sanctifying grace, is absent from the soul? If the "grace-presence" of God is missing from the soul, there could never be an understanding of Christ in the Eucharist, for the two are one and the same.

Also, the main purpose of Holy Communion is not only to have the way and the means to meet Christ and be united with Him, but to actually become *transformed* into Christ. To become one with Christ means to become Christlike in words, deeds and actions. And grace—a great deal of grace—is needed for that accomplishment. If a person keeps his soul in the state of mortal sin, and at the same time attempts to be united with Christ in the Eucharist, that person's spiritual state goes from bad to worse. One cannot be transformed into Christ unless the person's soul contains the vehicle for this transformation called sanctifying grace. Also, one cannot reach a higher degree of understanding the true presence of Christ if this presence is not already in the soul through Divine Indwelling and met again in the Eucharist. In other words, the Eucharist cannot benefit a "dead" soul (one without the life called grace).

Needless to say, then, there has to be the correct intentions when a person approaches Christ in the Eucharist. Many people make no intentions at all when they receive. I am not talking about prayers. They may indeed pray for themselves or others during the moments of the Eucharistic union with Christ. I am speaking of the person-to-person relationship allowed by receiving and the use of this relationship to have Christ assist the person's soul up that LADDER OF PERFECTION.

Marvelous, unbelievable things can happen to the person's soul if the Eucharist is received with the correct intentions, love and understanding. For example: the increase of sanctifying grace comes forth only to the degree of correct intentions. The more we desire grace and love from the Eucharist, the more grace and love comes to us. The more we give of ourselves to Christ when we meet Him in the Eucharist, the more He will transform us into Himself. The more we welcome Him as a guest in our souls, the more He will reveal His presence to us. The more aware we are of what He is trying to do for us, the more He will do for us. The more we pay attention to the spiritual insights which He wants to teach us, the more we will learn from our divine guest. The more we realize our commitment to the Mystical Body of Christ, His Church, the more we will accept our responsibilities as Catholics. The more hate we have for our sins and faults, the more grace we will receive to overcome them.

Just one Holy Communion contains a powerful force which will help to purify our souls, if only we would face and accept this force. Venial sins can be forgiven and even the temporal punishment due for sins committed and confessed can be taken away. In addition the force (or grace) from Communion can help to keep us free and preserve our souls from mortal sins. All these things, and more, can happen if we receive the Eucharist with the correct intentions.

Now to summarize the many reasons why we must also receive the Eucharist even though we have Divine Indwelling. The Eucharist is where we meet Christ in a very special way so as to become part of His Mystical Body. The Eucharist also gives to our souls an increase in sanctifying grace so we can better understand the God who dwells within us and whom we meet in the Eucharist. Holy Communion not only unites us to Christ in a very special way, but it helps us to become more Christlike. Then when we become more Christlike we can develop a very real, deep love for others as we practice virtues and overcome sins and faults. Finally, if received with the right intentions, Holy Communion can remit venial sins and take away the temporal punishment due for sins committed.

Also to be noted is the fact that both Baptism and the Eucharist have outward material signs of the channel of grace to the soul. This was no accident, on the part of Christ, when He instituted the sacraments. Christ might very well have asked Himself: "How can I reach out to a vast multitude of my children all over the world to give to each one personally my presence and to so unite them to me?" The answer to such a question was: to use common, universal elements as the way to bring them to Him. These common, universal elements became the water used in Baptism and the bread and wine used in the Eucharist. By means of these material, common substances Christ reaches out to all men calling them unto Himself. There was no limits, boundaries, barriers, to the way to union with Christ through the outward signs of Baptism and the

Eucharist. All men and women, from the King down to the lowly peasant, can reach a union with Christ by and through the common, everyday material signs of the Sacraments of Baptism and the Eucharist.

Even though the actual presence of God within the soul and the union with God are silent and unseen, the sacramental elements become a symbol of what is happening in our spiritual union with God. The water becomes a symbol of cleaning or cleansing the soul from all sin and darkness which allows God's light, grace and presence to enter. The bread and wine become a symbol or sign of feeding the soul to keep its grace strong and healthy. In other words, Christ calls us to Himself through the use of water and food for our souls.

Now to go back to the question I raised earlier in this chapter: How can you recognize the God who dwells within your soul? First of all develop a very deep love for Christ in the Eucharist and receive often with the correct intentions. Remember that in Divine Indwelling *you* are united with God. Think of each sacrament, especially Baptism, the Eucharist and Confession as your pathway to union with Christ. When Divine Indwelling occurs and also meeting Christ in the Eucharist, it is God who elevates *you* up to and into Himself, His grace, His ways. He does not come down to your level of material humanism. A true supernatural event takes place when your soul receives sanctifying grace and Divine Indwelling. Any supernatural event is "above nature" "above human ways." Realize the magnificent gifts which God bestows upon you when He allows, through grace, a dwelling place for Himself to be built within your soul.

As I said, many people may have Divine Indwelling through grace, but they keep their backs turned to the guest in their souls. They never really see Him although He is present. They never really recognize Him. They never understand what it means to have His presence within their souls or to have Christ present in the Eucharist. Thus, they don't know that God is with them every moment of every day when their souls are in the state of grace; but He is, recognize Him.

Chapter 4

THE SANCTIFIER, THE HOLY SPIRIT

In the 60's and especially in the early 70's, the Holy Spirit came "into His own." Equally divided between the Pentecostal movements and the T.V. preachers and faith-healers, according to some groups, the Spirit was "found" and released to pour forth His fruits upon a vast multitude of the "faithful."

However, no matter how often he was "found" in such a manner, His true identity as the third person of the Trinity and His true role of Sanctifier was somehow hidden or veiled behind the concept of what these multitude of faithful imagined this Spirit to be. In other words, most of the people who "found" the Spirit did not even know who it was they had found or what His role was which so greatly affected their own personal association with God.

This fact was made very clear to me when I had a conversation with a young woman, who claimed she had "found" the Holy Spirit after joining a Pentecostal group. She said, three times: "I never had the Holy Spirit before, but now I have found Him." Finally, I asked: "Tell me exactly whom you have found? Who is the Holy Spirit?" She went into a weak explanation which proved that she had no idea who the Holy Spirit was. But she mentioned that she had been "baptized by the Spirit." I replied: "But you were baptized as an infant."

She replied: "Oh that! That was nothing. Christ said to be baptized by the Spirit."

I replied: "You were baptized with the Holy Spirit, and you also received the Holy Spirit when you made your Confirmation. Now tell me who the Holy Spirit is?"

Again, she could not. She had no idea what her own Baptism and Confirmation had been or had done for her soul.

One day, before I started a Maryheart Crusader meeting, a woman came up to me and said: "Shall I give Witness?" I was puzzled and replied: "Witness to what?"

She answered: "Witness to the power of the Spirit!"

I replied: "But grace is the power of the Holy Spirit. Grace is what your soul needs for its own sanctification. Grace pours down upon our souls every moment of every day. In order to witness, as you call it, you have but to use this grace for the good of your own soul and for the good of the souls of others."

Then she was puzzled. She had no idea what grace was or how the Holy Spirit sanctifies the soul through grace, more so than through outward signs.

This chapter is not a discussion of the pros and cons of the Pentecostal movements. I will say here what I often tell people: if handled correctly, such spirituality can lead a soul to a closer union with God. If not handled correctly this same type of spirituality can be disastrous for a person's individual spiritual life by focusing all attention upon the outer, materialistic workings of the Holy Spirit and not upon the inner workings of God's grace within the soul.

One woman I talked to had a spiritually healthy attitude toward the workings of the Holy Spirit. She said: "People pay too much attention to the outer signs. The true miracles of the Holy Spirit are to be found within the soul." I agreed.

As I said, the main drawback of the whole "finding" of the Holy Spirit, through many Pentecostal types of religion and T.V. personalities is that such awakenings tend to make people believe that the world has been devoid or empty of the Holy Spirit until He "came" when such movements started. Yet, all the while, the Holy Spirit was present in a soul which was in the state of grace and He directed Holy Mother Church, as Christ has promised He would so direct: "But when the Spirit of truth has come, He will teach you all truth. He will receive of what is mine and declare it to you. All things that the Father has are mine. That is why I have said that He will receive of what is mine and will declare it to you" (*John* 16:7-15). Indeed, the Holy Spirit has never left the Church nor individual souls. The problem is that individuals do not understand who the Holy Spirit really is and what He has done for them.

For example, very often I heard about Catholics who went running to see and hear a T.V. personality who was said to be filled with the "Spirit," hoping that such "Spirit" would flow from this individual to them. At huge rallies, such a preacher would shout something like: "All who have found the "Spirit" here tonight come forth," and a large number of the ones who did "come forth" were Catholics. All were confused about who the Holy Spirit really is and how He daily works within their own lives and souls.

Most people, who become confused by some Pentecostal experience, make the mistake of believing that the Holy Spirit is only a feeling or an emotion, or worse, merely some outward sign or power. Yet all the while they fail to realize or to understand that a far greater wonder or miracle happened the day they were baptized when the Holy Spirit freed their souls from the darkness of original sin.

Granted, there are some genuine outward signs of the Holy Spirit working to show His power. We see Him as a dove above Christ's head when he was baptized. We see the Holy Spirit as tongues of fire on the first Pentecost, the birth of our Church; however, the Holy Spirit works His greatest miracles within the hidden depths of a person's own spiritual life. Such miracles are seldom seen or even felt, but they are there nevertheless.

I shall never forget the day I was the Godmother for a young adult. This woman was a convert and had never been baptized. She was radiantly happy and filled with joy before the baptism took place; but her joy faded after she was baptized. I asked her what was wrong. She replied: "I felt nothing. I thought a great change would take place in me that I could feel and see. I thought I would be different, but I am not. I am still me!"

I laughed and replied: "You made the mistake of looking for a physical miracle and change. That is not what Baptism is all about. It was your soul which changed, not your body. You cannot see nor feel this change, but God can see it. Now become filled with joy knowing that God Himself dwells within the depths of your soul."

Many people make this very same mistake. They have been taught to believe that the Holy Spirit is "there" only when extraordinary physical and material signs are present. Many Catholics who have fallen into this serious error concerning the Holy Spirit feel that anyone who has not had an experience like theirs is very much lacking in union with the Holy Spirit. They themselves often feel superior and believe that the only way to union with the Holy Spirit is for a show of some outward sign of the Spirit's presence. One such person told me that all Catholics are "no good" unless they belonged to a prayer group because the Holy Spirit is only in such prayer groups.

As I said, such Catholics are very sadly mistaken, and the proper knowledge about the Holy Spirit can correct their ideas and put them into perspective.

So, who exactly is the Holy Spirit and what exactly is His magnificent role as Sanctifier?

The answer begins with holy Scripture, the Bible. Christ referred to the Holy Spirit as a person: "But when the Advocate has come, *He* will bear witness concerning me" (*John* 14:26).

Because of that, we can be sure that the Holy Spirit is a *Person* and not merely a force or a power. Well, what kind of a person is He? Christ also answers that question when He said: "Go forth and baptize. . . in the name of the Father, the Son and the Holy Spirit" (*Matt.* 28:19).

Christ put the Holy Spirit on the very same level as Himself and His Father, so by such words we know that the Holy Spirit is not only a person, but a divine person as well. We see the Holy Spirit as the third person of the Trinity.

What does that mean, to be the third person of the Holy Trinity? It means that the Holy Spirit is not only God, but quite capable of acting and working as an individual person. In other words, He is not merely the so-called "spirit" *of God* or "power" *of God* or "promise" *of Christ*. The Holy Spirit *is* God, the third person of the Trinity.

All the misunderstandings concerning the Holy Spirit stem from the false notion or teachings that the Holy Spirit is merely a force or power or a "breath of God" which comes to us from God. The Holy Spirit does not *come from God*, The Holy Spirit is God! If that were not true, then Christ would have said: "I will send my spirit to you" or "I will send the spirit of my Father to you." But Christ did not say that. He said: "...it is expedient for you that I depart; for if I do not go, the Advocate will not come to you; but if I go, I will send Him to you" (*John* 16:7-9).

Christ called the Holy Spirit a person and then identified this person as a divine person of the Holy Trinity.

The Trinity, while difficult to understand, is nevertheless very real. The best way to comprehend the reality of the three persons in one God is to imagine that you are in a dark, empty room with three windows in it. Suddenly there is one beam of light; however, this one beam splits and enters the room through each window separately.

Now you see three different, separate beams of light on the floor of the room. Each beam of light is alone, separate. Each beam has its own light and its own warmth to the same degree. They are separate, yet exactly the same. When merged together they become the same one beam of light.

That simple example is, of course not all that can be said about the Trinity; but it does illustrate in a crude manner how the Trinity consists of three divine persons who are, at the same time, God and divine individuals.

God the Father is just that: the Father. God the Son is the Redeemer and God the Holy Spirit is the Sanctifier.

The most important roles of the Holy Spirit are to sanctify souls and to guide and inspire Holy Mother Church. That was why Christ sent the Holy Spirit to His infant Church.

The Holy Spirit can also guide and inspire individuals, but never will He guide them away from the Church which He has protected from the time of our first Pentecost.

Many, many people use the excuse that the Holy Spirit is "guiding" them or "telling them what to do" when they freely choose to go against Holy Mother Church and her teachings. That, of course, if far from true. The Holy Spirit does not tell the Church to teach one thing and then tell individuals to disregard such teachings and to do their "own thing." The Holy Spirit does not contradict nor change the truths of God. Sin is still sin, the sacraments remain the same. The doctrines will never change, such as the doctrines of heaven, hell, purgatory, etc.

So, the role of the Holy Spirit as the guide and protector of the truths of God must be clearly seen. So also, and perhaps even a bit more important, the role of the Holy Spirit as Sanctifier must be clearly seen.

Just exactly what does that mean, the Holy Spirit, the Sanctifier? You must fully understand what it means or else you will be fooled by the idea that the Holy Spirit has only recently been "discovered," or by the idea that unless you belong to a Pentecostal group and publicly exhibit all sorts of outward signs you cannot or do not possess the "Spirit."

True union with God is always a very personal, intimate experience, one not to be shared with others with outward signs of holiness or sanctity. No saint whoever lived (or whoever will live) wanted his or her union with God to show publicly. If such signs did come forth, such as healings or special gifts, the saint was the most surprised person on earth. They were amazed to think that a mere "nothing," as they thought themselves to be, could do such a marvelous thing or possess such marvelous gifts.

The truth of the matter is that the Holy Spirit seldom, if ever, reveals His presence through outward signs. He, daily, is present in millions of souls; yet these persons do not even know it because they lack the knowledge of who the Holy Spirit is and what He does within the hidden depths of their souls. In other words, the holding of hands, the healings, the speaking in tongues, the prophecies, all are not necessary when one wants to "find" the Holy Spirit. All that is necessary is grace: the grace which makes the soul and dwelling place of the Holy Spirit along with His gifts to that soul.

So in order to understand the Holy Spirit as the Sanctifier, you must first of all understand grace, but more: sanctifying grace.

Sanctifying grace is first given to a soul when the person is baptized. It is a true gift from God which has the power to transform the soul from the darkness of sin to the light of grace. Whenever a mortal sin is committed, this grace disappears and the soul becomes filled with darkness once again. This darkness can be removed in the confessional. After a good confession (with a firm purpose of amendment), sanctifying grace returns and the soul is filled with light once more. So you see here a simple explanation of how grace takes away the darkness of mortal sin.

But grace does much more than that. Grace prepares a dwelling place within the soul for the Holy Spirit. The fact is that the Holy Spirit and grace are as one. Where grace is, so also is the Holy Spirit. The Holy Spirit actually living within a soul that is in the state of sanctifying grace is called: Divine Indwelling.

It is this Divine Indwelling which the multitude of people fail to understand. Can you imagine the immense joy which would explode from your inner depths if you came into the full realization that the living God actually dwells within your soul?

I am reminded here of a very simple event which deeply affected me. One evening I was watching a program of Gospel music. It was being presented by a Protestant group. But I enjoyed the songs and the singers. Then a young woman started to sing a song which I had never heard before. I do not remember the title, but the words I do remember were: "If God is dead, who is this living in my soul?" Not only do I remember these words, but what impressed me the most was the look on the girl's face each time she sang: "If God is dead, who is this living in my soul?" Her face radiated with joy and happiness. She really understood what it was she was saying.

And if we could fully realize the truth that the Holy Spirit actually dwells within our souls when they are in the state of grace, unbelievable joy could fill our whole beings.

But more often than not, this realization is not there. That is why so many people look for outward signs of the presence of the Holy Spirit, and the main reason why they put so much importance upon only outward signs is because their own personal spiritual advancement is not developed.

When I first began to hear about the Pentecostal movement, the thing which bothered me the most was the fact that the people caught up in this movement seemed to think that they had reached a high or perfect union with God only after attending one or two prayer meetings. I would shake my head in disbelief and say: "It is *not* that *easy!*" or "It takes a lifetime to reach the union with God they say they reached in only a week or two or three."

The realization necessary for a deep understanding of Divine Indwelling cannot possibly come to a person overnight or in one week or in one year. Why? Because such enlightenment is the result of destruction of personal sins, faults and weaknesses, and the battle for perfection. The battle between temptation and the power of grace goes on for a lifetime.

An unpolished diamond is only a very poor sample of the diamond's true splendor. In much the same way, a person's realization of Divine Indwelling becomes only a very poor sample of understanding this magnificent mystery when this realization is not polished in the fires of spiritual battles. In other words, to perfect a union with God and to come to the full realization of the meaning of Divine Indwelling, there has to be a tremendous spiritual struggle to overcome sins, faults and weaknesses, and to replace them with the true virtues of sanctity. Realization of Divine Indwelling comes only to the degree of one's ability and willingness to overcome sins, faults and human weaknesses and to acquire holiness.

The Holy Spirit would never reveal Himself, in all His splendor, to souls not prepared to receive this gift simply because the soul would not be able or capable of handling such a gift. In much the same way that a soul which lacks grace could never enter heaven simply because the one element for enjoying the Beatific vision of God is missing; namely, sanctifying grace!

One of the big mistakes which the Pentecostal movement seemed to make is to teach people to experience the presence of the Holy Spirit only through physical and material signs, wonders and feelings, instead of teaching these same people that the *realization* of Divine Indwelling is far more important than all the outward signs and wonders.

It is the daily, the hourly growth of spirituality and putting into practice the gifts of the Holy Spirit which is far more necessary for a person's union with God than outward signs. It is the slow, painful climb up THE LADDER OF PERFECTION which is necessary for the final, full realization of Divine Indwelling.

That is why I often heard from people who were at one time caught up in the outward excitement of the movement, but who left because this excitement of having "found" the Holy Spirit faded away each time a prayer meeting ended.

Unless the inner workings of the Holy Spirit are clearly understood, great damage can be done to a person's spiritual life.

Chapter 5

THE GIFTS OF THE HOLY SPIRIT

In a previous chapter I mentioned Divine Indwelling. Just exactly what does it mean? The best way to describe Divine Indwelling is to say: "God dwells within my soul when it is in the state of grace." However, merely to say those words and to understand them are two different things. It is the understanding or the realization of what Divine Indwelling means and what it does for the soul that is important.

We can start to capture the true meaning of Divine Indwelling by referring to certain biblical passages. In the Gospel of St. John, Chapter 14, verses 15-19, there are these words: "If you love me, keep my commandments. And I will ask the Father and He will give you another Advocate to dwell with you forever, the Spirit of truth whom the world cannot receive because it neither sees nor knows Him. But you shall know Him because He will dwell with you and *be in you*. I will not leave you orphans."

Also, we find in Holy Scripture these words: "These things I have spoken to you while yet dwelling with you. But the advocate, the Holy Spirit, whom the Father will send in my name, He will teach you all things and bring to your mind whatever I have said to you" (*John* 14:25-26).

Now I will offer a little summary of what Holy Scripture tells us about the Holy Spirit using the passages I have already quoted and others.

First of all, the Holy Spirit is indeed a *person*, a divine *person*. Christ calls Him: "He," which He would never have done if the Spirit was merely Christ's own power or force or the

Father's own "spirit:" ". . .but you shall know Him because He will dwell with you. . ." (*John* 14:15-19). ". . .but the Advocate, the Holy Spirit, whom the Father will send in my name, *He* will teach you all things and bring to your mind whatever I have said to you" (*John* 14:25-26). "But when the Advocate has come. . .*He* will bear witness concerning me" (*John* 15:26). ". . .for if I do not go, the Advocate will not come to you, but if I go, I will send *Him* to you. . ." (*John* 16:7-8). ". . .but when the Spirit of truth has come, *He* will teach you all the truth. . .He will glorify me because He will receive of what is mine and declare it to you" (*John* 16:7-15).

Secondly, the Holy Spirit is not only a person, but a teacher as well. However, He remains a teacher of only what Christ taught. In other words, He, as God, cannot teach different doctrine than did Christ, who was also God: ". . .He will teach you all the truth. He will glorify me because He will receive of what is mine and declare it to you" (*John* 16:15). "He will teach you all things and bring to your mind whatever I have said to you" (*John* 14:25-26). Anyone who says that the "Spirit" has lead them into religious errors away from the Church and the truths of God, is sadly mistaken. They must remember that Christ not only left His truths to His infant Church (with Peter as the head of the Church) but He also sent the "Holy Spirit" to protect such truths by ". . .He will teach you all things and bring to your mind whatever I have said to you."

Thirdly, the Holy Spirit will come, as God, teacher and sanctifier to actually dwell within us. ". . .because He will dwell with you and *be in you*. . ." (*John* 14:15-19). Also: "If a man loves me, he will keep my word and my Father will love him and we will come to him and make our abode with him" (*John* 14:23). Here you see, not only the Divine Indwelling of the Holy Spirit, but the fact that this person, this "He" is also God. In *John* 14, verse 23, Christ speaks of "we," ". . .we will come to him and make our abode (home) with him." Compare: "He will dwell with you and be in you."

Fourthly, more often than not, the presence of the Holy Spirit is silent and unseen: ". . .the Spirit of truth, whom the world cannot receive because it neither sees Him nor knows Him. But you shall know Him because He will dwell with you and *be in you*" (*John* 14:15-19).

Those people who believe that the presence of the Holy Spirit is shown only by and through outward signs and wonders are sadly mistaken.

Lastly, the Holy Spirit is *not* a "power" or a "feeling" or an "emotion." The Holy Spirit *has* a power, a magnificent power to change a soul filled with the darkness of sin into a soul shining with the brilliant light of grace. He has the power to produce within a soul a wondrous rebirth and make this soul a fitting place for Him to dwell: "Unless a man is born again of water and the Holy Spirit, he cannot enter the kingdom of heaven" (*John* 3:5).

This rebirth takes place at Baptism. Baptism is the sacrament which brings sanctifying grace to the soul the first time. Note how the word sanctifying compares with the title of The Holy Spirit, Sanctifier. The Holy Spirit begins His job as the Sanctifier at Baptism when the grace of light floods the soul and He takes His place within the soul. He comes within the soul, the moment sanctifying grace enters. Grace is the gift from God which builds within the soul, the dwelling place of the Holy Spirit. The only time, thereafter, when this dwelling place is destroyed, is when mortal sin destroys the light of grace within the soul. But even then, even when that happens, the Holy Spirit works His wonders and uses His power to give to that soul the *actual* graces which the soul will need in order to return to the Sacrament of Confession, to rebuild His dwelling place by having sanctifying grace restored through a valid confession.

See now this main job or main power of the Holy Spirit: the job of bringing and giving grace to a soul! This is the most important function of the Holy Spirit as far as an individual soul is concerned. All outward signs are not as important nor as necessary as that one job of the Holy Spirit to build and maintain His dwelling place within each individual soul. If, for example, a person who refuses to repent, has gifts such as healing powers, prophecy, speaking in tongue, etc., these outward signs of the so-called "presence" of the Holy Spirit *mean nothing!* As long as a person refuses to see the main job of the Holy Spirit, His job as Sanctifier, then all the outward signs become useless and have no meaning. It is a great comfort to know that the Holy Spirit can be very much alive and very active within our souls even when we, ourselves, do not possess extraordinary signs of His so-called "presence." As long as our souls are in the state of grace (no mortal sins), then we can be sure that the Holy Spirit actually dwells within us and constantly works His wonders of grace within our souls.

But, as I said, just saying that the Holy Spirit dwells within us is one thing. Actually coming to the realization of what this means is another thing. How can we come to the realization of what it means to have God dwell within our souls? Well, let us start with the gifts of the Holy Spirit to us other than the main and first gift of sanctifying grace.

Remember that once the Holy Spirit takes up a dwelling place within your soul, He does not merely rest. He is not a placid inactive guest within your soul. The power of His love for you and of His grace is so intense that He wants to share with you His greatest spiritual treasures: the treasures which will last forever. He has an infinite, unlimited supply of spiritual gifts and treasures to give to you. That is one great mistake which some Charismatic groups make. They appear to stress only a very limited array of the gifts of the Holy Spirit in such a way that those who do not possess these special gifts feel sort of "left out" as if the Holy Spirit neglected or forgot them or worse: as if He left them or never came to them! Yet, the truth of the matter is that the Holy Spirit is indeed within a soul in the state of grace, and is very active and has numerous gifts to give to that person. Bear in mind the fact that many canonized saints never possessed special gifts or powers of healing, prophecy, etc.; yet they rose to the heights of personal sanctification with and by the powers of the Holy Spirit who dwelt within them.

Now, how do you possess the treasures of the Holy Spirit? First of all, some of His gifts to you come as infused gifts unbeknown to you. They come with the marvelous gift of sanctifying grace.

At Baptism you receive, along with grace, the infused virtues of faith, hope and charity (or love). These gifts enable you to know God through faith, to love God and others and to have hope and trust in God. That is why it is so easy for a baptized child to accept God and His ways. The child was given the gift of faith. This is one of the most precious gifts from the Holy Spirit to you: your faith. Equally as precious are His gifts of love for God and trust and hope in Him, His Church and His ways.

If you have faith in God, hope in God and love for God, such spiritual gifts are not accidental. You have these gifts because, at Baptism, the Holy Spirit made your soul His dwelling place and gave you these gifts.

There is more. Besides the first infused virtues of faith, hope and love (or charity as it is sometimes called), there are four other virtues which are infused into a soul at Baptism. These are: prudence, justice, fortitude and temperance. These are called the four cardinal virtues.

The moment you are baptized, you are given seven marvelous gifts of the Holy Spirit which you can use for the rest of your life to grow spiritually in holiness; for upon these seven infused virtues, all other virtues depend. In other words, you could never become holy or filled with sanctity unless you possess these seven gifts of the Holy Spirit! A baptized person does not have to search in darkness looking for the foundation upon which to build THE LADDER OF PERFECTION. By understanding the gifts of the Holy Spirit, the baptized person can be sure that he or she already possesses the materials needed to build that foundation, which are these seven infused virtues or gifts of the Holy Spirit.

That is the main reason why you can possess your faith in God even without trying. If God, His ways, His presence, His mercy, His love, His goodness to you are all clear in your daily life, you may have wondered why an unbaptized person cannot share such a faith with you. The answer is that an unbaptized person cannot possess these infused virtues which were the Holy Spirit's gifts to you when you were baptized.

See the marvelous, magnificent way that the Holy Spirit has

prepared your soul and your spiritual life for a very close, personal union with Him! He has given to you at Baptism all that is necessary for you to have, and also to understand, the paths which lead to your own salvation. There can be no greater gifts than these! If you never possess any extraordinary gifts of the Holy Spirit, if you never are chosen for a special job for God, *you can still reach* the holiness of the saints because you have all that is necessary to reach such an exalted state.

The Holy Spirit did not "slight" you nor "pass you by" if you do not possess outward signs of His presence. The most important gifts of the Holy Spirit, you do possess and have possessed since the moment of your Baptism.

Then there are more gifts which are given to you by the Holy Spirit. In order to protect the seven infused gifts which you received at Baptism, the Holy Spirit gives you additional spiritual gifts to help you keep and maintain and build up the grace within your own soul, this grace which is necessary for your holiness and salvation.

Included within the precious gift of sanctifying grace there are more wondrous gifts from the Holy Spirit who dwells within your soul. These are called the seven fruits (another name for gifts) of the Holy Spirit. They included: wisdom, understanding, counsel, fortitude, knowledge, piety and fear of the Lord. These gifts add to the spiritual treasures which your soul possesses. They also help to prepare you for spiritual battles on earth and also for life everlasting in God's kingdom of love. For example, the gift of understanding allows you to use the gifts of faith, hope and love for God. The gift of fortitude gives you the spiritual courage which you need when you battle sin, weaknesses and temptations.

So you see that the Holy Spirit has not neglected you nor "passed you by." You do possess, when your soul is in the state of grace, all that is necessary for you to reach the heights of perfection.

If you are not now striving for this perfection, the fault is yours, not the Holy Spirit's, because you may have hampered the action or activity of the Holy Spirit within your own soul by being careless, neglectful, lukewarm or ignorant of His gifts and ways. You did possess all that is needed for your personal union with God from the moment you were baptized; however, all these marvelous gifts to you can be pushed aside or even rendered useless by a neglected spiritual life or by mortal sin.

The Holy Spirit can work His wonders in your soul *only to the degree* that you allow Him to. If you care little about His grace and His gifts to you, He cannot give to you the holiness or sanctity which he desires you to possess. In other words, the Sanctifier cannot do His work of sanctification unless you cooperate with His grace and use the gifts which He has so freely bestowed upon your soul.

How can you do that? Use the gifts which the Holy Spirit has given to you? First of all by making sure that your soul is always in the state of grace. This is the most important concern of your life. All other things in your life must be second; grace for your soul comes first. Why? Because if you gain the whole world and yet lose sanctifying grace for your soul, you have lost everything, perhaps for all eternity. It is very important to know that if you commit a mortal sin, you must return grace to your soul as soon as possible. It must be remembered that when grace departs from your soul, so do many of the gifts of the Holy Spirit. That is why it becomes so easy for a sinner to continue to sin with no feelings of guilt for sins committed. When grace is gone from the soul, so are the fruits of the Holy Spirit. For example, the gift of understanding is no longer present. As Leo J. Trese explains in his book, THE FAITH EXPLAINED: "All things else being equal, a priest would much prefer to explain a point of doctrine to a person who is in the state of sanctifying grace rather than to one who is not. The former, having the gift of understanding, will be much quicker in grasping the point in issue."

The second thing which you must do in order to allow the Sanctifier to sanctify your soul is to increase sanctifying grace in your soul. The more this grace increases in your soul, the closer your union to God will become, the more realization you will have of whom it is who dwells within your soul, and the more virtues you will acquire and use. So it is very important, not only to make sure that your soul has sanctifying grace, but to increase that grace as well.

How do you do that? Increase sanctifying grace in your soul? You do that through prayer and the sacraments and living a Christ-centered life of virtuous deeds and actions. Each time you receive a sacrament, after Baptism (the initial flood of grace into the soul) the grace and gifts of the Holy Spirit within the soul multiply and increase.

It is questionable exactly how much grace a person would receive if, for example, he suddenly imagines that he is now a prophet, or if other outward gifts are "given" to him. The fact is, grace may not increase at all, but decrease if these outward gifts or signs of the "presence" of the Holy Spirit lead him into pride and self-esteem. Such a thing has happened many times. People imagine they are suddenly "chosen" and they build their whole spiritual lives around this so-called "mission" and end up utterly destroying their spiritual lives.

However, when prayer and the sacraments are used to increase grace within the soul, there are no doubts about the fact that this grace does indeed increase. These ordinary ways of sanctification have always been and will always be the surest and the safest ways to union with God.

So, it is very important to fully understand that the activity of the Holy Spirit within your own spiritual life goes on constantly and is very real even if you have not been chosen to do a special job or mission for God or to have special gifts.

Get to know intimately the Holy Spirit who dwells within your own soul when it is in the state of grace. Use prayer and the sacraments to obtain additional grace so that your realization of whom it is who dwells within your soul will become greater and clearer.

Learn how to recognize and use the magnificent gifts of the Holy Spirit which you do possess. Use these gifts to the fullest. Use them to protect your faith and to increase your faith. When you do, you will be doing what the saints did: allowing the Sanctifier to sanctify your soul and increase your holiness.

PART FOUR

BEGINNING THE PRAYER LIFE

Chapter 1

HOW TO CHOOSE A SPIRITUAL DIRECTOR

If a person is to attempt to climb THE LADDER OF PERFEC-
TION, he should place his spiritual life in the hands of a competent spiritual director. This spiritual director could also be the
person's confessor but that is not necessary. Sometimes a person
could have two spiritual directors and one confessor depending
upon the soul's needs. The ideal situation would be to find an
excellent confessor who, at the same time, is a competent
spiritual director.

Unfortunately, the task of finding such a priest may not be
easy. I am by no means downgrading the noble vocation of
priesthood when I say that not every priest has the talent nor
the ability to become a spiritual director. Although every priest
has a great deal more knowledge about the spiritual life than
the average lay person, such knowledge alone does not create
a competent spiritual director. For one thing, spiritual direction
could be time-consuming and most priests are too busy with parish duties to spend the time needed for weekly spiritual sessions
with individuals. Also, most all parish priests have had
experiences with emotional or fanatical or mentally unstable
people who bother them day and night with their spiritual problems. Such priests could be "turned off" at the very mention
of spiritual direction. Then there are priests who are themselves
far from the joys found in a deep spiritual union with Christ
who simply do not know how to teach other things they do not
know or practice. Their attempts at spiritual direction could
cause more harm to the person's quest for holiness than good.
Saint Teresa of Avila constantly prayed to God to deliver her

from poor, incompetent spiritual directors who did not have the proper insight into the needs of her spiritual life.

Then how is a person to find the best spiritual director for his or her needs? What should one look for when selecting a spiritual director? Sometimes God does the selecting and sends just the right priest to the person at the right time. But one cannot always depend upon receiving such a miracle. So how would the average lay person choose his or her personal director? Fortunately, the person can make the choice for himself, and if one director brings unsatisfactory results, a change can always be made. But how would one know that the results are unsatisfactory?

The first thing to look for in a spiritual director is to notice if the priest or person (a director does not have to be a priest unless he also becomes the person's confessor) is to pay close attention to the ways and actions of the selected person to try and see if this person is living the kind of spiritual life which you are seeking for yourself. Surely a priest who is beset with emotional problems or who is careless about his ministry or who angers easily or who shows little concern about people in need or who never wants to get involved with acts of charity, such as visiting the sick in their homes, will not make a good director. Often such a priest may know what he is supposed to do to become the type of priest Christ wants him to become but he does not have the spiritual strength needed to do just that. If he lacks spiritual strength and motivation to overcome his most glaring faults and failings, he could not help anyone else overcome theirs.

A good spiritual director must, of necessity, be very humble, holy and kind if he is to lead other souls along the paths of sanctity. One cannot teach others what one does not know. Unfortunately, many priests were never taught the secrets of sanctity during their long years of training. This spiritual void becomes very noticeable once the pressures of parish work fall upon their shoulders. So, the first step taken to select a spiritual director is to see the holiness and goodness in the person one thinks could be his or her director.

However, even this choice may still present problems. Sometimes a very humble, holy priest may not have the abilities to understand a person's spiritual struggles and battles and could think too lightly of serious problems which arise. One spiritual director I knew, who was humble and holy, used to tell people who came to see him for direction. "Oh! We will let the Lord take care of that," without explaining what was happening to the person. Such a "solution" did not solve any of the problems, it only made things worse. Such a priest will become a very poor spiritual director.

How would a person know that his spiritual director is most unsatisfactory, even if he, himself, seems to be most saintly? The best way to answer such a question would be to see the results in one's own spiritual life after a period of time. One person I knew said that she found more spiritual growth after one year's direction of a new spiritual director than she had found in ten years with her first director. Often a director cannot lead a soul up THE LADDER OF PERFECTION because he has no insight into the needs of the person, nor does he understand just what goals the person is trying to reach in his or her quest for "union with God."

What then would the qualifications be for a competent director to possess?

First of all, such a director should (as I already stated) possess holiness and many virtues. He should be kind, understanding yet firm in his direction. He should be most knowledgeable concerning spiritual growth and union with God; especially in the areas of problems which will arise as the soul struggles to climb that ladder. If the one you have chosen as a director seems to lack that knowledge by giving only vague, unclear explanations to your personal spiritual problems, such a director is not competent. An expert director will have the clear, correct answers in his mind before you finish asking the questions or explaining a problem.

There are "a million" spiritual problems; however, the basic struggles and stages of spiritual growth are more or less the same. That is why Teresa of Avila and John of the Cross or other great spiritual writers could agree upon answers that sound very much alike to certain spiritual ills or could give the same spiritual advice.

Not only should a director have such knowledge and possess moral qualities but he should also be a person of strong character who *will not* end up having the person *direct* him instead of he directing the person. Sometimes a spiritual director can become so caught up in the actions of the Holy Spirit within a person's soul, that the director could very well fall victim to a very sad spiritual state wherein he wants to believe that the person he is directing has some kind of a special "mission" from God. The director then imagines that he also has been "chosen" and eagerly looks for "signs," from the person as direct "communications" for him from God through the person. Many false visionaries will find a priest who will fit the role of that type of a director. When that happens, the spiritual director will find himself obeying the slightest wishes or commands given to him by the person *he* is supposed to be directing. Such a director will constantly praise and encourage the person in his or her "mission." Right then and there the person's whole spiritual life begins to fall apart and also the spiritual life of the director. A poor spiritual director can make the very same mistakes which the person is making. It would be sort of like "the blind leading the blind" situation.

I remember a case where a person who claimed to see visions had a very holy priest as her director. This priest was also a very gentle, kind person who could not bear to hurt anyone's feelings. No matter what the person, who said she saw visions, told him to do he did because he did not want to hurt her feelings. As a result, the person found it easy to gain control of the priest who was supposed to be directing her. If she told him to get out of bed to say a Mass at 4:00 A.M. so that the world "would not be destroyed" that night, he would be most obliging and do exactly what she commanded. Finally, he was under such pressure trying to do all the things she told him to do that his health broke down and he became seriously ill. Even though this holy, kind, gentle, understanding priest had some of the qualifications needed for a competent director, he was not a very wise one and failed his job and also the woman. It would have been far better if he had stopped such nonsense before it went too far. A wise director would do all in his power, in such a case, to bring the woman "down to earth" and along the ordinary paths of spirituality by firmly taking control of her spiritual life. One must always remember that visions and special "missions" *do not* a saint make. The surest way to sanctification is the ordinary way of grace, prayer, penance, the Mass and the sacraments.

Another quality which a wise spiritual director must possess in his ability to win the trust and respect of the person he is directing. It would be fruitless, to say the least, to place your spiritual progress under the direction of someone you do not trust nor respect, someone whose words or explanations you cannot accept nor believe.

If, for example, you are desperately in need of good, sound spiritual advice and your director does not care enough about nor has the interest in your problem and because of that gives you poor advice, you will begin to wonder how you can trust what he tells you.

I am not saying that your director must solve all your problems instantly but he must be able to guide you safely through your more trying spiritual struggles and battles; and you must be able to believe that he will do just that and place all your trust in his judgments.

A good test to use to decide whether or not you are receiving proper spiritual direction is to see if your director can put your mind at ease or if he only adds to your confusion and spiritual unrest. I am not saying that he must always agree with you; because there will be times when he might not. However, even at such times, does he give you good advice and clearly show you where you could be wrong or does he merely let you leave totally unsure of what is the next step to take up the ladder?

One of the most important duties of a spiritual director is to still the inner torments of the person he directs. When he does that, he is able to guide the person up the next step towards union with God. Often such torments will make the person give up the struggle for perfection. A spiritual director who knows what he is doing will be able to find the correct words and explanations which the person needs to continue the weary climb.

A final word about choosing the right spiritual director has to be a word of caution. A wise, prudent director never gets personally involved with the person he is directing. He can show kindness, care, interest in and even affection for the person he directs, but always in a very reserved sort of way.

He can become a dear friend of the person, but always the relationship must be and remain purely spiritual. At times, the person may in some way help or add to the director's own spiritual growth, but not if the relationship becomes dangerously personal. I do not have to explain the dire consequences resulting from a too personal relationship.

The reserved attitude is for *both* the person who is being directed and the director. Most priests could tell a story about someone who became very unspiritual about the relationship between himself as the spiritual director and the one he attempted to direct. In such a case, the director's kindness and interest in the person were misunderstood and the person began to care more about him than her own spiritual growth.

The best way to keep the relationship spiritual is to do just that: keep the relationship spiritual! Discuss spiritual subjects and problems. Do not tire your spiritual director by taking up all his time explaining over and over family problems, etc. If your appointments with your director become only one long, unending complaint about all your daily and family problems, then you are wasting his time and yours. In that case, you are not asking for spiritual direction, you only want a sympathetic ear. And do not be surprised if he makes the appointments for your spiritual direction further and further apart. You have a responsibility to your director as well as he having a responsibility to you.

Also remember that your spiritual director need not be your parish priest if you cannot find the right director for your spiritual needs there. You may even have to search to find the right director. How can you do that? Well, perhaps a friend can recommend such a director. If so, then call and make an appointment. Or you might find just the right director for you when you go to confession. I found mine by way of the confessional and he was not my parish priest. Try going to confession to several different priests. Chances are you will find the one who, you feel, will understand you and your spiritual quests. If he accepts the assignment, then it would be wise to receive direction during the time spent in the confessional or (as it is now called) the reconciliation room. This will enable you to receive spiritual direction at a time most convenient for him and you can be sure that you will have an appointment with him. Respect his time and the fact that he is a very busy person.

Holy Mother church had just that in mind when reconciliation rooms replaced the confessional boxes in the late 60's and 70's. The person could not only go to confession, but talk to the priest face-to-face and receive spiritual direction at the same time. While most Catholics were shocked when it was learned that you could talk to a priest face-to-face in the confessional, I was not. I had been doing that for years. Each time I had gone to confession to my spiritual director, I told him who I was and we had short, but most meaningful and helpful spiritual discussions. It is a pity that more Catholics do not take advantage of the spiritual direction they could receive in the reconciliation room.

Chapter 2

A LIFE OF PRAYER

Before I begin the following chapters on prayer, I would like to say a few words about a life without prayer.

Unfortunately, there are millions of people who never pray, and there are millions more who pray only when they want something from God. Most of these millions do not know how to pray or why a person should pray.

On the other hand, there are millions of people who do know how to pray, but who find "five minutes a day to talk to God," a chore they would rather not do. So they also live a life without prayer.

If all these millions of people could see their daily lives and understand a day with prayer compared to a day without prayer, they would be amazed to discover the vast difference between the two. A simple comparison would be a life with food and a life without food.

We all know what a life without food can do. Around the world, there are millions of people who do not get enough to eat every day. They slowly starve to death. Their bodies become weaker and weaker as each day passes. They are susceptible to all sorts of bodily ills and diseases. They lose their desires to live. They no longer smile or laugh. They retreat into a tiny world of hopelessness until they completely lose all contact with their surroundings. They no longer care if night turns into day or day turns into night. They become crushed, beaten and filled with despair; so much so, that they no longer want to be part of the human race which has treated them so cruelly.

Now, take that analogy and apply it to a soul which never

tastes the sweet spiritual food of a person's union with God through prayer. Then add the possibility of the person, who does not pray or who prays poorly, spending all eternity in hell simply because that person never asked God to help him save his soul. The tragedy of a human body starving to death could never equal the tragedy of a soul losing its eternal salvation.

Actually, the need for prayer is planted deep within the soul of every person. It is not God who disrupts or destroys the line of communication, between Himself and man, called prayer. The Almighty, Infinite God has made Himself available to hear the voices of His children; but they must speak if He is to listen. And, if they refuse to speak to Him, by and through prayer, He cannot give to them the wondrous spiritual blessings and gifts which He desires them to possess.

Prayer means: talking to God. A person must try to analyze what that statement really means. Think of what it would be like if God never allowed anyone to talk to Him, except every ten years! When your turn came, to talk to God, what would you say? Would you have a long list of all the things you wanted God to know about your personal, private life? Would you have a long list of requests? Would you include in your talk a few words of praise to Him or thanksgiving? Or would you consider the very idea of "talking to God" something worthless and not even bother to stand in line when your turn came?

Unfortunately, a great many people do consider "talking to God" a worthless act, so they find all sorts of excuses why they should not pray. They rather imagine that they do not have to pray because they cannot see whom it is they pray to or they cannot "hear" God answer them or they cannot believe that there is a God who does exist, who is ready to listen to their words. As a result, when they do not pray or pray very poorly, they actually bring to their souls the disaster of spiritual starvation.

Now, what exactly is prayer? Why is it so necessary? How does a person pray so as to benefit his or her own soul?

First of all, the subject of prayer can become very complex. Whole books, and there are many of them, have been written about prayer. There are many different types and kinds of prayers. I, myself, did write a book just on the subject of prayer. But because this book is a complete spiritual guide, I can only write a few short chapters on prayer. There are many excellent books written about the different types of prayer, so I suggest that the reader of this book, broaden his knowledge about prayer by obtaining books written for that purpose (See Vol. II).

Prayer has been defined as "the lifting up of our minds and hearts to God." However, that is not all that prayer is. Prayer should be not only the way and means to lift up our minds and hearts to God, not only to talk to Him when we pray, but also to encounter Him.

The need for prayer is so great, that theologians teach the fact that there is no salvation without prayer. Then, a person's need for salvation becomes the most important reason why a person must pray. In that case, the first prayers we learn and use should be prayers of repentance or sorrow for our sins. With that start along the paths of prayers, the next step taken is to use prayer to acknowledge God's greatness and His mercy.

When we tell God we are sorry for our sins, when we acknowledge His greatness and His mercy, we are not merely "trying to become a saint" (as people who pray are often accused of doing). We are doing what we, who are children of God, must do. We are paying a debt which we owe to God simply because He, the Creator, created us. In other words, we owe a debt to God because He so lovingly created us to be His children. The first payment made, to lessen that debt owed, is to acknowledge that there is a God who created us, to thank God for all He has given to us, to tell Him how sorry we are for our sins and to thank Him for His mercy and love. Why? Because God did not create us for hell. He created us so that we can one day share all the treasures He wants us to share in His home called heaven. If we lose our souls, we will have no one to blame but ourselves. God never intends for any soul to be lost. He only desires to enrich the soul with "a million" spiritual treasures. But how can anyone accept treasures from a God whom he does not believe exists? How can anyone receive these treasures when the person's soul is submerged in the mire and slush of mortal sins?

Mortal sin does not just disappear from a person's soul. It must be washed away by the person's confession of guilt combined with an expression of sincere sorrow. This is done in the confessional where the person's words become prayers to God.

Many people think that the sacrament called confession is used only to "tell the priest" a person's sins. That is not true. The person, while confessing his sins to a priest, is actually uttering prayers to God: prayers telling Him how sorry he is for his sins, asking God for His love, mercy and forgiveness, and acknowledging God's greatness and power.

So, if you have never prayed before or prayed poorly, then start a prayer life with prayers of sorrow for sins, asking God for His mercy and forgiveness and acknowledging God's greatness.

These prayers will lead you into an encounter with Christ. That means that Christ (God) becomes very real to you. You will realize that He does exist, that He does love you and that He does listen when you talk to Him by and through prayer. You will begin to want to know more about this Christ whom you discovered. Then your prayer life can expand into areas of vocal prayer, mental prayer and meditation; as I explain in Volume II of this book.

Chapter 3

FIND TIME FOR PRAYER

One of the first things to learn about the prayer life after knowing how important it is to pray, is that prayer is one way to gain numerous merits, or treasures, for heaven: treasures that will last forever.

Merits and grace are what determines your quality of glory in heaven. Needless to say, common sense tells us that there are different degrees or stages of glory in heaven, from the Heaven of No Merit to the highest degree enjoyed by the most perfect of all God's creations, Mary. A person can save his soul on his deathbed after a lifetime of sin. But such a last minute conversion, while marvelous in what it accomplishes, is devoid of the merits which could have been gained had the person obtained these treasures by and through a lifetime of close union with God through prayer.

Merits are gained through holy actions, prayers or good deeds done which are deserving of an *eternal reward*. The word, eternal, is very important. Many people do good deeds and are looking for or else receive only a material reward, say, a hundred dollars or a merit badge or medal. However, such material rewards are not meant to last forever. They quickly fade away and disappear never to return. On the other hand, eternal rewards or merits will last forever and they become the spiritual treasures Christ told us to gain. So these merits are not only necessary to enrich the soul's eternal glory, but should be sought after at all times.

Now, please do not imagine that it is selfish to want to gain as many merits as possible while on earth. It is not selfish, providing you do so knowing that the more merits you gain, the more glory you will give to God for all eternity. It is God who told us to gather unto ourselves the treasures which will last forever (*Matt.* 6:19-20). He has an infinite amount of these spiritual treasures which He wants to give to His beloved children. It is His joy and pleasure to give many spiritual treasures to His children. It is up to us to prepare our souls to receive these gifts from so loving a God. One way to prepare our souls to receive what God longs to give us is through prayer.

Now, when we speak about prayer and praying, there are many misunderstandings. People misunderstand what prayer is for, why we pray or how prayer is used to worship and glorify God. That is why so many Catholics say: "I don't need the Church, I can pray in my own closet!" Even if a person could pray "in his own closet" without the Church and the sacraments, would such poor prayers be "enough"? The answer is "No!" If a person truly wants to live as Christ wants him to, that person must follow His examples and live a life of prayer which includes many different types and kinds of prayers. It is never "all right" for any Catholic to substitute the Church and the sacraments for a few, poorly said "closet prayers."

Now, what exactly is a prayer life? It is imagined by many that only nuns and priests can live a prayer life or a life of prayer. Lay people, more often than not, are inclined to say: "I am too busy to pray all the time."

In one way that statement may be true. An average lay person's life leaves little or no time for prayer. A nun or priest's life includes certain hours for prayer. However, that does not mean that lay people cannot find such time in their daily lives. If they closely examine their lives, they can indeed find precious moments for prayer without changing their state of life or interrupting important schedules. All they have to do is to put first things first and to make a few sacrifices. All they have to do is to find the time in their daily lives *which belongs to God*. It is there, it just has to be found.

Within each daily life, there is time which belongs to God. When a person finds this time which belongs to God, he will learn how to share each day with God. Finding this time is the beginning or the start of a prayer life. How does a person do that?

The person can start with finding the time to go to Mass at least once a week and on holy days. So many Catholics say: "I don't have time to go to Mass." What they are really saying is: "I do not want to find the time to go to Mass." They take the time which belongs to God and use it as if it were their own. They ignore God's call to their souls simply because they refuse to share their lives with God. Yet they manage to find time for the things they love to do, such as golf, no matter how busy they are.

After the person finds time for Mass, he can begin a program of morning and evening prayers. These simple vocal prayers can bring the person into a realization that God created him for a life of union with God which begins on earth and reaches its fulfillment in heaven. In that way, the person acknowledges that there is a God who offers to him that eternity of peace, joy and happiness.

The simple morning prayers, for example, are ones of faith, love and hope. Faith is needed to know and believe that God exists, love is to love the God who exists, hope is to know that if one does believe in and love God and follows His teachings, then he can one day be with God in His heaven of eternal joy.

Then the person can go a step further and learn that faith also means that he or she has certain religious duties and obligations to carry out daily. Love goes into the area of faithfully following and believing all the Church teaches because in that way, a persons proves his or her love for God. Hope then expands as a person learns that many of the spiritual joys to be found in heaven, such as being very close to God, can be experienced now while one lives a life of prayer and union with God.

Now, it is just as important to know how to pray *well* as it is to know what prayer is.

Do we pray well? Most people will say: "I do try...but!"

It really is not very easy to pray well or correctly. Prayer does not come in a way that we just automatically fall into a state of recollection needed for prayer. It is often very difficult to get our hearts, minds and wills down to the business of praying. There are just too many distractions, too much noise, too little time, too many other things to think about rather than God. It often becomes a real struggle just to say a morning or evening "Our Father" or "Hail Mary." But these problems will disappear when one learns how to deal with distractions during prayer.

Chapter 4

DISTRACTIONS DURING PRAYER

Distractions, distractions, distractions! We all know what they can do as we try to pray. No one is immune from this spiritual plague, not even the greatest of saints. Saint Teresa of Avila spoke of this trial during her prayers; and this was when she was an expert of experts in the prayer life.

Spiritual writers tell us that no one can entirely rid themselves of distractions; but, on the other hand, everyone can develop methods to diminish them or at least to cope with them.

The first thing to remember about distractions is that they begin in the mind or intellect. So does prayer. We begin to pray when we think about God, the Mass, Mary or a saint. But all too soon, our minds are somewhere else: on the golf course, in the kitchen wondering what to cook for supper, with a problem which has surfaced, with our friends and what they told us, with a T.V. story which deeply affected us, etc.

Now notice one very important fact about all these distractions during prayer. Within the mind, there can be only *one thought at one time*. If you think about God, that one thought is in your mind, if you change your thoughts and start thinking of other things, you lose the thoughts of God. There is much hope in knowing that one fact because it places within our own reach a solution to distractions. It puts *us* in control of the situation. We do not have to rely upon anyone else to control our own thoughts. We can do that ourselves with the help of God's graces.

This controlling of our own thoughts is a virtue called interior mortification. This virtue is not an easy virtue to acquire and practice, but it is there and because it is there so is the hope that we can do something about distractions.

Now, how can we begin to acquire and use this virtue? First of all, we must attempt to learn the difference between voluntary and involuntary distractions. A voluntary distraction is one which the person willingly brings into his or her own mind. Once the thought is in the mind, after being sought, the person dwells upon it. In other words, the person wants to think about the idea or subject matter more than he wants to think about God and the prayer being said. He quickly puts aside all thoughts of God and allows himself to think about whatever he has chosen to replace God and prayer in his mind. Voluntary distractions during prayer are sinful (venial, if not mortal) because they are used to deliberately take one's mind off of the subject of God and prayer. In other words, the person actually insults God by turning away from Him after God so lovingly bends forth to hear what the person has started to tell Him.

On the other hand, involuntary distractions are not sins because they do not come into the mind with the person's own approval. They are not wanted, they become only annoyances. The person really wants to think about God and to talk to Him, but the little distractions keep popping up. I call them little mosquitoes buzzing around one's prayer life.

But, what to do about all these distractions? First of all, the more a person practices and polishes prayer, the less he or she will be disturbed by distractions. The more of a love-filled encounter a person has with Christ, the less that person will fall into the pits of distractions. So, there is hope that distractions can become less and less; and conquering such distractions can become one of the wondrous rewards for a person who is faithful to daily prayer. I, personally, know one person who has so conquered distractions, after years of faithful prayer, that she can sit through a whole Mass or say a whole Rosary without one distraction bothering her. This is a great joy for her.

That is the end or final result of a long battle with distractions. How does a person start this conquest? First of all, a person who will not prepare himself for prayer by a short period of interior recollection, should not be surprised if his prayer time becomes nothing more than a battle with distractions. A person simply cannot rush into a room or a church with a "million" thoughts whirling around in his or her mind and expect these thoughts to stop instantly as soon as the person is in the room or the church. This is just not going to happen.

Then, how does one get into the mood (or recollection) for prayer? There are several ways. One of the most important ways is by and through spiritual reading. I, personally, never begin a period of prayer without first reading a few pages from a spiritual book. I have had this habit for years and it is a most powerful method of preparing the mind, heart and soul for a love-filled encounter with Christ. When you start this method, you will quickly discover how the "million" thoughts whirling around in your mind will disappear.

Be very careful about your choice of spiritual reading. Some people may want to use the Bible, but that may not be a wise choice for a beginner. The Bible is excellent for study, but may not be so excellent to prepare the person's mind for prayer, simply because it can become most involved and complex, especially if the person knows little or nothing at all about the Bible. It would be wiser to read booklets *about* the words of Christ in the Bible and then look up one passage at a time to bring oneself into the state of recollection needed for prayer.

There are many excellent spiritual books which can help a person fight distractions. A good one would be an adult catechism which explains such things as grace and merits. Then there are very inspiring stories of the saints or books about Mary or heaven, etc. All such spiritual reading takes the person's mind out of the material world and brings it into the supernatural world of grace and union with God. That is the whole point of spiritual reading. To let the person's heart and mind associate with God's world.

Another method of preparing for prayer or the Mass or the Rosary is to realize to whom you are praying and to think deeply about what you want to say to Christ or Mary during your period of prayer. When you do that, you will cast aside a great many distractions which may otherwise come freely to your mind. Allow yourself the time to think deeply about the spiritual encounter with the one to whom you pray and what you will say.

If you were going to speak to the President of the United States or to the Pope, think what a tremendous honor that would be! How you would prepare yourself! Carefully you would select your words. Over and over you would practice these words so that you will not make one mistake when the big moment came. Then think what a disaster it would all become if you were presented to the famous person and forgot what you wanted to say or did not pay any attention to what you were saying or allowed distracting thoughts to interrupt what you had started to say.

Now think of talking, not to the President, not to the Pope, but to *God!* You actually have the wondrous privilege of speaking to God or to Mary, His Mother, or to a great saint when you pray.

Do you really know what that means?

Can we humans, with our limited, finite intellects comprehend what it means to be able to converse with God, the Almighty, Infinite God, Himself, who bends forward to hear what we want to say to Him?

That one realization that you are going to talk to God when you pray, can help you enter into the proper state of recollection needed so that your prayer will become fruitful, meaningful and filled with merit.

For example: when you go to Mass, whom do you go to talk to? Do you know to whom the prayers of the Mass are said? And if you know, do you care enough about God to prepare yourself for that wonderful encounter with your Eucharistic Lord? Do you go to Mass to talk to your friends or members of your family or do you go to Mass to talk to God? Do you go to love Him, to worship Him, to see before you, in the Eucharist, the Christ who died upon that cross for your sins? Are you prepared to talk to that very same Christ? Or do you go to Mass just because it is the thing to do with a "million" other thoughts racing through your mind? If you realize to whom it is you talk when you pray, you will discover that you will be better able to control the distractions during prayer.

Another method to use in order to lessen distractions is to prepare yourself, not only to talk to Christ when you pray, but to adore and worship Him as well. We can run to Christ when we feel a personal need for His assistance but prayer is far more than a simple cry for some kind of help. It is far more than a greeting or a gesture which we decide to do when we "feel like praying." We must think deeply about the fact that this God who will listen to our prayers is also the same God who deserves the highest respect and worship from us. While it may be a fad or fashionable for a person to be on very friendly terms with the Lord such as yelling out "Jesus," "Jesus," or calling the Lord "my Brother" or a "Super Star," such a way of approaching the Lord is devoid of the respect He deserves. It would be very bad manners to go up to the Pope and slap him on the back and shout something like: "Well, how are you doing today?" When one is in the presence of the Pope, one must show him the proper respect and act accordingly. Likewise, when a person prepares himself for prayer, he must do so with much respect and quiet dignity. Placing yourself in such an environment will help you control the distractions which could disturb your prayer.

Finally, a tremendous help in controlling distractions is to learn how to say little prayers as you carry out the duties and responsibility of your daily life. If you form a habit of raising your heart and mind to God, with a little prayer of love, often during the day, you will find less distractions when you go to Mass or kneel down to say a Rosary. You will be more able to go from active duties into the quietness required for longer prayers or the Mass if you already feel "close" to God before you pray.

Chapter 5

DRYNESS OF SOUL OR ARIDITIES

There is another spiritual illness which can cause as much, if not more, havoc with the prayer life as can distractions. It is called dryness of the soul or aridities. I have had more people mention this problem to me than the problem of distractions. The main reason is that distractions can be more easily tolerated. Dryness of the soul can become devastating especially when a person does not understand what is happening.

There is a vast difference between distractions and dryness of the soul. Aridities are also much more difficult to prevent or get rid of. The word is taken from arid which means dry, lifeless, unproductive. When this dryness hits a person's soul, it means exactly the same thing, dry, arid and unproductive. The person is thrust into a state of darkness as far as the spiritual life goes. In this darkness (often called the dark night of the soul), all light from heaven seems to disappear. All joys and consolations once found in prayer are gone, often overnight. The person feels abandoned by God. To make matters worse, the person is attacked and assaulted by the devil with temptations of all sorts. Often the person begins to question the value and purpose of prayer and even finds that to say a simple prayer is repugnant.

Very often, after a period of ecstatic joy found in praying, dryness of the soul will suddenly strike and the person's whole spiritual life will seem to disappear into an inky blackness. Then, unless properly directed, the person could struggle for years to try to recapture that joy once felt, usually not succeeding.

That happened to a young woman I met. She had "found" Christ through a Charismatic prayer meeting. She had been filled with tremendous joy. She had been "on fire" to serve her Lord. But when I met her, she was not filled with joy as she spoke bitterly against her Catholic faith. She threw at me one question after another asking about the Mass, etc. Her actions and words puzzled me at first until I found out what happened to her. She had indeed experienced the joy of "finding Christ," but all too soon (as often happens) her joy disappeared into a darkness which she did not understand. She did not have the proper spiritual direction and so for *five years* she had, on her own, attempted to recapture that wondrous joy she had once felt. She roamed from religion to religion trying to "find Christ" again, all the while blaming her Catholic religion for the plight she was in. If someone had only explained to her what aridities were and how they can be used for the good of the soul, she would have been better able to weather the storm.

Aridities not only come to simple folks trying to improve their spiritual lives, but to great saints as well. A basic example is the case of Saint Therese, the Little Flower. After she entered the convent at an early age, the first wondrous joys of being with Christ suddenly disappeared. Then she lived most of her life as a nun in a state of spiritual dryness and darkness. Saint Teresa of Avila also, at times, lived through spiritual darkness when she could find no joys or consolations in her prayers or even in her visions, which had also disappeared into the black night of the soul.

One reason why aridities or darkness of the soul are so difficult to cope with is that they produce a spiritual pain for the soul unlike any other pain. This type of hurt can be compared to that suffered by a heartbroken man or woman whose beloved one left and never returned. While the beloved one was near all sorts of physical pain could be borne with ease. Just a word of concern or sympathy from the loved one made the cross easier to carry. However, who can really console a broken heart when the loved one leaves and is unfaithful? This type of pain burns into the heart and soul and no one can ease this suffering.

In much the same way, all sorts of crosses can be carried by a person who feels deeply the sunshine of God's love ever burning brightly near them. But, put out that light, and the person not only still has crosses to carry, but suddenly no one is near to help bear these burdens which become twice as heavy and painful.

In addition, there is a feeling of guilt experienced by the person who starts to wonder what he or she did wrong: Why did God leave? Where did He go? What did I do that made Him stop loving me? All sorts of questions pop up which have no answers.

Now, why would God allow such a situation to develop? There are several answers to that question. First of all, it may be the person's own fault which brought about such a situation. A person may imagine that he or she is on top of THE LADDER OF PERFECTION after experiencing the first feelings of joy and love for Christ, when in reality the person may have not even begun to construct the platform upon which the ladder will rest. Very rarely will there be an instant ascent from the bottom of the ladder to the top. One example was the good thief who hung on a cross next to Christ. Some people want to believe that this same miracle will happen to all of us and we will become instant saints ready to immediately enter heaven (without a purgatory) when we die. But common sense tells us such is not true. If Christ allowed the good thief to enter heaven immediately, it was mainly because of his sorrow for his sins and his complete, perfect willingness to accept his punishment, which was his death on a cross. Very few of us would be willing to accept such a punishment for our sins.

It is the idea of instant sanctity so prevalent within the Charismatic movement which I have always objected to. I have said many times that it is just not that easy to rise up from a life of human weaknesses to the pinnacle of sanctity by attending a few "praise the Lord" meetings. Granted, these meetings may be a good beginning if they stir a person to becoming a better Catholic or returning to the sacraments; but they are just that: only a beginning. After such a start, there is a great deal of work to be done to live an active prayer life and to understand the different stages of that prayer life.

One of these stages involves aridities, and as I have already explained with the story about the young woman trying to recapture the joys she once experienced, a person has to have proper spiritual direction to pass through each stage successfully.

So, when searching to find the cause and remedy of aridities, first of all try to discover, with the help of your spiritual director, if you have been at fault because you had thought your spiritual life to be far more developed than it was. If this is the cause, then go back down to the beginning of your encounter with Christ and try to discover the many obstacles to a closer union with God which you may have overlooked. Try to find out what stage of spiritual development you really are in and not what you think you might be in.

For example, have you imagined that you already have a close union with God, yet you never really tried to overcome a sin which you are most attached or attracted to? Is a love for a material object or hobby, etc. greater than the love you think you possess for Christ? If it is, then the problem of losing the joy of "finding" Christ might have a simple solution of removing the material love which you have placed above the love for Christ in your heart.

Other reasons for aridities and the darkness of the soul may not be so easily solved. Great, often violent, temptations can suddenly surface and plunge the soul into spiritual darkness. These temptations usually start when the person had found a beautiful tranquility in his or her prayer life. Almost overnight, the storm comes and it can last for weeks, even months. The soul no longer finds joy, comfort or peace in prayer. Instead, temptations, many of which the person never had before, come forth to make the spiritual life a living nightmare.

Many people have come to me completely devastated by such temptations, totally unable to understand what had happened to their beautiful union with Christ or where the temptations come from, or what they did to bring them into their spiritual lives.

The first thing to know about this type of spiritual darkness is that if it happens, the person, himself, did not do anything wrong. The fact is, the person was doing everything right. He or she was becoming closer to God, slowly, but surely, climbing each step of THE LADDER OF PERFECTION. Naturally, the devil never likes to see any soul's advancement. Remember that his mission is at all times to take souls away from God. I always say that the devil never bothers his own. Most sinners who do not hide their evil deeds, go about their daily lives appearing quite content with life and living. They do not struggle against temptations simply because they are already doing what the devil wants them to do. However, let them make one move towards God with one act of repentance and they will soon become a victim of the devil's fury. Likewise, any person who decides to overcome sin and acquire virtue will find himself a victim of the devil's fury.

The best way to handle the problem of the devil's temptations, is to expect them. Don't let them take you by surprise. Know that the devil will do all in his power to interfere with and attempt to stop your prayers. If you give up praying because you are tempted while you pray or after your prayers, then you have made the devil victorious because that is exactly what he wants you to do.

Also, try to find out what you did or said or saw just prior to the onslaught. Remember that the devil will always strike you at your weakest point. Holy Mother Church shows such wisdom when she tells us not to allow ourselves to go or become involved in an occasion for sin. The devil always presents to us, in beautiful disguises, situations wherein we can commit sins, often serious sins. If you are aware that being in a certain place or with certain people could cause you to sin, then by all means do not go to that place or allow yourself to associate with such people. Don't be foolish enough to say: "I can handle it and not sin." Remember, the devil is far more powerful than your petty, good intentions. Run away from occasions of sin, not because you are a coward, but because you know your own weaknesses.

On the other hand, if you have temptations which you never had before, do not despair. No temptation is ever a sin no matter how vile or against your nature it might be. Such temptations are used only to attempt to have you give up your prayer life. When you show the devil that you *will not give up*, such temptations will gradually disappear; and they could help to purify your soul by the struggle not to give up.

That brings up another reason for darkness of the soul and aridities. Often God uses such a means to help purify a person's soul.

Often a person may find so much joy and consolations in prayer that the motives for prayer become selfish. That is, the person seeks the consolations and joys more than making prayer an opportunity to give joy and consolation to the Heart of Christ. A purely selfish motive destroys a person's union with God no matter how much he or she prays. That does *not* mean that a person cannot find joys in prayers. One of the signs of true prayer is that it brings joy to the soul in spite of daily crosses and problems. What I am speaking about is when the person starts to wander away from the true and pure motive for prayer. Many fanatics have the wrong reasons for praying. They rather imagine that they are the only ones on earth who pray correctly, so they love to "show off" when they pray, thinking that everyone is admiring them. Or else they will say ten Rosaries instead of one a day to "show" everyone how holy they are. Such prayers bring no or little merit to the person's soul. The motives are very self-centered.

Even if a person is not fanatical about prayer, he or she can taint the true motives for praying. Or else, the person's motives may be pure, but God decides that the person's soul should be purified to allow an even closer union with Him. He will then throw the person's spiritual life into a sea of darkness.

When people I know, who do have true motives for prayer, come to me with this problem of sudden spiritual darkness, they come filled with grief and sorrow asking what they did wrong when everything about their prayer life seemed so right and "all together."

I tell them that the good Lord has given them a wonderful opportunity to express love for Him, asking *nothing* in return. It is only natural to delight in prayer when one expects much joy, consolations and satisfaction. But can that same person still

pray as fervently when there are no joys, consolations and satis-
factions? Can the person pray to express deep love for Christ
when the person feels no love in return?

That is the secret of understanding this type of aridities. To give
to Christ a pure, a holy, a loyal love when the person feels no love
in return is a giant step up THE LADDER OF PERFECTION. It
is to become more understanding of Christ who may sometimes
desire your love and consolations as a free gift to His Heart.

Usually, advanced prayer is a love-for-love relationship, but
when it becomes a one-way act of pure love for Christ, then
a wondrous purification is being poured upon the soul. You can
call this a test of the person's love for God and also a test of
his or her motives for prayer. Can the person still smile and
continue to pray, just to tell God that He is loved, or to thank
Him or to worship Him, when the person's whole being rebels
against the very idea of praying due to aridities? Can the person
light up God's Heart with words of love, when the person's own
heart and soul have been thrust into spiritual blackness? Can
the person console the Heart of God, when the person, himself,
feels no consolation in his union with God and in his prayer life?

Would a person be willing to serve God, to live a holy life,
to pray when there is no delight in so doing? The answer to
all the questions I just raised is yes, if the person allows God
to purify his or her soul by and through a period of spiritual
darkness.

I also tell the ones who come to me with this problem that
there is more merit in praying and serving God when the light
of heaven has been hidden, than when the person finds great
joy in praying and serving God. Why? Because, as I said, in
that case, the person does so asking and expecting nothing in
return. That to me is pure love and also pure joy: to freely give
and desire nothing in return.

However, the person actually gains far more than he gives.
God is never outdone in love and generosity. While it may seem
that the person receives nothing in return, he or she is given
wondrous graces of purification so that the next step to closer
union with God can be taken.

Chapter 6

A DEEPER PRAYER LIFE

Everything I have explained so far, about living a more active spiritual life and climbing THE LADDER OF PERFECTION speaks of a life which is centered around Christ, your love for Him and prayer. However, just to say that is one thing, understanding the way a person can pray is another matter altogether. There is a vast difference between merely praying, as one does when he or she goes to Mass or says the Rosary, and actually using prayer to improve a spiritual union with God. If one is to climb THE LADDER OF PERFECTION, the person must know many important facts about prayer and the prayer life of someone who wants to live a more active spiritual life.

In the following chapters about prayer, I propose to open up for you a pathway which, if followed, could bring untold opportunities for advancement up the ladder. Just to know these facts about prayer can open up for you new spiritual horizons along with the desires to reach out to a closer union with Christ.

Before I begin this explanation of how to develop a deeper prayer life, I assume that you are well aware of the fact that the Liturgy (the Mass) remains the greatest and most perfect prayer to offer to God and that the Eucharist becomes your greatest source of grace. In other words, any prayer life must first of all be centered around the Mass and the Eucharist before it can become deeper and more meaningful. Only if illness (or other valid reasons) prevents one from going to the Church for Mass and the sacraments (Confession as well as the Eucharist) only then can one try to develop a prayer life apart from the Liturgy. (But do not give up just because you are prevented from attending Mass. The Eucharist can still be brought to you).

I also assume that you do have a set of prayers which are said daily, such as morning and evening prayers, along with the Rosary or a favorite Novena. You must already have a prayer life before you can deepen and develop it.

However, unfortunately most people think that because they do go to Mass, receive the Eucharist, say a few daily prayers, including the Rosary, that their prayer life is full and complete. They will be shocked to learn that all that is but a foundation for a prayer life which is in its infancy. Even the magnificent treasures of the Mass and the Eucharist can remain hidden behind a wall of complacency if the person does not realize that only a deeper prayer life can reveal such treasures and bring them forth so they can be used to hasten the perfection of union with God.

So, I am assuming that you already have a steady prayer life which, as I said, must include the Liturgy and the sacraments. Where does one go from there?

The first step is downward into the virtue of humility. Even if a person goes to Mass faithfully and has a daily prayer life, this person may have a very deep conceit about all this praying. The person may not even realize it, but he may compare his "noble" deeds to ones done by a less spiritual member of society and deem himself a rather special person. Such an attitude is, of course, most damaging to any quest for a closer union with God. But, even if you personally do not have such an exalted opinion of yourself, the first step to take is still downward into the virtue of humility. Why do I say that?

Well, for one reason, holiness, sanctity and union with God must begin with the precious virtue of humility. Only a truly humble person can cast himself upon his knees and admit that someone greater than he exists and demands from him obedience and love. You could go to Mass and say the Rosary everyday of your life, but if you are not humble enough to obey God, His ways, His laws and to love God with a pure holy love (one that asks nothing in return) then your prayer life is but a false replica of what it should be and you do not possess the virtue of humility. This virtue is a must because only while kneeling within the virtue of humility, can you, not only acknowledge God and His greatness but also acknowledge yourself and your nothingness. Only then can you start to develop the prayer life which will lead you into a deeper union with God. You must see that all you are, all you have, all the virtue which you do possess are but a gift to you from the God who created you. And this admittance must be completely genuine; otherwise, each time you think you have taken a step up THE LADDER OF PERFECTION you will discover that you will be thrown back downward into the virtue of humility, and you must begin all over again to accomplish what you thought you had gained in the first place. Make no mistake about it, only a truly humble person can deepen his or her prayer life.

What is the next step? It is to understand what prayer is all about. Does that sound strange? Well it is not. Many people who go to Mass faithfully, who say prayers at home, such as the Rosary, may not know what prayer really means or how to use it most effectively. For example, most people think of prayer as something they do when *they want to do it*. As a result, they pray or go to Mass only when they feel like doing these things or only when they are in the mood or when things go well in their daily lives. However, if they are given a heavy cross to carry, such as the death of a loved one, nine times out of ten, they will stop going to Mass or say: "I can't pray anymore. I am too filled with sorrow to pray" or "Why did God do this terrible thing to me? I am not going to pray or go to Mass anymore" or "What did I do to deserve this?" Many people think they "punish" God, if He gives them a heavy cross to carry, by not going to Mass and by no longer praying to Him. Actually what they do is to only punish themselves and not God.

The very first fact to know about prayer is that it is a vital part of every Catholic's life. It becomes an absolute necessity if we are to live a true Christian way of life and if we are to reach the shores of heaven. Prayer is not given to us to toy with. It must become the cornerstone upon which our relationship with God is built. If it is removed, the structure will collapse. That is why Catholics who stop going to Mass, who give up this greatest prayer of all, soon have a "million" doubts about their religion to fill their minds. Then they think that a few "closet" prayers are all they need to build some kind of a communication with God. I have talked to hundreds of fallen-away Catholics, who still want God and heaven, but who live in a spiritual world of doubts, fears and confusion. All such doubts, fears and confusion would be eliminated if they had remained faithful to prayer, especially the prayer of the Liturgy. Why? Because the grace needed to preserve one's faith comes from the sacraments and prayer.

There you can see why prayer and the Mass are so necessary to each and every one of us. We *need* the grace which comes from prayer and the sacraments so that we can continue to live an active spiritual life and climb that LADDER OF PERFECTION to a closer union with God. It is *grace* obtained through prayer and the sacraments which becomes the stabilizing force in our quest for a closer union with God.

See how foolish are the Catholics who attempt to "punish" God by no longer going to Mass or praying. Also, see how equally foolish are the Catholics who go to Mass or pray only when they are "in the mood."

The next thing to know about prayer is that it is not only a necessity for our personal spiritual lives, but it is also a duty and responsibility which we must accept and perform. The moment we are baptized a child of our Church, this duty and responsibility is placed upon us. We are then expected by God to live a true Christian way of life because we now have the magnificent grace, obtained through Baptism to do just that. No longer are we pagan children of the world adrift on a sea, floating without a guide or a compass. We have been called into a union with God, which only can be obtained by way of sanctifying grace. But this call is not without our own duties and obligations. The greatest of all obligations is for us to keep within our souls the precious grace freely given to us by our loving God. How can we do that? Through prayer and the sacraments.

The next thing to know about prayer is to realize that there are many different stages or degrees of prayer and several types of prayer. Most Catholics who do use prayer tend to think of prayer in the terms of going to Mass once a week, saying the Rosary or a few daily prayers. Such people can pray for years, or even a lifetime, and never advance beyond the Mass-daily-prayer stage. That can be enough as far as salvation and receiving grace go. People can receive and even increase sanctifying grace, to a certain quality, if they never add to their initial prayer program. However, a person cannot climb very high, or even start the climb, toward a closer union with God unless there is a noted advancement in his or her prayer life. That is a spiritual fact which was known by all the saints who struggled for years to develop remarkable prayer programs for themselves under the proper direction of a competent spiritual director. A slow development into the different degrees and types of prayer becomes a must for anyone desiring a closer union with God. There is no other way. There should be added components to the spiritual program such as reading and charity; however, prayer becomes the number one element for advancement because prayer remains the vehicle used by God to bestow His most intimate tokens of love upon the soul. When one is in the advanced stages of union with God, then that person's every breath becomes a pure act of love for God. That is the highest form of prayer.

Before I continue, I wish to make a note, stating that if you do wish to advance into the higher degrees and stages of prayer, it is wise to get a spiritual director who is knowledgeable concerning such matters. You will need the proper guidance because many mistakes can be made along this perilous route. The greatest danger for you is to imagine that you have reached the final stages of union with God, because of a moment of exultation, when in reality you have barely begun the climb. Also, you could very well imagine that our Lord has chosen you for a special mission which in reality is only a fragment of a very active imagination. I have personally seen individuals bring a well-started prayer life to ruination by desiring and accepting special "blessings" from God which He never gave to them. Remember that the more your prayer life progresses, the more the devil will attempt to stop it. One such method used by the Father of Lies is to bring you a subtle feeling of pride as you believe that you have advanced into a world of "messages" from God, "visions" and "divine missions." It is well to know that in the advanced stages of union with God, the communication of love between Him and the soul is so exquisite that there is no need for visions or other extraordinary manifestations. The fact is, such showings would interfere with the soul's song of love heard in the quietude and stillness of a magnificent abode, deep within the soul in which God has chosen to dwell.

But that is the end of an active prayer life, what is the beginning? Well, after Mass and daily prayers are a fixed part of a spiritual program, what comes next? There are very definite stages or uses of prayer which I will explain as follows:

FALLING IN LOVE WITH GOD

The very first use of prayer or reason for prayer is to fulfill the First Commandment: you should love God with your whole heart, your whole soul, your whole mind. What exactly does that mean, to love God with your whole heart, your whole soul, your whole mind? It means that you must fall deeply in love with God to the point where you constantly want to do, say or think only what pleases Him. It means that you love Him so much, that you would do all in your power, with the help of His grace, to avoid all sins, venial as well as mortal, to correct all your human weaknesses and faults, to accept all crosses He wishes to send to you and last, but not least, to obey all His laws and rules and teachings. It means a total, complete abandonment to His holy will. It means to allow Him to give to you the tremendous joy and peace which comes when He returns to you pure love for love.

All that sounds like an impossible task, but briefly, that is exactly the road which has to be taken if one is to climb THE LADDER OF PERFECTION to a closer union with God. And it can be done through prayer and the use of grace.

Now, how does one fall in love with God to the extent which I have just explained? Or to put it another way, do you really love God?

Most people say, yes, they do love God. But do they really? Do they "prove" their love for God by going to Mass and saying daily prayers? Yes, they do. But are they really "in love" with God? Judging from the average lay person's spiritual life, the answer has to be no they are not. Why do I say that? Because I know that there are numerous Catholics who faithfully go to Mass and say daily prayers who truly love God until a heavy cross is placed upon their shoulders or until they decide that they will no longer accept and obey a rule or law of God or of our Church. There are an equal number of good practicing Catholics who constantly complain that they "get nothing" out of the Mass or their daily prayers. Others say that they will accept and believe the doctrines of God and the Church *except* the ones they *think* are "wrong." Then we have the large number of fallen-away and lukewarm Catholics who insist that they do love God; however, they are not willing to prove in any way that they do indeed love Him. Finally, a large percentage of Catholics, practicing or fallen-away, are unwilling to make any effort to acquire virtue and overcome sins, faults, weaknesses or bad habits. All such Catholics are not *in love* with God no matter how much love they say they have for Him.

To really fall in love with God is far different than merely to say that you do love God. Again, how can a person really fall in love with God? Is this a gift from God or something you acquire yourself? It is both. It can become a precious gift from Him if there is an initial call to the soul from God. However, this call is only a slight opening of the path leading to falling in love with God. It is a tiny taste of what being in love with God means. The walk upon this path to the very heart of God can only be done through prayer which brings to the soul the grace necessary to fall in love with God.

There are two basic or fundamental ways which are used to fall in love with God. The first way is the direct action of God the Father, Christ or The Holy Spirit which suddenly touches a soul with a powerful experience of falling in love with Him. This happens a great deal when a person is suddenly converted from a life of sin into a life of grace. This also happens when a dying sinner suddenly repents and confesses his sins on his deathbed. In addition there is, as was prevalent in the 60's and 70's, a type of suddenly falling in love with God experienced by Catholics and non-Catholics alike who found Christ or The Holy Spirit by and through the Pentecostal or Charismatic movements. Apart from the deathbed conversions, such a way of falling in love with God is not by any means the best one. I prefer the second way which is the slow, but sure, gradual preparation of the soul so that this falling in love with God has a better chance to grow into a permanent close union with God.

God does indeed have His own reasons for suddenly touching a soul with an experience of love for Him; however, more often than not this experience can lead into a great deal of abuse and confusion unless (and this is so important) the person seeks the correct spiritual director. Without this proper director, the person simply cannot handle this powerful experience. That is why, the saints who were converted or felt the touch of God upon their souls in such a way *immediately* sought proper spiritual direction; and would not *even accept* this gift from God unless and until they were assured that such an encounter was indeed from God. They knew that human emotions were involved in such an experience and because of that, it becomes very easy for the devil to create a *false imitation* of this true gift from God. Also, without the proper spiritual direction, the falling-in-love-with-God experience can be most consuming for awhile, but will fade away when the cares, crosses and hard work of daily life come back into view.

So, the first thing which a person must become aware of after such an experience with Christ or the Holy Spirit is to realize that the encounter—as powerful as it may be—is but a faint, tiny call from God who wants to draw the individual into a closer union with Him. In other words, it *is not* the beginning and end of union with God all wrapped up into one beautiful package which most people, who had such a meeting with God, want it to become. It is only the *first step* up that LADDER OF PER-FECTION and not a magical flight to the top. A person simply cannot reach instant perfection. Why? Because, before perfection can be obtained, there must, first of all, be many a hard-fought battle to overcome sins, weaknesses and faults and acquire virtues. There is no "easy" way to the top of the ladder.

Unfortunately, many people, who had at one time or another actually felt the touch of God upon their souls, could become so engrossed and wholly occupied by the experience that they tell themselves that nothing else is needed in their personal relationship with God. They could convince themselves that they have "made" it and refuse to either seek spiritual guidance or else they become involved with groups of people who had this same type of experience who agree that they are all on "top" and can go no higher.

I have seen such situations develop numerous times and such people involved developed the very same mistakes. They, first of all, believe that they are the only ones on earth who truly love Christ (or the Holy Spirit) and receive love in return. They refuse spiritual direction because they feel that as long as the Holy Spirit is leading and guiding them they need no human director. Most Catholics with such an attitude will leave the Church and the sacraments because they feel no need for them as long as they "have" the Holy Spirit. They also want nothing to do with doctrines or the Holy Mother of God, again because they have the Holy Spirit and need no one or nothing else. They focus so much attention upon their "rebirth" that they reduce their whole spiritual programs to a very narrow circle and never find out what the next step up THE LADDER OF PERFECTION is. As a result, they remain in a rather simplistic, infantile state of union with God for they close all the doors to a more adult union. They fail to note that a more complete union with God is a very personal, quiet one which *cannot* be shared. They also look for, and think they have, all the gifts which they expect from this encounter with Christ or the Holy Spirit, not realizing that the greatest gifts anyone can receive from God are the Eucharist and grace through the sacraments.

As can be seen, such people are on very unstable spiritual grounds and the inadequacies of such an immature spiritual life can clearly be seen.

For example: I have received several letters from or talked to people, who no longer want to be called Catholics, who severely criticized me for my love for The Holy Mother of God. They said: "We do not need her, we go right to Christ."

They also criticized my work with the Crusaders: "Why bother to learn doctrine? We have the Holy Spirit that is all we need." They called me rather unpleasant names in the process (you are nothing but a "glory-seeker"); but, at the same time or in the same letter, they called me their "dearly beloved sister-in-Christ whom they will pray for" because they "so cherish" me.

One man even sent me a beautiful get-well card. Needless to say, such diverse attitudes or emotional feelings on their part left me in a state of confusion until a friend of mine offered a good explanation of why such a thing could happen.

Having known many such people, he noticed a most unusual thing about them. They all try to follow their basic rule of extending to everyone they meet or know a pure, holy, brotherly-love which they themselves are totally unable to give because they have not as yet overcome their most glaring faults and weaknesses. As a result, they are under a self-imposed strain to maintain the I-love-you-attitude even when they are angry and do not agree with a brother or sister-in-Christ. They, due to human nature, will severely criticize or disagree with another person, even call him all sorts of names; but, at the same time, they feel compelled to tell the person how much they "love" him. Confusing? It is unless you understand the fact that in order for a person to profit spiritually from the touch of God upon the soul, there has to be the correct knowledge of how to take the next step up that LADDER OF PERFECTION.

Of course, not all who have been involved in a personal religious experience act or think as I have described. There are many who do have the proper direction and many who have the knowledge of how to take the next step. However, the ones who do not have this knowledge or direction miss the whole point of what it really means to fall in love with Christ.

That is why I said that I prefer the second way of falling in love with God. So, if you have never experienced the touch of God's love upon your soul, do not become discouraged. There is a better and much safer way. It is called the ordinary road to holiness, and this road begins with the sacraments and prayer.

Sometimes this way becomes so ordinary that many Catholics fail to notice it. That is why it becomes easy for a Catholic, who is bored with ordinary prayer and who gets "nothing" out of the Mass to become impressed with all the excitement found in the Charismatic prayer groups. But remember that such excitement is not holiness and sanctification. It is to be noted that most Catholics who do have an advanced union with God and a beautiful prayer life are not the least bit interested in all the loud noises, the loud shouts, the gifts and the public witnesses of the prayer groups. They know that true, lasting spiritual development is a very precious, personal thing which lies hidden and becomes a wondrous secret between the soul and God.

As I said, the ordinary path to falling in love with God may be so ordinary that it can go unnoticed; however, there is no better, safer, or quicker way. So, do not go searching to find the way to fall in love with God. You already have that way, now understand it.

The first thing for you to do is to get to know the God who dwells within your soul when your soul is in the state of grace. How do you do that? By understanding "Divine Indwelling" (see Chapter in this book) and understanding the presence of Christ in the Eucharist. Then pray for the graces which you will need so that you can truly meet and fall in love with this God, this Christ, this Holy Spirit who already dwells within your own soul. Remember that God must have a tremendous, infinite love for you to actually want to dwell within your own soul. He must have an equally infinite love for you to actually give to you the holy Mass wherein Christ becomes present in the Eucharist. Surely, God, who so loves you, can be loved in return by you.

Then polish this virtue of love-for-love each day with prayers of love. They do not have to be long. For example, a simple prayer such as, "My God, I love you, teach me how to love you more" will bring to you a most beautiful awareness of God's personal love for you.

TO KNOW HIM

Prayer is also used to know God and to understand His ways. It is true, the more you love God, the more you can understand Him, the more you understand Him, the more you will love Him. This is basically the same way that human love and friendships develop. It is true that people can fall in love at the first sight as with the instant touch of God upon the soul. However, it is never wise to accept such an instant encounter as true or lasting. As I have already explained, there can be many hidden inaccuracies in such a love which, when they surface, can very well destroy it.

The reason why prayer is used to get to know God is simple. Prayer increases sanctifying grace within your soul. The more this grace is increased, the more you are going to understand and know God.

What does it mean to know and understand God? That means not only to know the historical Christ (who is and was God) and what He did by dying on the cross for you and also His teachings, but to know how He is working in your daily life and in the world.

It is very necessary to get to know Christ through the Bible and how He is revealed in Holy Scripture. That is called Bible reading and becomes a form of prayer all its own. But do be careful with Bible reading. You cannot understand what the Bible tells you without the proper guides. A Catholic who picks up the Bible and leaves the Church saying that the Bible is all he needs is sadly mistaken. Such a Catholic can only find what is in the Bible. That does not mean that he will understand the God whom the Bible talks about.

The best way to begin the prayer of Bible reading is to find the proper adult catechism, suitable to your own level of comprehension. (These can be found in any Catholic bookstore or can be obtained from the local Parish.) Then as you learn more about the teachings of God and of the Church, check your Bible to find the reference passages mentioned. In that way, you will better understand what you read. You will also begin to become aware of the fact that the good Lord planned your salvation and the start of our Catholic church with infinite love and care. Then you will understand God in a way which you never understood Him before. You will also be more able to understand many aspects of your own daily life. For example: Christ told you to take up your cross and follow Him. That explains why you will find many daily crosses to carry. Bible reading also explains or shows you why you must use the sacraments and prayer.

There is another way to get to know and understand God. It is to become more and more conscious of His presence and action in your own personal daily life. It is to see and even look for His holy will as you go about your daily duties and obligations. What is His holy will? It becomes things like unexpected illness; however, there is much more to His will than that.

To accept, love and follow God's holy will every day of your life is to do everything that will please Him. What pleases Him? Well, prayer and receiving the sacraments please Him a great deal. To acquire and polish virtues and to get rid of sins, weaknesses and faults. That pleases Him, also, very much. Charity, brotherly-love, kindness, concern for others, all such please God. It is God's will for you to have you develop a very good, active spiritual life, one that you live every moment of every day. (And, believe me, when I say that just attempting to do that is far from boring.) God is also pleased when you faithfully follow and obey all the teachings of His and of His Church. In addition, you love, accept and follow God's holy will when you carry out the duties and obligations of your daily life.

Remember, a very important fact about God, your love for Him and obeying His holy will: You cannot separate that love from the structure of the Church or from daily, religious duties and obligations. They all go together. The Church is needed to help you fulfill the commands of God and your daily duties are needed so that you can fulfill the role or purpose which God created for you alone. That helps you know God better.

Many people make serious mistakes about this love for God bit. They believe that in order to love God completely they must leave the Church, to do it on their own, or leave their daily duties and obligations.

So we have the Catholics who take the Bible in their hands and refuse to go to the sacraments. And we have the Catholics who will actually break up their own families and leave to go someplace where God never intended them to go in order to prove their love for God. I know of several families that were left in dismay when the husband or wife ran away to "work" for God. Of course, I am not talking about a vocation of those who follow the call to become a brother, sister or priest who have no family obligations and responsibilities. What I am referring to are married people who run away because they cannot face nor accept the daily responsibilities of their lives. Remember, it is more meritorious to face each day with its grinding problems with a true love for God's holy will than it is to run away to a deserted island to pray in peace and quiet. Living your daily life as God intended you to live it becomes a prayer all by itself.

So, through prayer, when you ask to know, love and follow God's holy will in your daily life, you get to know Him better and to understand His ways.

Prayer also brings to you extra graces so that you can better understand God's ways in the world. While you cannot accept that will for the world in general, you can avoid the great mistake of blaming God for all the wrongs, evils and catastrophic disasters of mankind. Many people do. Then they sit and wonder how a good God could do such terrible things or allow such evil to exist. Such an attitude is a very huge barrier to spiritual advancement. But by means of prayer and the grace which it brings to your soul, you will have a clearer view when you look out at suffering humanity. You may not know all the "reasons for" and the "whys" of all that happens, but you will know that God does have His own reasons for allowing certain events to take place. You will also see clearly that not all of mankind's ills come from Him. Man and the devil can interfere with God's will, and often do, because God gave to man a free will. Man can choose good deeds or evil deeds. If he chooses evil deeds then he, not God, is responsible for the natural results of such actions and ways.

TO WORSHIP HIM

To know God is also to know why He must be worshiped. In order to put God first, as He commands, He must be worshiped as He deserves to be worshiped. We need a very special kind of prayer for that.

It must be clearly understood, before I explain more, that there is a great difference between merely *praying* to and actually *worshiping* God. Sinners often pray even when they have no intentions of freeing themselves from the life they live; but they do not worship God with such prayers. Nor do the people who say they can pray in their own closets as well as in a Church. Also, just reading the Bible, no matter how sincere one is in this type of prayer, does not constitute an act of worship. That is why we pray *to* Mary or the saints, but do not worship them. In addition, it becomes a delusion to attempt to pray in only "one's own way" without adding to a prayer life other duties and obligations such as the personal responsibility to assist at the Holy Sacrifice of the Mass. Man can indeed pray alone; however, it is also his duty to take part in formal prayers with the community; and the home prayers cannot become a substitute for the Sunday (or Saturday evening) Mass.

Why is that so? Because when a person uses prayer or wants to pray, he must know that there are many different aspects of and reasons for prayer. Anyone who believes that a person prays only to ask for something is very much mistaken. Prayer must also be used for adoration, for repentance, for praise, faith and thanksgiving. In addition, prayer is used to tell God you love Him, to accept His holy will, to share your joys and sorrows with Him. But even more important than these reasons for praying, prayers must be used, as part of the activity of worshiping God by means of one holy sacrifice: The Mass.

Unless all these different types of prayers are included within a person's prayer life, he or she is not fulfilling religious obligations which center around prayer.

How can that statement be true? If you examine all the different types of and reasons for prayer, it can be clearly seen that each one is needed for its own special purpose. If one uses prayer to love God, such a prayer is far different than one which begs God for His mercy for a sinner. There can be no substitute for a certain prayer which is used for a specific, precise reason. Because of that, there has to be a variety within each person's individual prayer life; and the very first type of prayer must become an act of true worship of God so that the first commandment of God's can be fulfilled.

The Catholic Church has this true act of worship. It is called the Holy Sacrifice of the Mass.

The Mass becomes the supreme worship of God. There is no other way to truly worship God. No amount of home prayers, Bible readings and, I dare say, even some Protestant services can worship God as He deserves to be worshiped. You can *pray to God* in your own home or when you read the Bible or in a Protestant Church; but you may not be worshiping God by and through such means. Why? Because to pray to God is far different than to worship Him. That is why it is so foolish to say that we Catholics worship Mary and the saints. We pray to them, we love them, we honor them but we could not worship them even if we tried. Because in order to worship, one should have a sacrifice which is offered, not by just anyone, but by someone who has the power to offer such a sacrifice.

The greatest sacrifice offered to God in worship must be of a nature that it is alive and can be destroyed during the act of worship by someone (the priest) who has the right to do that in the name of the worshipers or assembled group. From the beginning of the human race, man has given to God worship by and through the means of destroying upon the altars a living sacrifice.

So, in order to give to God the worship which He commands, there must be a sacrifice worthy enough to be offered to Him, by a priest who has the power and authority to offer such a sacrifice in the name of the community.

That being the case, all the shouting, singing, Bible readings and home prayers of those who do not attend Mass, no matter how sincere they are, cannot worship God because these people *do not have* the perfect sacrifice needed for such worship: the living Christ, who becomes the sacrifice upon the altar! It is Christ, who, once again, offers His own life as an act of worship to God, His Father; and He does that only through the Mass.

Chapter 7

THE DEVIL'S TORMENTS

Before I explain the different types of prayer, I would like to write about the devil, his temptations and his torments. The reason is obvious. Anyone who tries to reach a closer union with God will encounter the devil, his temptations and experience his power, especially his agonizing torments.

I shall lightly skip over the usual, ordinary temptations of the devil. I do not have to explain them. We are all quite familiar with the temptations to steal, cheat, lie, become angry or do other things which can result in sin. We know that sin does exist so we can be sure that the devil is always around with his tantalizing suggestions to do something we know is wrong. More often than not, we listen to him and then commit a sin.

Many people wonder why the good Lord allows the devil to tempt us to sin. The simplest answer is that the good Lord also knows we can conquer such temptations by using grace, and in that way gain many merits for heaven which will last forever. If we do not use grace to fight and conquer temptations, it is our own fault and not the fact that God allows us to be tempted.

Temptations come in many and varied ways, but behind each and every one is a spirit which is 100 per cent evil and filled with total hate for God. The motive which brings about the reality of all temptations is always the same. It never changes. It encompasses the reasoning that every sin, no matter how small, is an expression of someone's hate for God and His ways. So the tempter never ceases to attempt to plant the seeds of that hate within the thoughts, words, deeds and actions of us, God's own beloved children. Even a very tiny sin, a "little white lie," becomes a triumph for the fallen angel who lost his place in God's kingdom of love. If heaven is the pinnacle of pure love, then hell has to be the shadowy depths of total hate. The pathway to hell is always constructed with little bricks of hate created when temptations are not rejected.

Many people attempt to convince themselves that they do "nothing wrong" if their sins are seen by themselves through rose-colored glasses. I have heard a "million times" the time-worn excuses for one's sins which go something like this: "What do I do wrong? Nothing!" "Whom did I hurt? No one!" "What I do is my own business!" Yet mingled within the self-complacency of such placid remarks is the hate which brings joy to the heart of the tempter.

However, there are many people who do use grace and who resist temptations. They are the ones who receive the greatest onslaughts and the most vigorous attacks from the devil. The reason why is plain to see. The devil hardly, if ever, attacks his own. The sinner, who finds delight in his wrongdoings, is lulled to sleep by the comforting, reassuring, stroking hand of the master of deceit. The devil knows well how to still the pangs of a guilty conscience. He knows how to turn the sinful pleasures of the world into ornate jewels which sparkling glitter hides the hideous face of sin from the eyes of the sinner. But what if the sinner accepts grace and wants to free himself from the bonds of a life without grace? What then? What price must be paid for resistance?

The price is one which always brings some sort of a suffering to the person. The greatest tool the devil uses, when he is afraid that he cannot win a soul to his unscrupulous ways, is mental anguish so as to discourage a person's quest for union with God.

This tool of the devil's, mental anguish, comes in all ways, for a wide variety of reasons and often can totally ravage a person's whole spiritual program.

Why would the devil want to cause such spiritual havoc? Why would he even bother anyone who makes an effort to live a more spiritual life and seek a closer union with God? Why would a plain, ordinary, not-so-important person experience the same type of mental torment as say a great saint whose life occupation is to snatch souls from the devil's grip by and through prayer and penance?

Once again, the world hate must be brought into the picture. The devil is the supreme personification of hate. The one thing which infuriates him the most is the type of pure love which gives glory to God and saves souls.

It can be said that the devil just wants people to join him in his hell for all eternity. That is true. However, the devil, at all times, not only seeks the destruction of grace within souls; but more so, seeks the destruction of love for God which souls in the state of grace possess. To that end, he uses all sorts of temptations, sufferings and mental torments. One drop of pure love for God burns deeply into the being called Satan and causes him torments so great that the outer fires of hell seem mild in comparison. If he could succeed in eliminating each and every drop of pure, holy love for God, his own torments would become less. Of course, he will never be able to do that; however, he never stops trying. Even if a person has only one tiny ounce of love for God there is an attempt by the devil to destroy that love by way of temptation and sin. Every sin committed, no matter how small, is a way for the devil to relieve himself of the burning torture of someone's love for God through the person's display of hate for his or her Savior by the sin.

Very often the devil does an excellent job in destroying all traces of a person's love for God by and through temptations and sin. It is a well-known fact that little sins, called venial, can lead to mortal sins and a life lived without God and His grace. If you let one "little devil" into your life and do nothing about it, chances are many more devils will appear to take up residence. If you become comfortable with "little sins," chances are you will become comfortable with mortal sins. If you feel no guilt for your sins, you have destroyed your love for God.

The ideal situation in regards to the devil and his temptations, is to reject the smallest temptations by calling upon the power of the grace of God. A person must always be on guard and never forget that he is on a spiritual battlefield. The devil never sleeps in his quest for souls, nor should you ever sleep in your quest for grace and virtue.

But what about the devil's torments which still come even when you have done your best to resist temptations and not to sin? Let us now examine such torments.

TORMENTING THOUGHTS

Say, for example, that you know you are not a great sinner. Yes, you do have faults and weaknesses, but you make sure that you never allow yourself to fall into the state of grievous, mortal sin. You go to the sacraments often, you may even go to Mass every day. You are faithful to your daily prayers. You love Mary and say the Rosary. You do a great deal of spiritual reading. In other words, you do live an active spiritual life. You do try to polish your virtues. You feel very safe under the protecting mantle of God's love and Mary's love. You have found a certain peace which brings joy to your heart and soul.

Then, suddenly, you are plagued with violent, crushing torments from the devil. All sorts of wild, uncontrollable thoughts flash through your mind. You are tempted to think the most terrible thoughts about someone or a situation. You begin to form imaginary pictures in your mind which you want to believe are true, even if they are not. Your whole safe world of peace and security begins to fall apart as you imagine the worst. Once such thoughts start they go from bad to worse. There seems to be no relief from the devastating torments. They go on and on, sometimes for days or weeks.

Any number of things or situations can trigger such thoughts. Perhaps you heard that a relative has a fatal disease and you begin to imagine that you also have the same illness. Perhaps, someone makes a remark about someone you love and all sorts of wild thoughts begin to flash through your mind. Perhaps the very fault or sin you thought sure you had conquered starts to show its ugly head and you find that this problem becomes worse than ever.

Sometimes such a display of uncontrollable thoughts can be comical. For example, there is a story told about a person who had not seen his best friend for some time. The person begins to imagine all sorts of uncharitable thoughts about the person. Where was he all this time? Did he visit all his other friends except me? What did I ever do to him, etc. Then one day the person meets his best friend who greets him warmly ready to tell him all about the trip he had to suddenly take for his company. But the person, with all the wild thoughts in his mind yells out: "Oh! There you are, you low-down so and so! Some friend you are! I never want to see you again!" End of a precious friendship.

However, most of the cases of such torments from the devil are not the least bit funny. These torments can destroy not only spiritual programs, but also a person's union with God. They can destroy marriages and cause rifts in families which are never healed. They can throw people into uncontrollable fits of rage, anger or jealousy, all of which have no cause or foundation. Innocent people can be accused of doing all sorts of terrible things which they never did do. We have all heard about the remark: "Well, if *that* is what you think I do, I might as well go out and do it."

This problem of the devil's torments which brings all sorts of wild, imaginary thoughts to the person is very common. It strikes almost all of us at one time or another. I am never surprised when someone I know, who has a very beautiful relationship with God, suddenly begins to tell me about such torments. Why is that so? Because we all have our one special spiritual weak point, the weakest link in the chain. Once the devil discovers that flaw, watch out! He will use it for his own purposes.

What to do? Yes, what can be done about this trick of the devil? Fortunately, there are many things which can be done about this serious spiritual problem.

WEAK POINTS

The first thing to do is to pay very close attention to your greatest, most prominent weak point. A soldier never goes out onto the battlefield without weapons. Be prepared for every attack of the devil upon your most vulnerable human weakness.

And do not be fooled if this weakness has not bothered you for some time. The day will come when the devil will suddenly bring it into sight and this could cause disastrous interior conflicts.

What is your greatest weak point? Only you can answer that question, but here are some examples of weak points which may help you decide what yours is.

One woman I knew found her weak point in her mother-in-law who often was very unkind to her. The mother-in-law caused her all sorts of sufferings, so that when the mother-in-law was not in her company, her mind was filled with tormenting thoughts about her. She had "a million" imaginary conversations with the woman, telling her all sorts of things which she never dared tell her mother-in-law face to face. The poor woman would torture herself with all sorts of thoughts about her mother-in-law until she could not sleep at night.

Yet, the truth of the matter was that she did not see her mother-in-law very often. Still, daily, she had her in her mind and suffered greatly from her thoughts about her mother-in-law. Another person thought she had reason to believe that her husband had been unfaithful; although, she never had any proof. But constantly she worried about the situation, becoming more and more possessive of him, demanding that he explain everything he did, where he went and who he was with. He tried to tell her that her fears were groundless, but she would rather torture herself with all sorts of wild thoughts about him, becoming more and more consumed with jealousy.

The truth of the matter was that her husband loved her dearly and never would be unfaithful to her.

Another person thought he had truly conquered a very serious sin. He had not been bothered with the temptations for some time. Suddenly the temptations started again to fill him with torment as he first fought them. He fell once again into sinful habits. Night and day he struggled, yet it seemed that the devil and temptations became the constant victor. Fortunately, a good confessor helped save his spiritual life with the correct information. Then, just as suddenly, the devil's torments vanished.

Other people are tormented by the devil because they constantly feel a very deep guilt for their past sins, which have already been confessed and forgiven. They have inner conversations reminding themselves what a "terrible," "horrible" person they are. The torture goes on for days, weeks, months, perhaps even years.

Still other people love to play the part of the martyr, torturing themselves day and night, thinking about how unloved and unwanted they are.

Then there are the people who feel that a slight remark by someone is in reality a vicious attack against them; and they spend days seeking revenge in their minds, pondering over and over their own "get even" plans.

Finally, we can see the weak point in someone who flares up into a fit of anger for no apparent reason. The slightest thing which is said or which he does not like can cause a violent outburst.

All such examples of the weak points show one very important fact. The person *allowed* the devil to enter into the weak point of his or her spiritual life by not recognizing the most open, vulnerable place therein which could trigger an attack. So the very first thing to do to stop the devil's torments is to be in control of the situation and to be on guard when you know a situation will develop which can bring on the devil's attacks.

For example, if the woman who had the mother-in-law problem would have realized that seeing the woman or hearing her name or thinking about her would build up in her mind agonizing thoughts, then she would have been better able to *put a stop* to such thoughts as soon as they began. In other words, she should have instantly recognized her weak point in such a way as to be able to control her thoughts the minute they started so that her thoughts would not go on and on for days, torturing her.

If the man, who had the misfortune to be tormented by temptations he thought were long gone, would have recognized the hand of the devil who wanted to gain control of his thoughts by entering into the weakest point of his spiritual life, he would have been better to use grace to strengthen that point so that the devil could not use it as a means of torment and torture.

If the person who flared up in a fit of anger for "no reason at all" would see his weakness and be prepared for the "no reason at all" situations which arise in his daily life, he would be better able to control his feelings instead of allowing the devil to torment him with such feelings.

If the person who had been tormented by past sins confessed, would only realize that this is a weakness in his spiritual life being used by the devil to torment him, he would be better able to realize that past sins are indeed confessed and forgiven; and if they really bother him, then a program of daily penance can easily still all the tormenting feelings of guilt.

So, it is not only up to the person to see the weakest points in his or her spiritual life, but to realize that certain situations could bring about an attack of the devil's torments. In that way, the person will be better able to stop the torments as soon as they start and not allow the devil to enter in with his suggestions and self-torturing thoughts.

This is a parallel to the Church's teaching to avoid the occasions of sin. If you know you will commit a sin by going to a certain place or being with certain people, then the wisest thing to do is to stay away. Once you learn that given situations, which may or may not be sinful, trigger wild, uncontrollable, tormenting thoughts in your mind then the wisest thing to do is to be prepared for the devil's onslaught you know is coming so as to stop the thoughts as soon as they start.

LOSS OF FAITH

The main reason why the devil comes with his tormenting thoughts is to get the person to completely lose faith in God. Loss of faith can become a very serious sin and this sin delights the cold, loveless heart of the devil.

I have noticed, during the years of helping people live a more active spiritual life, that the ones who have the most beautiful spiritual union with God, who find great joy in praying and going to Mass are the ones most likely to be a candidate for the devil's tormenting thoughts. At first, I used to wonder why these people would allow themselves to be swept up into such a devastating situation. One woman had so many torturous thoughts about her face that she actually began to hide herself away from the world refusing to leave the house because she thought she was so ugly. The truth of the matter was that she was a very attractive person with a beautiful smile, when she smiled. Fortunately, the correct spiritual guidance brought her out of her self-created shell back into the world. She began to enjoy life. She returned to the Mass and sacraments. She even got a little part-time job. And her charming, fun-loving personality revealed itself.

After I heard about case after case concerning that type of a person who developed interior, mental torments, which actually had no foundations, I realized that what the devil was attempting to do was to destroy the person's faith in God. It became so clear as I analyzed each incident. During the periods of mental torment and anguish, the person's whole relationship with God and union with Him began to change. The people so affected would tell me that they could no longer pray. Some stopped going to Mass. Others began to speak against God. Still others said they would never go to Mass again. They could no longer even think about God as the all-consuming thoughts took control of them every moment of every day.

However, the pathetic, ironic truth of the matter is that neither God nor the devil can be completely at fault for the sad situation. True, the devil triggered the thoughts by and through certain situations, but once the torture started, the person was left on his own. As the thoughts, the agony, the torment continued, it was *the person who kept* them going in his or her own mind. In other words, after the devil touched the person's weak point with his suggestions, the person began *to torture himself or herself* with more and more thoughts. The person then was more in control of the situation than either God or the devil.

That is one reason why this spiritual illness can so easily destroy the person's faith in God. The *will of the person* allows the illness to fester and spread into the areas of trust and faith in God; until, the person destroys his or her spiritual union with God. *It is the person* who will not do anything to rid himself of such torture when, indeed, he can! All he or she has to do is to recognize the situation at once and *stop* the thoughts as soon as they start.

People who find that they do have periods of such tormenting thoughts should pray daily to increase their trust and faith in God or Our Lady. They should use that trust and faith to stop the torments the minute they begin to show themselves. They should be able to say to the Dear Lord: "I will trust you. I will put the whole matter in your loving hands. I will accept your holy will. I will never allow this situation to take me away from you or the Mass or the sacraments."

It is also wise to have trust and faith in the ones you love: members of your family, your husband, your children, your best friends. Do not allow yourself to imagine all sorts of dire, unfounded thoughts about them. Do not accuse them of things they never did. If there is a problem, try and find the correct solution, even if the solution is painful. Remember with Christ and Our Lady on your side, you will always have the strength to bear any cross placed upon your shoulders.

A WASTE OF TIME

An excellent way to stop the tormenting thoughts as soon as they start is to fully realize what a waste of precious time they are. There is a story told about a soul who appeared from purgatory to a certain person. One of the things said by this holy soul was something like this: "If you, on earth, only knew and realized how precious time is! So much time is wasted which could have been used to serve and love God and gain the merits which will last forever."

Time wasted! You can well imagine how much time is wasted with useless, tormenting thoughts which have no real value, nor serve any good purpose. Truly wasted moments which quickly extend into wasted hours and even wasted days! What a shame! Think of all the good which could be done if these wasted moments were used to pray, to love God, to gain merits which will last for all eternity.

Not only do such thoughts waste time, but they also lead a

person into areas of selfishness and self-love. Ninety per cent of all tormenting thoughts concern the person himself or herself. So the thoughts are filled with ideas that the person was wronged or slighted or pushed aside or ignored or hated. They squeeze the person into a tiny corner of his world where enormous self-pity takes over the tormenting thoughts adding to the person's sufferings.

All these sufferings are really not meant to be and they become a cross which the person created and not one which God asked the person to carry.

Also, the tormenting thoughts which the person allows to dominate his or her whole mind could become a very bad habit. The person could become so accustomed to falling into the moods of tormenting thoughts, he or she could become so consumed with that type of self-pity that nothing or no one could change or break the habit.

Needless to say, a person gains no merits from carrying such a cross. However, this type of spiritual suffering can have one type of value.

THE SPIRITUAL VALUE OF THE DEVIL'S TORMENTS

Chances are the person, who does want to live an active spiritual life, who does not want to lose faith in God, finds such tormenting thoughts a burden to get rid of. He would rather be free from them and get his spiritual life back on an even course without that type of a detour.

Such can be done by, as I said, stopping the thoughts as soon as they start. I realize that, at first, one may not have the grace nor the ability to do that. As with all phases and stages of development of an active spiritual life, one must remember that "practice makes perfect." But, at least, the person will know how to achieve the desired goal.

Here, now, are a couple of suggestions which should be a great help in the struggle to stop tormenting thoughts as soon as they start. I often give this advice to people who come to me with this spiritual problem.

First of all, fully realize that you and only you can keep the tormenting thoughts in your mind. So if you have the power to keep them going on and on, you also have the power to halt them with words such as: "Wait a minute! Here I go again, but this time I am not going to fall into that trap! Forget it! Why waste all that time feeling sorry for myself. I have better and more important things to think about. I will think about the way God loves me and how much I love Him."

Then, after such a positive decision, turn to the devil and say: "Okay, keep coming at me with all these tormenting thoughts! But I tell you, the more you torment me, the more souls I will save because I will use this suffering to help save souls!" If you really mean what you say, you will find out how quickly the devil and his tormenting thoughts will vanish. He is not about ready to help you save souls.

In summary, I hope that I have given you enlightenment about this spiritual problem, which could destroy your whole union with God. If you have this problem, follow the suggestions I have given and it should disappear from your spiritual life. Also follow the instructions from your spiritual director. It may take awhile to rid yourself of this problem, but he should be able to help you do just that.

Chapter 8

VOCAL PRAYER

An active prayer life must, of necessity, start with vocal prayer. After the start, a prayer life must continue to include vocal prayer, no matter how advanced the prayer life becomes. Vocal prayer, then, is not only the beginning of the prayer life, but the chain which binds all other forms of prayer together. A person can have a prayer life which consists only of vocal prayer, never adding any other type of prayer; however, a person must include vocal prayer within the most advanced form of prayer life. In other words, vocal prayer never ceases to have a very important part to play in all forms of the prayer life.

What then is this vocal prayer which is so versatile? Prayer is, in general, getting in touch with God. There are many different ways to get in touch with God or to realize that God exists. We can suddenly "feel close" to God while watching a breathtaking sunset. We can realize that God exists when we witness the power of a miracle. Or we can believe in a God who actually bends forth to listen when we want to talk to Him.

Vocal prayer is one way of talking to God, telling Him what we want to say to Him. Usually, when one is a beginner in the art of praying, a person does not know what to say to God. So he or she picks up a prayer book and starts to pray using words written by someone else. That is vocal prayer: saying or reading prayers which have a set formula and were written by someone else. More often than not, such prayers better express our sentiments than any we could write ourselves.

So, Holy Mother Church has given to us, for our use,

numerous vocal prayers which are said and have been said daily by millions of Catholics.

There are prayers which every Catholic should know by heart, such as The Our Father, The Hail Mary, The Glory Be, The Apostles Creed, The Confiteor, An Act of Faith, An Act of Hope, An Act of Love, An Act of Contrition, Grace before and after meals, The Angelus, Morning Prayers, Evening Prayers, Litanies, the Rosary and the prayers during Mass. In addition, there are approved devotional prayers to the saints, the Sacred Heart, the Holy Spirit, the Blessed Virgin, novenas, etc.

All such prayers are called vocal prayers because they were written by someone else for our use. Many of these prayers were written by saints who mastered the art of praying. Others, such as the prayers said during Mass, were composed by Church authorities who knew what to say to the Lord and how to say it for very special occasions.

Now, the purpose of all these vocal prayers is not only to give to us Catholics words which express our love for or hope in God, etc., but also which bind Catholics together as one community, praying as one unit, all saying the exact same words. So it is possible for Catholics in thousands of different cities to say the exact same prayers as a community, during Mass. It is possible for a Catholic, who lives in Boston to go into a Catholic church in California and hear the very same familiar words which are spoken during a Mass in his local parish Church. It is also possible for hundreds of thousands of people to kneel at the same hour, to say a Rosary, and all of them will say the exact same prayers. That is one reason why vocal prayers are so important and also why, as I said, they are necessary for the advanced prayer life as well as for the beginner.

As can be seen, by what I just said, all public or common prayers are necessarily vocal. The highest form of public prayer for a Catholic, is, of course, the Mass.

Many people who say that they get "nothing" out of the Mass fail to realize that the vocal prayers said during the Mass by the priest and the people, combine to give to God the highest, most perfect act of worship which it is possible to offer to Him.

No matter how lofty a person's own private prayer life may seem, if he is able to go to Mass but does not, such a prayer life remains empty if the Mass is not part of that prayer life. There can be no substitute for the vocal prayers of the Mass; and if a person wants to believe that his own prayers, said in his own home, are more pleasing to God than the prayers said during Mass, that person is sadly mistaken. He can say as many "home" prayers as he wants, but the prayers of the Mass should always be first upon his list.

The best way for a person to begin an active prayer life is to start by learning the simple vocal prayers found in a Catholic prayer book. If the person was born and baptized a Catholic, he or she will be surprised to discover that these prayers have never changed since he or she was a child and first learned them. They are still the same "old" Our Father, Hail Mary, or Apostles Creed. That is another reason why vocal prayers are so important. Most of them remain the same and can be memorized and said for a whole lifetime without changing one single word. The Rosary has not changed for centuries. Once I was delighted to discover, in a store, the exact same Rosary Novena booklet which I had used 35 years before, and lost.

The Mass, the most perfect vocal prayer, has had some of the spoken words changed during the centuries, as was done during the 70's and 80's. That does not mean that the Mass is "new" for it remains the same Holy Sacrifice wherein the bread and wine are changed into the body and blood of Christ. Different prayers have been added, however, the Mass, itself, is the very same perfect vocal prayer which Catholics join together to say as a community with the priest.

Now, a Catholic can use only vocal prayers for a whole lifetime and still have an active prayer life. He or she is on solid ground, spiritually praying, as the Church teaches such prayers as the Rosary and ones found in prayer books. With Mass added to these vocal prayers, the person can gain many graces and climb THE LADDER OF PERFECTION to a wonderful union with God.

I dare say that most Catholics never go into an advanced

prayer life and feel at ease only in the vocal prayer stage. That is fine, except for the dangers of limiting one's prayer life only to the vocal prayer stage. The main danger is, by doing that, the person may fall into the very bad habit of repeating over and over words of vocal prayers which have lost their purpose and their meaning for the person. There can develop a very vicious habit of merely repeating words learned by heart without actually encountering God or telling Him what you really want to say to Him. For example, a person may go to Mass faithfully but never really pay attention to the prayers said during Mass. The person may even learn the prayers of the Mass by heart, yet never really understand what they mean. Or a person may say the Rosary every day, and still feel that Mary "never hears" the prayers or the requests.

Fortunately for us Catholics, Holy Mother Church has given to us the way and the means to enter into other stages of the prayer life, while still keeping the vocal prayers which are so necessary to spiritual growth.

In Volume Two of this book, I have explained fully the different types and stages of a more advanced prayer life. But before a person can enter into such stages, he or she must understand the most perfect of all prayers: the Mass.

Chapter 9

THE MASS; THE PERFECT WORSHIP OF GOD

In order to understand the Mass, as it should be understood, in order to gain the fullest spiritual treasures which can be gained from the Mass, a person has to know the difference between private prayer and liturgical prayer. In addition, there has to be some knowledge about worshiping God as perfectly as He deserves to be worshiped with a sacrificial type of worship.

The word worship is often used for different types of encounters with God. We hear such expressions as: "Worship together every Sunday" or "Let us honor and worship God in our own Church" or "I can worship God in my own way."

We have been taught that we can worship God by acts of faith, hope, love and charity and by praying to Him.

The first commandment obliges us to, not only, know and accept the truths of God, but it puts upon us the obligations to worship God as He deserves to be worshiped. So we try to fulfill that commandment by performing some act of worship.

However, when a person wants to actually worship God, often there arises a great deal of misunderstanding due mainly to lack of knowledge.

While it can be said that an act of hope or a prayer of love is in some way worshiping God, the most important thing to consider when worship is brought into the picture is: by means of such an act or prayer is the person worshiping God as *He deserves* to be worshiped? In other words, if a person sincerely wishes to worship God as perfectly as it is humanly possible, what must the person do? What would be the most complete, the most perfect act of worship?

Many people like to believe that, no matter how poorly their private prayers are said, they do worship God perfectly. They forget a very important fact. There is a vast difference between merely *praying to God* and actually *worshiping Him* as He deserves to be worshiped.

I would like to explain now, the way we worship God in the most perfect act of worship and the only way we can worship Him as fully as He deserves to be worshiped.

The most essential and perfect act of divine worship is to be found in the Catholic Mass. When a person is baptized, he or she becomes part of the community, working and praying together, called the Church. This Church gives divine worship to God. This divine worship of God has a certain, definite form. It is called the Liturgy. The Mass is part of the prayers of the Liturgy. As I explain the form of divine worship called the Liturgy, you will understand that the holy Sacrifice of the Mass is the principal act of Christian worship.

That being the case, any Catholic who claims that he or she loves God would want to show that love by and through the most perfect, the most complete act of worship. To say that you love God, but you do not have to go to Mass to prove your love, is to say that you do not really want to worship God in a way and manner which best expresses that love.

If a person believes in God and wants to pray to him, that person must, of necessity, include the Mass as the most important part of his or her prayer life. But, just as important, the person must understand what worshiping God, by and through the Mass, is all about.

The whole core, around which a person's prayer life must revolve, is the Mass or as it is formally called: liturgical prayer. Liturgical prayer is when the complete family of God unites to give public worship to Him. This type of prayer is far different than private prayer. Private prayer, no matter how devout or sincere, can never take the place of liturgical prayer. Unless there is a grave reason, such as illness, for not attending Mass on holy days and Sundays, (or Saturday evenings) liturgical prayer must become a part of a person's spiritual life.

As I said, in the last chapter, many people like to think that saying a few "home" prayers or reading the Bible takes the place of the Mass. Many Charismatics believe that because they "have the Holy Spirit" they do not need the Church, the sacraments or the Mass. But just learning a few simple facts about prayer and worship will show the great need for two very different and distinct types of prayer. One is the prayer of petition and the other, the prayer of worship. Within the prayer of petition there are to be found the prayers of thanksgiving, asking for forgiveness for sins committed, and so forth. Such prayers are understood by most people who pray. Also these kinds of prayers can be said by anyone, anyplace.

However, it is the prayer of worship which is so often misunderstood or not even known to the vast majority of people. The prayer of worship and the prayers such as asking for forgiveness or thanking God are two entirely different types of prayers and one cannot take the place of the other.

The next time someone tells you that he or she does not have to go to Mass because anyone can pray at home just as well as in a Church, ask the person this question: "But, do you worship God as He deserves to be worshiped?"

If the person says yes or merely stares in surprise, ask this question: "Do you really know what it means to worship God as He deserves to be worshiped, to place Him first in your life, to keep holy His day?"

Chances are the person will not have the slightest idea what you are talking about.

If the person, who refuses to go to Mass to worship God as He deserves to be worshiped, could be asked, as was Abraham, to kill a beloved child as an act of worship to God, that person would begin to understand what worshiping God really means (*Genesis* 22:1-15).

The offering of true, complete, perfect worship to God requires much more than a few poorly said prayers in one's own home (or closet). Such worship is not possible by an individual who merely prays in "his own way." Why? First of all, the most complete worship of God is always a sacrificial worship. That means that there has to be given to God something called a sacrifice. The sacrifice or gift to God becomes the essential element in the sacrificial worship of God. So the first requirement is something offered to God, which will become a sacrifice. In the story of Abraham, God said: "Take your only son, Isaac whom you love, and to into the district of Moria and there offer him as a sacrifice. . .to me" (*Genesis* 22:2). Abraham was willing to offer to God this complete act of worship. But when the angel of the Lord stopped him, he found a ram caught by its horns, in the bush. This ram became the living sacrifice in place of Isaac (*Genesis* 22:11-14).

Many people, who care enough or are interested enough in Abraham's story to attempt to figure out why God would command Abraham to do such a horrible thing, could never understand either God's command nor Abraham's obedience unless these people understand what it means to worship God to the fullest. Abraham knew that when God called for an act of complete, lawful worship, there had to be a sacrifice. When God commanded Abraham to kill his beloved son on an altar, Abraham knew that God had a right to demand such a living sacrifice as part of an act of worship.

The first Catholic Martyrs, who willingly gave up their own lives rather than worship a false god, also knew what worshiping God was all about. If they took a living sacrifice, an animal, and killed it upon an altar in a complete act of worship, that would mean that they accepted a false god and rejected the one true God. This they would not do.

If any person, who no longer goes to Mass and who tells himself and others that he can worship God just as well in his own home as in Church, would think deeply about Abraham's plight and a Martyr's death, that person would begin to catch a glimpse of the confounding, awesome nature of sacrificial worship offered to God. There can be *absolutely no substitute* for this perfect act of worship! To worship God in this way becomes the only worship of God which is the type that He deserves. To say that one can worship God, in his "own way" without the Holy Sacrifice of The Mass, is to attempt to tell God that

He has no right to expect the type of worship which He rightfully deserves.

Sacrificial worship, then, becomes an act offered to God which we, His children, make to Him to acknowledge that He alone is worthy of supreme adoration, love and worship.

I said "an act" and that is what complete, perfect worship becomes. It is a combination of prayer and bringing to God a gift which will be put upon an altar to be killed or sacrificed and then offered to God.

In addition to a gift that will be sacrificed to God, there must be other parts incorporated into this type of divine worship. This has to be an offering made before a gathered community. That is why the Mass is a public act of worship to God offered in a public place such as a Church.

Finally, there has to be a priest who has the power and the right to offer the sacrifice as an act of worship to God, in the name of the whole community.

In private prayer, the three important, essential elements of an act of complete worship are missing. There is no sacrifice to be slain upon an altar. There is no public gathering of the community. There is no priest who has the power to offer the sacrifice to God in the name of the people. There you have a simple explanation of why it is impossible for a person, who refuses to go to Mass, to worship God as He so deserves and to fulfill His commandments to worship, honor, love Him and place Him first, above all others. No amount of Bible study, private prayers or "praising the Lord," no matter how sincere, can take the place of the perfect, complete act of worship known as the Holy Sacrifice of The Mass.

The history of sacrifice and worship as one act, is as old as humanity itself. The Bible tells us that Cain and Abel offered sacrifice to God. The first murder occurred when Cain thought that God was more pleased with Abel's sacrifice than his (*Gen.* 4:1-11).

Wherever man found himself, from the dawn of time right up to this present day, there he offered sacrificial acts of worship to whatever or whomever he thought was a god. This act of worship had to be performed by someone who was chosen for the role of a priest. In the name of the gathered community, the act of worship was sent to the sun-god or rain-god and so forth.

The three simple rules concerning sacrificial worship have never been changed. Today, among primitive people called pagans, there can be found the ageless rituals handed down from countless generations which are used to worship a god. To the sacred huts or caves or woods, the high priest will carry the sacrificial gift, given by the people (which is usually an animal) to be slain and offered as an act of worship so that the god's blessings can fall upon the whole community.

When the Jewish people were taught to worship, not gods, but the one true God, they quickly offered to Him sacrificial worship. The Old Testament worship of God was best given by and through the use of living sacrifices, slain on the altars, then offered to God by the High Priest who did so in the name of the Community. God not only approved these sacrificial acts of worship, but encouraged them as well.

The story of Moses and the Exodus tells how important sacrificial worship of the one true God was. We are told: "...Moses then erected at the foot of the mountain an altar and twelve pillars for the twelve tribes of Israel. Then, having sent certain young men of the Israelites to offer holocausts and to sacrifice young bulls as peace offerings to the Lord..." (*Exodus* 24:4-5). (The actual killing could be done by other men; but only the priest could offer the sacrifice to God.)

It was the act of killing or destroying the gift, then the offering to God, which made the worship complete. That became a sign or symbol that the gift had been taken from human possession and had actually been given to God. Often, after the animal was slain, it was also burnt. That is why there is a term called a "burnt sacrifice" or "burnt offering."

When an animal was the sacrificial victim, all of the blood had to be poured out and sprinkled about because the blood was considered to be the life of the animal and belonged to God in a very special way. If the blood was sprinkled on the people, that was a way of sanctifying them. This act became one of extending outward to the people the means of personal purification so they could do what the Lord wanted them to do.

That is exactly what Moses did. As the High Priest, he: ". . .took half of the blood and put in large bowls; the other half, he splashed on the Altar. Taking the "Book of the Covenant," he read it aloud to the people, who answered: 'All that the Lord has said, we will heed and do.' Then he took the blood and sprinkled it on the people, saying: 'This is the blood of the covenant which the Lord has made with you in accordance with all these words of His' " (*Exodus* 24:6-8). By sprinkling the blood upon the people, Moses sealed the Covenant which the Lord (God) made between Himself and His chosen people. In other words, the people were now ready to live a life of holiness according to the rules and laws of God as given to Moses by Him.

Finally, often the slain, roasted animal was given to the people to eat as a sacred meal: ". . .that same night, they shall eat its roasted flesh with unleavened bread and bitter herbs. . ." (*Exodus* 12:8).

Now to summarize all I have just explained about sacrificial worship of God. When there is an act of complete sacrificial worship, there must be a gift or sacrificial victim given to God by His people. The gift is then slain. Finally, it is offered to God by a priest who has the power to offer the gift to God in the name of the community which is present. Not just "anyone" can do this, but only a priest. In the Old Testament, the Levitical priesthood was charged with offering sacrifice in the name of the people as an act of worship to God. The killing actually changes the complete nature of the offering so that what once belonged to the people, now belongs only to God. Blood was sprinkled upon the people as a means of their purification. The flesh of the animal was also eaten for the same reason: that which was once owned by man had been changed into a magnificent gift which God now returns to His people for their spiritual benefit.

Now let me break down that explanation into only a few pertinent facts:

1. In order to give to God complete worship, there has to be a sacrificial victim or gift.

2. The people present this gift to God.

3. Then this victim is killed or destroyed upon an Altar, which was set up for the worship of God, and then offered to God.

4. The priest does that in the name of the people, who are gathered to take part in this act of worship by their presence before the altar.

5. The blood of the victim is sprinkled on the people so they can, in this way, accept God, His rules and His laws.

6. Then the roasted flesh of the animal is given back to the people as a magnificent gift from God, who is pleased with their gift to Him, for their personal spiritual advancement.

When you have all these elements present, you have the means to offer to God complete worship and you also have the Holy Sacrifice of The Mass: the most complete, perfect act of worship.

Now compare the worship of God in the Old Testament with the worship of God in our Catholic Mass.

The Mass is a sacrifice, hence its name: The Holy Sacrifice of The Mass. The Mass is held in a public place where the Community gathers to participate by its presence and its prayers. There are the gifts, which the people bring, which are to be used in this act of worship. There is the priest who has the power to offer these gifts to God. Then there is the meal given to the people which, when eaten, is their way of accepting the laws of God and desiring personal purification.

The sacrificial act of worship has never changed but the sacrificial victim has. No longer are animals slain upon the altars in an act of worship. We no longer need animals nor their blood or meat to purify and sanctify us; because, we now have Christ!

Now note the following facts. As complete and lawful as the Old Testament sacrifices were, as pleasing to God as they were, the sacrifices of the Israelites were never perfect enough to repair the damage done by our first parents. When Adam and Eve sinned, an enormous chasm developed between God and His creation called man. Who could ever repair this break and

bring man and God together again into the supernatural relationship which had existed before the fall? Could an animal
sacrificed upon an altar redeem fallen mankind? The answer had
to be, no. Could Abraham's beloved son repair the damage and
become man's savior? Again the answer had to be no because
Isaac was himself fallen. There was only one perfect sacrificial
victim who could be offered to God, not only in an act of worship, but also as the one gift so pleasing to God that He would
be able to accept it as total reparation for the sins of mankind.
That gift, that perfect sacrificial victim was Christ.

Not only was Christ the perfect sacrificial victim, but He also
became the High Priest. As in all acts of worship, it was not
the killing which needed a High Priest, but the offering.
Although, He was slain by others, He offered Himself upon the
Altar of the Cross, to God so that the break between Creator
and creation could be mended. This combination of the perfect
victim and the perfect High Priest became the height or pinnacle
of sacrificial worship. Until the end of time, no other victim,
no other High Priest could possess the perfection of Christ's sacrifice of Himself as an offering to God for our redemption.

Saint Paul fully explains this truth with these words: "For if
the blood of goats and bulls, and the sprinkling of a heifer's
ashes can sanctify those who are defiled so that their flesh is
cleansed, how much more will the blood of Christ, who through
the Holy Spirit offered himself unblemished unto God, cleanse
your conscience from dead works, to worship the living God?"
(*Heb.* 9:12-14). He adds: ". . . but He, because He continues forever has an everlasting priesthood. . . for it is fitting that we
should have such a High Priest, holy, innocent, undefiled, set
apart from sinners. . . He does not need to offer sacrifices daily
(as the other priests did) first for his own sins and then for the
sins of the people. . . for this latter He did once and for all in
offering up Himself. For the Law appoints as priests men who
are weak; but the word of the oath, which came after the Law,
appoints a Son who is forever perfect" (*Heb.* 7:24-28).

With Christ's sacrifice of Himself for mankind's sins, the door
of our redemption should have been closed. There was nothing

lacking in Christ's perfect act of worship, done for us in our name; nothing more to be accomplished. The final curtain should have been drawn tightly. There was no longer any need for sacrifice or worship; or was there?

Were we to believe that after the crucifixion, we no longer would have to worship God, or share in the redemptive act? Some false biblical religions teach that Christ's sacrifice on the cross ended man's responsibilities to live a holy life and to continue to worship the one true God. They try to tell us that man is now free to do anything he wants because Christ died for all sin, and no matter what sins we commit, we are automatically saved.

There are many mistakes contained in such religious nonsense. Christ died for our sins, yes; however, we must freely accept and participate in our own redemption. The redemption becomes a useless act unless and until each individual gathers unto himself its fruits. Christ's perfect sacrifice meant *not the end* of worship or personal sanctification *but the beginning* of a more complete union with God. The Crucifixion poured down upon mankind sanctifying grace; but man has to recognize, accept and use that grace. Only when he does, only then can the perfect act of worship, by Christ, draw man into the eternal rewards of that act. In other words, Christ's perfect sacrifice, His perfect offering, for our redemption, continues as long as there is one person on earth who must gather its fruits. Christ did His part, now it is our turn to make use of the redemptive power which Christ made available to each and every one of us. The way to our personal salvation has been made open; but we, ourselves, must walk that path.

How do we know that we must gather the fruits of the redemption, individually, and in that way participate in our own redemption? Why can we not say, as do false religions, that Christ "did it all" and we are automatically saved no matter what we do or how many sins we commit? The answer to such questions is to be found in the teachings of Christ. Nowhere does He say, or is it recorded, that Christ's death took away from us the personal responsibility to save and sanctify our own souls. The contrary is true. The free will which God gave to Adam and Eve and the fallen angels is still ours. We can either respond to and accept the fruits of the Redemption or ignore and refuse them. The same question which God asked the angels and repeated to Adam and Eve, He also asks us: "Will you follow and obey me and my holy will for you?" Christ was obedient until death; but are we?

Christ wanted His perfect sacrifice, on the cross, to be with us in such a way that we can constantly gather its fruits and use them to help us follow and obey God's laws and His will.

When Christ sent His apostles out to bring His teachings to the people, He said: "Receive the Holy Spirit, whose sins you shall forgive, they are forgiven them; and whose sins you shall retain, they are retained" (*John* 20:22-23). "Thus it is written; and thus the Christ should suffer, and should rise again from the dead, on the third day; and that repentance and remission of sins should be preached in his name to all the nations" (*Luke* 24:46-47). "Go into the whole world and preach the gospel to every creature. He who believes and is baptized shall be saved, but he who does not believe shall be condemned" (*Mark* 16:15).

To follow Christ and His teachings would never be possible for us, God's children, because we have a weak human nature. The act of redemption did not take that away from us. Christ knew that His sacrifice was perfect, but He also knew that those, who would benefit from it, were not. To help us gather the fruits among all the thorns of human living, Christ gave us the way and the means to participate fully in our redemption: by and through the sacraments. Not only did He give us the sacraments, but He made it possible for His sacrifice on the cross to be daily present to us. This He has done by giving to us the perfect worship of God called the: Holy Sacrifice of The Mass.

The very first Mass was offered by Christ Himself at the Last Supper in the upper room. There He gave us the Blessed Eucharist. After He said: "Do this in remembrance of me" (*Luke* 22:19), He walked to the altar of sacrifice: the cross. The apostles continued to say Mass, after Christ had taught them and given to them their priestly powers. St. Paul tells us:

"...For I myself have received from the Lord that the Lord Jesus, on the night in which He was betrayed, took bread and giving thanks broke it and said: 'This is my body which shall be given up for you; do this in remembrance of me...' in like manner also the cup...For as often as you shall eat this bread and drink the cup, you proclaim the death of the Lord until He comes. Therefore, whoever eats this bread or drinks the cup of the Lord unworthily will be guilty of the body and the blood of the Lord" (*1 Cor.* 11:23-27).

Now, as you begin to understand the Mass, in the light of all I have explained in this chapter, you can easily see why it is called the Holy Sacrifice of The Mass and why it is the only perfect worship of God.

Why is it a sacrifice, when Christ's sacrifice occurred on the cross? Because Christ, under the appearance of bread and wine, continues to offer up to His Father the sacrifice of His life which he first offered on Calvary. This He does in a now bloodless sacrifice whereas before the blood flowed from His wounded body. But because it is bloodless does not take away the fact that Christ, body and blood, is present upon the altar of worship. When the priest acts, through the power bestowed upon him when he was ordained (the same power which the apostles had) he changes the community's gifts of bread and wine into the body and blood of Christ. Then, there upon the altar lies Christ, His sacrifice of the cross continuing. He is still not only the sacrificial victim, but also the High Priest who offers Himself to the Father in the name of all who are gathered together.

There you have the complete, perfect worship of God: our Catholic Mass. All the essential elements are there for worship.

1. The people gather in a Church, or other public place (or in a home) before the altar of God to worship Him as He deserves to be worshiped.

2. They present their gifts of bread and wine to the priest.

3. The priest accepts these gifts and places them upon the altar.

4. The priest then has the power to change these gifts into the body and blood of Christ.

5. Christ then becomes the sacrificial victim which the priest accepts and offers in a perfect act of worship.

6. Christ's role of the sacrificial victim continues when He, as the High Priest, offers Himself to God in the name of the people who are gathered before the altar.

7. Finally, God returns to these people the way and the means for their personal sanctification which is the Holy Eucharist.

Also, incorporated into this act of divine worship, there are other truths of God. At Mass, the community gathers and although there are many individuals, they all become one body with Christ. This one body is known as the Mystical Body of Christ. This Mystical Body of Christ lives and exists for the purpose of offering to God divine worship. That is why the Mass and the Eucharist become the core around which our Catholic religion revolves. That is also why the Mass or the Liturgy is the highest form of vocal prayer and the official public worship of God.

The Mass, then, allows us to fulfill our personal responsibilities to God so that we can acknowledge Him as divine, adore Him, worship Him, and thank Him for His favors and blessings to us. In reverse, God uses the Mass to show us His love and concern for us; and as the way and the means to bring His spiritual food to us for the good of our souls. That is why the Mass is not only the bloodless sacrifice of Christ continuing to this very day, but a sacrament as well.

So, our Catholic Mass began at the Last Supper, then continued upon the wood of the cross; and now is brought to us daily for our spiritual welfare. By and through the endless flood of graces which the Redemption released upon mankind, we become one with Christ and gather the fruits for our personal redemption. This makes the Mass the greatest miracle which we can witness.

Unfortunately, many people go to Mass only to "get something" out of it. This "something" usually is an emotional feeling of great peace, joy and closeness to God. When they get "nothing" out of the Mass, they stop going.

However, although there are numerous graces to be received

during each Mass (graces which cannot be seen or felt), the main reason why one should go to Mass is to participate in the divine art of worship. It is to *give* to God the recognition which he deserves as our God and heavenly Father.

Do you understand now why a few poorly said home prayers could never take the place of a Mass? Do you understand why there has to be the gathering of the people before the altar of God? Do you understand why the priest must be present? And do you understand the difference between merely *praying to* God and actually *worshiping* Him?

Know also why the Catholic clergymen are called priests. Only a priest can take part in the sacrifice of the Mass. That is why non-Catholic clergymen *are not* called priests. They do not offer sacrifice in an act of worship. They do not believe in this sacrifice. They can *pray* to God, but they cannot worship Him as He deserves to be worshiped. Non-Catholic clergymen are called pastors, ordained ministers, elected representatives or elders, but not priests. The meaning for the word priest has never changed. It remains the same today. Priest means someone who offers sacrifice in true worship to God.

When the Protestant leaders broke away from the Mother religion, they did not take the power of priesthood with them because this power was with the Catholic bishops. Having no bishops with the power to ordain priests, Protestant religions have no priests.

Also, and this is very important, do you now understand why we Catholics *do not* worship saints as we are so often accused of doing? We *could not worship* saints or Our Lady, Mary. That is why the Church allows us to have pictures and statues of Mary and of the saints. We can love them, honor them and *pray* to them; but we cannot *worship* them in the same way that we worship God, because we do not offer sacrifices to them. When the pagans of old worshiped false idols, they offered a sacrifice to these idols such as a living animal which was slain upon the altar. That is worshiping false idols. Never do we do such a thing before a statue or picture of Our Lady or of the saints. It is forbidden by the first commandment to worship false idols and false gods. The words about worshiping false idols are these: ". . .I am the Lord thy God. . .you shall not carve idols for yourself. . .you shall not bow down before them, worshiping them" (*Eph.* 20:2-5). Offering sacrifices and burnt offerings to idols would be the sacrificial act of worshiping them.

When you go to Mass and really get involved in worshiping the true, living God, you will quickly know the difference between just *praying* to God and actually *worshiping* Him. You will know why Christ is called the "Lamb of God" sacrificed upon the altar; and you will gather unto yourself all the wondrous fruits of your own redemption.

Finally, when you do attend a Mass, pay close attention to the following words. Perhaps they are familiar to you, but you never paid too much attention to them. Now see the way these words, which are part of our Catholic Mass, retell the story of worship and sacrifice which I have just related to you in this chapter.

The words are to be found in the part of the Mass called the Liturgy of The Eucharist. Before our gifts, the bread and wine become the body, blood, soul and divinity of Christ, the priest prays: "Blessed are you, Lord, God of all creation. Through your goodness, we have this bread and this wine to offer. They will become for us the bread of life and our spiritual drink. Pray, brethren, that our sacrifice may be acceptable to God, the Almighty Father." The priest continues: "Bless and approve our offering, make it acceptable to you. . .let it become for us the body and blood of Jesus Christ your only Son, our Lord."

Then the Last Supper, the first Mass, is retold by the priest: "The day before He suffered, He took bread in His sacred hands. . ." and so forth. During this part of the Mass, our Lord becomes present on the altar. No longer are there upon the altar gifts of bread and wine, but the Lord, God, whom the priest and Christ, as the High Priest, will offer to God as the sacrificial victim.

The Liturgy of The Eucharist continues with the following prayers included: "We offer to you, God of Glory and majesty, this holy and perfect sacrifice, the bread of life and the cup of eternal salvation." The priest is, at that moment, along with Christ, offering to God, the Father, His beloved Son for us who are gathered before the altar. Now note the fact, that this perfect worship of God is bringing back the memories of the true worship of God in the Old Testament. We hear these words: "Look with favor on these offerings and accept them as once you accepted the gifts of your servant Abel and the sacrifice of Abraham, our Father in faith." The priest continues to pray: "Almighty God, we pray that your angel may take this sacrifice to your altar in Heaven."

Then comes the offering of the sacrificial victim to God the Father. (Remember only a priest can make the offering): The divine worship of God.

The priest holds up the chalice and the Host, now the body and blood of Christ, and says: "Through Him, with Him, in Him, in the unity of the Holy Spirit, all glory and honor is yours, almighty Father, for ever and ever." Here you see the sacrificial victim, Christ, along with the priest, worshiping God as He deserves to be worshiped.

Then, the people, who are present at the Mass, join in the act of worship by praying the Our Father.

Then the words "Lamb of God..." are used. It must be remembered that the most perfect sacrificial victim, in the Old Testament was a pure, white, male lamb. So we call Christ the "Lamb of God."

Finally, the communion of the faithful: "Then, as we receive from this altar, the sacred body and blood of your Son, let us be filled with every grace and blessing." (Eucharistic Prayer 1) There, within the words of our Catholic Mass you can find the story of the sacrificial worship of God, the most perfect worship of God.

Note

The full explanation of prayer and the prayer life is continued in Volume II of *Come Climb The Ladder And Rejoice.*

BIBLIOGRAPHY

A CATECHISM FOR ADULTS
Rev. William J. Cogan
Adult Catechetical Teaching Aids
4848 Clark St., Chicago, Illinois 60640

A CATHOLIC DICTIONARY
Third Edition 1961
Edited by Donald Attwater
The MacMillan Company, New York

CONTEMPLATIVE LIFE
IN THE WORLD
A. M. Goichon
Translated by M. A. Bouchard
B. Herder Book Co., St. Louis, Missouri

CONVERSATION WITH CHRIST
Father Peter Thomas Rohrback, O.C.D.
Fides Publishers Association
Chicago, Illinois

ENCYCLOPEDIC DICTIONARY OF
THE BIBLE
Louis F. Hartman, C.SS.R.
McGraw-Hill Book Co., New York,
New York

THE FAITH EXPLAINED
Leo J. Trese
Fides Publishing, Inc.
Notre Dame, Indiana

HELPS AND HINDRANCES
TO PERFECTION
Thomas J. Higgins, S.J.
The Bruce Publishing Co.
Milwaukee, Minnesota

A HANDBOOK OF
THE CATHOLIC FAITH
Van Doornik, Jelsman, Lisdonk
Image Books, A Division of
Doubleday and Co., Inc.
Garden City, New York

CATHOLIC EDITION OF
THE HOLY BIBLE
Confraternity—Douay Version
Catholic Book Publishing Co.,
New York

THE JERUSALEM BIBLE
Doubleday and Co., Inc.
Garden City, New York

THE NEW AMERICAN BIBLE
Saint Joseph Edition
Catholic Book Publishing Co.
New York

OUR WAY TO GOD
Dr. Franz Michael William
Translated by Ronald Walls
The Bruce Publishing Co.
Milwaukee, Minnesota

THE PHILOSOPHY OF
ST. THOMAS AQUINAS
Etienne Gilson
B. Herder Book Co.
St. Louis, Missouri

THE STATES OF PERFECTION
St. Paul Edition
By The Benedictine Monks
Daughters of St. Paul
Boston, Massachusetts

THE TEACHING OF CHRIST
Edited by Ronald Lawler, O.F.M. Cap.
Donald W. Wuerl, Thomas C. Lawler
Our Sunday Visitor
Huntington, Indiana

INTERIOR CASTLE
St. Teresa of Avila
E. Allison Peers
Image Books, A Division of
Doubleday and Co., Inc.
Garden City, New York